THE WORLD SAYS NO TO WAR

Demonstrations against the War on Iraq

Stefaan Walgrave and Dieter Rucht, Editors

Preface by Sidney Tarrow

Social Movements, Protest, and Contention
Volume 33

University of Minnesota Press
Minneapolis • London

D0188061

Published by the University of Minnesota Press
111 Third Avenue South, Suite 290
Minneapolis, MN 55401-2520
http://www.upress.umn.edu

Library of Congress Cataloging-in-Publication Data

The world says no to war : demonstrations against the war on Iraq /
Stefaan Walgrave and Dieter Rucht, Editors.
p. cm. — (Social movements, protest, and contention ; v. 33)
Includes bibliographical references and index.
ISBN 978-0-8166-5095-8 (hc : alk. paper) —
ISBN 978-0-8166-5096-5 (pb : alk. paper)
1. Iraq War, 2003—Protest movements. 2. Peace movements—History—
21st century. I. Walgrave, Stefaan. II. Rucht, Dieter.
DS79.76.W674 2010
956.7044'31—dc22
2009046761

Printed in the United States of America on acid-free paper

The University of Minnesota is an equal-opportunity educator and employer.

18 17 16 15 14 13 12 11 10   10 9 8 7 6 5 4 3 2 1

THE WORLD SAYS NO TO WAR

Social Movements, Protest, and Contention

Series Editor   Bert Klandermans, Free University, Amsterdam

Associate Editors Ron R. Aminzade, University of Minnesota
        David S. Meyer, University of California, Irvine
        Verta A. Taylor, University of California, Santa Barbara

For more books in the series, see page 305.

Contents

Preface

Sidney Tarrow

The first decade of this new century witnessed a number of events of global importance, from the World Trade Center bombing to the wave of terrorism that followed, from the attack on the Taliban and al-Qaeda in Afghanistan to the war on Iraq, and from the electoral revolutions in the old Soviet bloc to the expansion into that area of the European Union, followed by its constitutional failure; and from the launching of the Iraq War in 2003 to the American withdrawal promised for 2010. These events and others like them have fundamentally changed global politics.

With the exception of the electoral revolutions, however, most of these episodes have been bad for humanity and destructive of human rights. The World Trade Center bombing alone produced a militaristic turn in American foreign policy and retractions of human rights, both at home and abroad. It also brought a crisis in the Atlantic alliance and splits in the European Union, a renewal of Islamist terrorism, and a diversion of the world's attention from the grave problems of Darfur, HIV/AIDS, and global warming. And it led the United States to fail to follow up on its initial victory in Afghanistan and to a recrudescence of Islamist power in both that country and in Pakistan. From the optimism that greeted the turn of the new century, there has been a turn to profound pessimism for advocates of global progress and human rights.

Yet not all has been bleak for advocates of world peace, global solidarity, and popular politics. On February 15, 2003, millions of people around the world combined in the largest example of collective action in history to protest against the impending war on Iraq. These demonstrations had three main properties that marked them off from previous peace campaigns:

- Their vast geographic reach
- The enormous numbers of participants they attracted, many of them with little previous experience of contentious politics
- Their coordinated transnational nature.

Let us not exaggerate. These demonstrations, however vast, did not stop the rush to war, which had been, in any case, decided long before. And they did not draw on as broad a range of social groups as was maintained at the time. Nor did the campaign against the American-led attack on Iraq lead to a sustained social movement against a conflict that—at this writing—continues to destroy people and take treasure and lives from both proponents and victims. But it was something new in the history of contentious politics: a concerted campaign of transnational collective action—using the new tools of the Internet and more conventional means of mobilization—which brought millions of people together around common goals and against common targets.

Of course, there have been transnational campaigns of collective action before. From the transnational network formed in support of the Chiapas rebellion in the early 1990s (Olesen 2005), to the "Battle of Seattle" against the World Trade Association (Lichbach 2003); from the campaign against land mines in the late 1990s (Cameron, Lawson, and Tomlin 1998) to the wave of global justice protests that followed (della Porta et al. 2007); from the justice cascade against ex-dictator Augusto Pinochet of Chile (Lutz and Sikkink 2001a and b; Roht-Arriaza 2006) to the campaigns against global warming from 2006 on: in the new century, contentious politics has begun to escape the boundaries of the national state (Tarrow 2005).

But much of this activity has been organized by well-financed NGOs and lacked a mass base. The most successful operations—like the landmine campaign—depended on the support of allied states (in this campaign, Canada, for example). Moreover, many of the activities that activists think of as global have actually taken bilateral form—as in the "boomerang" campaigns documented by Margaret Keck and Kathryn Sikkink (1998). Much of these have been carried out by domestic constituencies in the name of global values, as in the Battle of Seattle, which drew largely on American trade union supporters who quickly disappeared from the global justice coalition after 9/11 (Hadden and Tarrow 2007). Coordinated transnational campaigns on the part of non-state actors, like the one that burst on the world on February 15, 2003, are still a relative rarity in global politics—thus the great importance of this book.

But that is not all. In addition to documenting a major new threshold in the transnational coordination of contentious protest, *The World Says No to War* is important for three other reasons: methodological, contextual, and dynamic.

First, methodologically, the book demonstrates conclusively the potential for the use of coordinated survey techniques for the study of contentious politics in action. Until recently, with the exception of a pathbreaking strand of research in France (see Favre 1990), survey research on contentious politics drew on surveys of the mass public, not activists themselves, or depended on the memories of activists long after their actions ended (McAdam 1988). Instead, the organizers of this study accessed the activists in the act of protesting—or very soon afterward—when their images of participation were still "hot" and not yet warped by selective memory or disillusionment (see appendix A for details). It will be important to see whether other scholars take up their method, applying it to other types of protest campaigns, perhaps digging more deeply into the biographies of the activists and following up with detailed studies of their itineraries after the protest is over.

Second, from the point of view of comparative contextualization, the study's coordinators were neither too far from nor too close to their subjects. They made a reasonable compromise between commissioning separate analyses of the protestors in the eight countries they studied (which might have produced in-depth but noncumulative case studies) and carrying out a context-free examination of their massive dataset of roughly 4,500 respondents (which might have produced a context-free exercise in number-crunching). Their decision was guided by the heuristic process model (see Figure I.1) that organizes the book. They asked each of their authors to focus on either the independent, the intervening, or the dependent variables in their model. This intermediate strategy allowed them and their authors to use comparison creatively, relating the findings of the study to their national contexts, as well as to the sociodemographics of their populations and the framing of the protest.

Third, although the study took place at only one point in time—one in which American hegemonic overreach was at its height—the book provides us with elements for a process analysis of a transnational movement against it. It shows how the mobilization of a vast transnational protest campaign was planned, organized, framed, and carried out. In the process, it shows that the Internet combined with more conventional means of mobilization, but did not replace them. It also demonstrates the key role of activists from the then-powerful global justice movement in founding the emerging antiwar movement. And it shows how key factors in mounting the demonstration were the European Social Forum in Florence, Italy, and the World Social Forum in Porto Alegre, Brazil. Though taken at one point in time, the survey provides precious information on the dynamics of contention.

The book is particularly valuable for the light it sheds on individuals. It shows how key activists with "complex identities" were close to the core of the mobilization (see W. Lance Bennett, Terri E. Givens, and Christian Breunig's chapter in this book). It reveals the mix of common and diverse factors producing the demonstration in the eight countries under its analytical lens. Finally, it reveals a workable model of cross-national collaboration permitting the exploitation of a common dataset by scholars with diverse research perspectives.

Critics might complain that there is little information here about the diffusion of information in the weeks and months before the protest. And students would also have profited from more information about the interaction between protest organizers and institutional actors in the various countries in which the demonstrations took place. This would have been particularly useful in the United States, where the Bush administration did all in its power to "sell" the war to the public, succeeding in stilling the voices of protest that were so insistent before the first bombs fell on Baghdad. Future researchers using protester-based survey techniques may wish to add a subsequent phase of follow-up research on public opinion after the demonstrators go home.

Walgrave, Rucht, and their collaborators have given students of social movements, antiwar movements, and activism a precious example of how multicountry research can be carried out by many players, through theoretically based empirical research on the formation and execution of a transnational protest campaign. That alone is a significant achievement that deserves praise and replication.

Works Cited

Cameron, Maxwell A., Robert J. Lawson, and Brian W. Tomlin, eds. 1998. *To Walk without Fear: The Global Movement to Ban Landmines.* Oxford: Oxford University Press.

della Porta, Donatella, Massimiliano Andretta, Lorenzo Mosca, and Herbert Reiter. 2007. *Globalization from Below: Transnational Activists and Protest Networks.* Minneapolis: University of Minnesota Press.

Favre, Pierre. 1990. *La Manifestation.* Paris: Presses des Sciences Politiques.

Hadden, Jennifer, and Sidney Tarrow. 2007. "Spillover or Spillout: The Global Justice Movement in the United States after 9/11." *Mobilization* 12: 359–76.

Keck, Margaret, and Kathryn Sikkink. 1998. *Activists beyond Borders: Advocacy Networks in International Politics.* Ithaca, N.Y.: Cornell University Press.

Lichbach, Mark I. 2003. "Global Order and Local Resistance: Structure, Culture, and Rationality in the Battle of Seattle." Unpublished paper, University of Maryland Political Science Department.

Lutz, Ellen, and Kathryn Sikkink. 2001a. "International Human Rights Law and Practice in Latin America." *International Organization* 54: 249–75.

———. 2001b. "The Justice Cascade: The Evolution and Impact of Foreign Human Rights Trials in Latin America." *Chicago Journal of International Law* 2: 1–34.

McAdam, Doug. 1988. *Freedom Summer.* Oxford: Oxford University Press.

Olesen, Thomas. 2005. *International Zapatismo: The Construction of Solidarity in the Age of Globalization.* London: Zed.

Roht-Arriaza, Naomi. 2006. *The Pinochet Effect: Transnational Justice in the Age of Human Rights.* Philadelphia: University of Pennsylvania Press.

Tarrow, Sidney. 2005. *The New Transnational Activism.* Cambridge: Cambridge University Press.

Introduction

Stefaan Walgrave and Dieter Rucht

On February 15, 2003, following the global time zones from Australia in the East to Seattle in the West, a massive flood of protest conquered the streets throughout the world. Millions of people in more than six hundred cities worldwide protested against the imminent war on Iraq. This massive demonstration was the culmination point of a sustained protest wave against the Iraq War starting in late 2002 and lasting for several months. At that time, the United States and the United Kingdom were busy preparing for war with Iraq, but it seemed as though war could be avoided, as the United Nations Security Council was still debating a potential resolution. Some of the protests staged on February 15 were small-scale, only local marches consisting of a few neighbors banding together; others were large-scale national protest demonstrations. In Rome, Italy, for example, an estimated record crowd of 3 million people expressed their anger about the imminent war, in Barcelona, Spain, more than 1 million demonstrators appeared, while in Warsaw, Poland, only ten thousand people exhibited their resistance. Together, the February 15 demonstrations were the largest protest event in human history. Journalists, observers, politicians, social movement scholars, and political scientists alike were stunned by the magnitude of, dispersion of, and apparent similarities among the global February 15, 2003, events.

The astonishment on the part of social scientists regarding these protest events reveals first that these antiwar protests, indeed, were extraordinary; and second, that social science seems to lack appropriate models to grasp transnational protest phenomena of their size. This book tackles both these challenges.

First, the study aims to significantly enhance our empirical understanding of what happened that day, who took to the streets and why, and how such a protest event resulted in mobilizing as large a crowd as it evidently did. Much has been said and claimed regarding the February 15 events; political actors, movement leaders, journalists as well as social scientists have frequently voiced opinions pertaining to the lessons to be learned from the protests. February 15 did become a myth quickly. For example, claims were made that people from all walks of life participated, that February 15 essentially was a global social justice action, that the Internet was pivotal in coordinating the protest events and mobilizing the people involved in them, and that local political conflicts conflated with the antiwar issue. However, there was no empirical base for these contentions. Drawing on an original protest survey directed at a great number of February 15 participants, combined with a broad variety of other materials and sources, our book offers the necessary solid empirical base.

Second, and more important, this book embarks on a quest to improve general understanding of protest events in a comparative perspective. Considering the February 15 case, our goal is to enhance general knowledge of the background, nature, and significance of protest politics. Many aspects of protest are insufficiently understood. To raise only some of the questions: To what extent and why does the composition of protest events differ across issues and nations? How do divergent mobilization patterns affect the composition of protest events? What is the relationship between the social movements' infrastructures and the types of protesters that take to the streets? What determines a protest's dominant mobilization pattern? How and why do people initially participate in protest? What is the role of the Internet in persuading people to participate in protest? We do not claim to provide conclusive answers to all of these questions; our main contention is that contextualizing protest can help us make important inroads toward better comprehending it.

One of the main limitations of the mainstream empirical literature of protest is the lack of comparison. The bulk of collective behavior scholarship, in particular that of students of social movements, engages in single or multiple case studies. This limits the researcher's capacity to thoroughly test existing theories by confronting them with diverse cases and to generalize findings. To not compare cases rules out the possibility of systematically taking into account the very context in which contention takes place. This leads to a second stream in literature: political participation studies, which have been flourishing in the political sciences since Barnes and Kaase's study on political action (Barnes and Kaase 1979). Essentially comparative in nature, these studies draw on *general* population surveys across several countries, allowing for more rigorous tests of theoretical propositions and broader generalization.

However, political participation studies tend to completely decontextualize protest behavior, as they do not contain any evidence of participation in specific events and merely characterize protest participation in general terms. While the case studies often lack a comparative angle, the studies drawing on general population surveys are, in part, comparative, though they entirely disregard the context.

A massive wave of similar demonstrations in many countries, the events of February 15 offer scholars a unique opportunity to go beyond single cases and adopt a truly comparative perspective, taking context into account. In this study, we systematically compare antiwar demonstrators and demonstrations in eight Western democracies. On February 15, 2003, the authors of this book, in a collective effort and using the same template questionnaire, conducted protest surveys at eleven different locations. The surveys compare demonstrations and demonstrators in the United States (New York, San Francisco, and Seattle), the United Kingdom (London and Glasgow), Spain (Madrid), Italy (Rome), the Netherlands (Amsterdam), Germany (Berlin), Switzerland (Bern), and Belgium (Brussels).[1] These nations represent most of the largest Western countries in the months leading up to the war and allow for a comparison of the mobilization against the different positions that Western governments adopted vis-à-vis the war: from active participation and initiation (United States and United Kingdom), to limited military collaboration and verbal support (Spain, Italy, and the Netherlands), to silent opposition (Switzerland) or raucous critique of the United States (Germany and Belgium). The eight countries are highly diverse in their protest cultures, public opinions, systems of interest mediation, and in (involved) political institutions.

What makes the February 15 protests particularly interesting from an analytical perspective is that a number of crucial variables can be held constant when comparing the protests and protesters in the countries studied. In all venues, demonstrators opposed the imminent war on Iraq; and all events occurred on the same day (and thus in the same stage of the conflict's build up), relied on the same protest repertoire of peaceful demonstrations, targeted the same war-preparing countries (the United States and the United Kingdom in particular), and appeared to shout the same slogans and carry similar banners. While holding constant the issue, time, and action type, with a focus on the variety in institutional structure—the diverging political stances of government and opposition, the differences in political cultures, protest repertoires, and social movement strengths in the eight countries under study allow for a strong comparative design. The essential research question that our study raises is: *What are the core differences and similarities across the February 15 protest events in the eight nations, and what factors account for them?*

The main empirical claim upheld throughout this book is that—although similar in timing, action repertoire, set-up, slogans, banners, atmosphere—the February 15 demonstrations differed considerably across countries. Under a surface of apparent similarity a host of differences was concealed. The demonstrators displayed substantial variation across countries; people taking to the streets in Madrid, for example, did not exhibit the same characteristics, attitudes, and convictions as those protesting in Glasgow, at the same time and against the same war. Confronted with such findings, the predominant theoretical claim relevant throughout this volume is that political context does indeed matter for protest events. Distinct political contexts mold dissimilar protest events. Protest correlates as the composition, target, amplitude, radicality, and claims of the contention differ in relation to the diverging political context.

That political context matters in terms of social movements can hardly be considered a new assertion. In fact, it is the core claim of one of the most influential accounts of social movements. More than two decades ago emerged the political opportunity structure (POS) approach, stressing that social movements are dependent on the political environment in which they operate (Kitschelt 1986; Tarrow 1998). The book fully endorses the core claim of the POS approach, yet, simultaneously acknowledges that the classic version of this approach was devised to study not specific protest events but rather social movements at large. Movements have an organizational structure and a certain continuity based on an ongoing interaction with power holders, while protest events, although often staged by social movements, can be one-shot actions without any organizational backbone (Tilly 1994). The protest wave against the war on Iraq that reached its apex on February 15 exemplifies this fact; it declined quickly after the war broke out, with only a few protests in most countries just one month later. The dynamic of social movements may be determined by the ebb and flow of protest events, the movement itself can survive without collective action and remain alive for years in a state of abeyance. In a similar vein, a social movement may be weak—with only a few core activists, light structures, and hardly any visibility—but its protest events may be large. Particularly with regard to issues of war and peace, a distinction between the peace movement and the protest events staged to support the peace cause seems crucial. Accounts reveal that the relationship between peace movement and peace protest is complicated, at least in Western Europe, as specific peace organizations may not be well developed, while their demonstrations often receive ample support from the entire associational spectrum of the Left resulting, occasionally, in huge mobilizations (Rochon 1988).

Devised to comparatively account for the strength of social movements—their constituency, organizational structure, mobilization level, turnout, militancy—the POS does not make claims regarding the features of individual activists or demonstrators. Yet, this study focuses on the individual demonstrators and asks who they are, why they participated, and how they had been activated. As we opt to concentrate on protest politics and individual participants rather than on social movements and movement strength, we cannot simplistically assume the classic explanatory factors associated with the POS approach. We believe, for example, that social movements are only one of the determinants of protest events. The POS approach states that political opportunities determine the strength of social movements; we maintain that a protest event is affected by the broader political context and that movement strength is only one of the intervening variables between the political context and characteristics of individual demonstrators.

What, therefore, is the theoretical argument buttressing the book? Our focus is on similarities and differences among demonstrators in eight nations. This is the dependent variable, that which we strive to fully understand and explain. We focus on three features of the demonstrators: their sociodemographics, attitudes, and (political) behavior. The relevant context of protest events such as February 15, the independent and intervening variables, consist of five sets of explanatory factors, which are derived from key social movements and political participation theories:

1 On an overall level, the *sociodemographic composition* of the population—especially age, class, and education—predetermines the constitution of the protest and accounts for cross-country differences and similarities. This argument draws on theories about "social centrality" as suggested in general participation theory (Verba, Schlozman, and Brady 1995). Trivial as it may seem, a generally high educational level in a given country is mirrored among the protesters.

2 Structural features of the *political system* play a role more concretely in the channels of access to the decision-making system, the distribution of decision-making power, and the prevalent mode of interest mediation. This dimension corresponds to the central claim of the POS approach, as developed in the social movement literature (Kriesi 2004). Note that the classic POS approach focuses on permanent and stable arrangements that structurally mold general protest behavior in a given country; it is not meant to inherently explain variable traits of specific protest events or campaigns, let alone to account for the traits of individual protesters.

3 More specific *issue-related* political context variables have an impact on the protest. These are the concrete and volatile political opportunities, such as sudden changes in political elites' support for a protest cause. This specific "interaction context" will be operationalized in three dimensions: (a) the position of government and opposition regarding the issue at stake, (b) mass media's coverage of the issue and the protest, and (c) the supportive or nonsupportive attitude of the general public (Kriesi 2004). This middle-range context dimension can be traced back to several theories, among which are those of "relative deprivation" (Gurr 1970) and the framing literature on social movements (Gamson 1992, Snow et al. 1986). We expect this context to influence the composition of the demonstrations. In countries where political elites are not supportive of the protest's cause, media are ignoring or marginalizing the protest, and public opinion is unaware of or manifestly opposed to the protesters' goals, the protesters are likely to differ from those in countries where elites, media, and the public opinion endorse the protest.

4 On a more concrete level, *social movements* that organize an event come into play. Having distinct constituencies, structures, goals, and strategies, these movement organizations affect the profiles of the protesters. This argument coincides with the central contention of resource mobilization theory, that social movement organizations and the existing structure of the social movement sector affect a protest's mobilizing force and the type of people that show up for it (McCarthy and Zald 1977). As applied to the February 15 protests, we expect that the demonstrators will basically mirror the traits of the social movements behind them that staged the events. Different social movement sectors lead to different people on the streets.

5 Finally, and most closely linked to protest events per se, the actual strategies and channels of *mobilization* utilized by organizations and participants affect the demonstrators' sociodemographic characteristics, attitudes, and behavior. This dimension, serving as the macromicro bridge, corresponds with a vast body of literature stressing the importance of mobilizing agencies, motivations, and networks for both social movements and, more generally, political participation (Klandermans and Oegema 1987; Rosenstone and Hansen 1993; Diani and McAdam 2003). In terms of February 15, we expect to find different mobilization patterns across countries, which ultimately lead to different types of demonstrators.

Thus, we argue that protest politics can only fully be understood in a multilayered and multifaceted context (such as the one we have described). These five context dimensions are not entirely independent from one another. Political system arrangements, for example, are a prior condition for the issue-specific political context that, in turn, influences the structures and strategies of social movements. An additional example: the presence and strength of certain social movements similar to and supportive of peace groups, combined with the media's stance and predominant public opinion, has an effect on the type and scope of the mobilization processes. Therefore, we conceptualize the first four dimensions as independent variables, as shown in Figure I.1 below. The one remaining dimension—mobilization processes—can be considered as a set of intervening variables that are influenced by the independent variables and have a direct effect on our threefold-dependent variables: the sociodemographic characteristics, attitudes, and behaviors of the protesters in the eight respective nations. These three blocks of variables correspond to the three chapter groupings of this book.

As the reader may have inferred, our theoretical framework is twofold, as it draws on two strands of research that have largely remained separate, although often studying the same phenomena: the political participation literature (see factors [1] and [5]) and the social movement literature (see factors [2] to [4]). Methodologically, the individual actor-level evidence we collected in surveys resembles the emblematic design of the participation studies. The contextualization of the data in a movement-staged campaign or event, by contrast, is typical for movement studies. Focusing mostly on movement organizations (mesolevel) or country features (macrolevel), quantitative individual-level data (microlevel) are rare to find in social movement research.

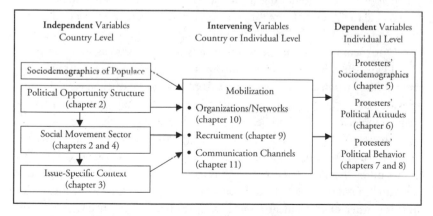

Figure I.1. Explanatory model and organization of the book

Our theoretical and methodological blending of both approaches is warranted, as we deal directly not with individual participation or social movements but with protest events found in the middle of the spectrum. These are precisely the instances and mechanisms that connect movements to participants. Protest events are a micro-macro bridge in action.

Obviously, our simple argument cannot be considered as a fully integrated and rigid theoretical model. For example, we do not specify the interactions among the different independent variables or among the dependent variables, nor do we arrange the independent variables in a distinct causal chain. The model we present is rather a heuristic device; it serves as an organizing or sensitizing tool that the authors of this book will use selectively. No chapters systematically integrate all context dimensions and factors of the model. The reasons for this are twofold. First, as research on specific protest events and moreso research using surveys of protesters is rare, we do not have much data to build on. Our study is explorative, aimed at detecting new theoretical insights instead of testing precise hypotheses. Second, it does not appear useful to design an elaborate and detailed theory, as we are unable to test it systematically. The more numerous the independent and dependent variables and the more precise and nuanced our propositions and hypotheses regarding their mutual relationships and dynamics, the more cases are necessary to test these hypotheses. Though our surveys cover thousands of respondents, we compare on a country level and, as a result, have restricted ourselves to eight cases only. Even our simple heuristic model with three independent, two intervening, and three dependent variables cannot be tested conclusively with eight cases. That is why, additionally, we organize this book in chapters, each focusing on at least one of the eight variables or factors proposed above. We concede that in this stage and with our available data, it is impossible to fully weigh the different explanatory factors against each other and to systematically explore all relevantly mutual interactions and dynamics.

Our theoretical argument is essentially as contextual as it is comparative. Depending, however, on the target at hand and on the selection of the cases, a comparison can take two forms. Applied to our particular case, if countries are very different but the phenomena to be explained—protesters' sociodemographics, attitudes, and behavior—are similar, it appears to be of greatest value to search for certain similarities within the dissimilar countries that account for these similar "outcomes." If cases are generally similar but outcomes different, the standard strategy is to search for certain case differences that can be used to explain the differences in outcomes. The present study does not use either of these ideal typical comparative designs. It covers a broad range of countries with large institutional, political, and cultural divergences, but we did not select the countries based on any theoretical design. Clearly, though, ours comes closest to a most-similar-systems design, as it merely focuses on Western, postindustrial democracies—even if it compares systems such as the United States, Italy, or Switzerland that differ in some respects. Whether outcomes are similar or dissimilar cannot easily be established in our study. Remember that the outcomes, or the aspects of them that we are particularly interested in, are features of demonstrators, and these form a continuum. We hardly have an external benchmark that allows us to conclude that the demonstrators in a given country score high or low on any certain variable.

In their chapters, the authors have employed different strategies. The book's main angle is comparative—assessing and explaining dissimilarities and similarities among the protesters in eight nations—yet not all chapters deal with an explicit comparison to the same extent. Some authors stress similarities, that is: they primarily search for commonalities across the demonstrators. They use comparative evidence to submit existing theoretical, mostly noncomparative, propositions to a test (Do they hold across all countries?) or to derive new theoretical claims (Do we obtain similar findings in all countries?). Authors following the similarity logic do not explain differences but focus on similarities stemming from theoretical arguments (see chapters 7 and 11). Other authors depart from the differences across countries. Their aim is to account for the discrepancies in outcome—namely features of the demonstrators—relying on contextual differences between countries (see chapters 6, 8, 10, and 12). These authors explicitly draw on comparative arguments as those we presented above. Some chapters combine both logics; they test general theories across nations to assess whether they hold under all circumstances, and they focus on explaining the remaining differences (chapters 5 and 9).

The chapters in this book make use of more than the heuristic model described above. Depending on what needs explanation, they apply—and in part further develop—major approaches in current social movement theory by emphasizing aspects such as resource mobilization, structural opportunities, movement networks and cultures, and framing. Therefore, apart from contributing to the exploratory model we propose, nearly all the chapters of this book introduce their own theoretical arguments and test corresponding propositions. However, as far as the dependent variable is concerned, all chapters rely on the same core data set.

The main empirical source for this book is a comparative protest survey addressing participants in the eleven demonstrations in the eight nations. We will present our methodology in more detail at the end of the book; in this introduction, we will briefly sketch our approach. Protest data were collected that rely on an innovative protest survey methodology consisting of directly questioning participants at demonstrations, a rather uncommon research technique. Favre and colleagues even speak of "a strange gap in the sociology of mobilizations" (Favre, Fillieule, and Mayer 1997). To the best of our knowledge, protest surveying has only been used in few studies (Jasper and Poulsen 1995; Waddington 1988). Most elaborate is the work of the French research team including Favre, Fillieule, and Mayer, who developed a method designed to offer every participant an equal opportunity of being interviewed (Fillieule 1998; 1997). Stefaan Walgrave and Peter Van Aelst refined their method further and tested it on seven Belgian demonstrations in the 1998–2001 period (Van Aelst and Walgrave 2001; Norris, Walgrave, and Van Aelst 2005). The essence of the method is to take a random sample of demonstrators, distribute postal questionnaires to the demonstrators selected, and ask them to fill out the questionnaires at home and send them back to the researchers (postage paid by addressee). This technique has been also applied in surveying protesters against unemployment and welfare cuts in four German cities in 2004 (Rucht and Yang 2004). In general, protest surveys result in quite high response rates, and tests of response bias for the most part yield encouraging results. We will report on the precise fieldwork method, sampling strategy, response rates, and response bias tests at the end of the book.

Regarding the February 15 protest survey under study here, war against Iraq was still an open matter in December 2002. The authors of this book, an international team of social movement scholars, began preparing for comparative data collection and created the International Peace Protest Survey (IPPS), should protests against a potential war occur. Drawing on an existing questionnaire and fieldwork method developed by the Belgian team working with Stefaan Walgrave, they prepared themselves and waited for the "Big One." The researchers did not expect it to be as big as it was. On February 15, the authors and their students distributed about ten thousand questionnaires in eleven different protest venues in eight countries, resulting in 5,838 successful postal interviews, with response rates varying from 40 to 55 percent. We also managed to conduct 913 oral interviews with demonstrators in Belgium, the Netherlands, Switzerland, and the United Kingdom. In the United Kingdom (Glasgow and London) and the United States (Seattle, San Francisco, and New York), we covered several demonstrations. As differences among the demonstrators in these different venues within the same nation were minimal, we decided, unless explicitly mentioned otherwise in specific chapters, to consistently draw on a collapsed data set on a country level. Taken together, the IPPS is perhaps the largest data set available on actual protesters to date. The IPPS questionnaire ascertains key variables, such as sociodemographics, political attitudes, political behavior, and organizational affiliation. The majority of available survey data do not focus on one specific protest event, since they are measurements of general participation. The IPPS, though, contains event-specific questions on attitudes, mobilization processes, network structures, and organizational background. Therefore, our data allow us to make significant progress in connecting protest with its context and forerunners.

This book both draws on the core protest survey and utilizes as well as relates it to a broad range of other data, such as general population surveys, surveys on social movement activists, media reports, flyers and calls for action, and speeches held during the event. Together, these put the core survey data into context and help answer all relevant questions initially raised.

Our study is organized in analytical chapters, since we are interested not in individual country results but in comparison. All chapters are related to the model that guides our book. The first chapter of the book introduces the case to be analyzed: the worldwide February 15 protest event. Second, from general to specific, the first several chapters present three layers of the contextual approach that form the theoretical core of the book. These independent variables will be used throughout the book, serving as a theoretical toolbox to help us better understand similarities and differences between countries. From a POS approach perspective, general regime features regarding elite-challenger relationships predetermine the existence, size, and outcome of contentious political action. Therefore, the first contextual chapter outlines the general regime features for the eight nations (chapter 2). At the middle-range level, these general characteristics are supplemented with a specific set of explanatory factors related directly to the Iraq War and to the citizens who joined the protest. We chart the respective governments' positions on the Iraqi issues, illustrate the position taken by public voices and the population at large in the eight nations vis-à-vis the war, and analyze the media's coverage of the Iraqi conflict and of the protest against the war (chapter 3). More concretely, from a resource mobilization perspective, previous protest and its organizational remnants could potentially be an important resource for renewed mobilization. This resource approach applies particularly to the peace movement, a movement exemplifying oscillating mobilization levels with long-lasting latent phases and sudden outbursts of massive activity. Hence, one chapter is devoted to previous peace protests in the eight nations (chapter 4). Chapters 2 to 4 are influenced by the fact that regimes, issue specifics, and peace mobilization are mutually associated; the chapters succinctly explore these mutual links. Not drawing on IPPS data but relying on other primary and secondary evidence, these are mainly descriptive. But they also raise questions and generate hypotheses about how and to what extent "their" context layer might affect one of the dependent variables, be it sociodemographic characteristics, attitudes, or behavior of the demonstrators.

Chapters 5 through 8 are devoted to the protesters. Who are they? What are their backgrounds? To what extent did they participate in previous protests? What do they believe in, and why did they participate in the February 15 event? These chapters draw extensively on IPPS data and address the classic individual-level features that are central to all participation studies: sociodemographics (chapter 5), political-attitudinal characteristics (chapter 6), and political-behavioral characteristics of demonstrators (chapter 7). In other words, these chapters concern the dependent variables: they describe them and draw on the contextual elements presented in the first four chapters to account for intercountry differences, testing the usefulness of the contextual approach of protest events. Against the backdrop of certain theories, each of these chapters tests the hypotheses revolving around diversity and normalization of protest, the centrality of the peace issue versus government opposition in the demonstrators' motivational structure, and the determinants of participation. Chapter 8 follows a slightly different logic and deals with the possible political spillover of the protest by developing an informed guess about the demonstrations' potential impact on subsequent elections in the eight nations under study.

The remainder of the book focuses on mobilization. Which channels and means were used to inform and motivate people? What was the underlying organizational infrastructure of the event? Were many protesters recruited via social movements? In terms of the contextual model structuring the book, these chapters examine the intervening variables, namely movement structures and mobilization processes. These variables can be considered both independent and dependent. Mobilization and movements are to be explained by more general context layers as well as they help explain sociodemographic characteristics, attitudes, and behavior. These chapters tackle the mobilization puzzle, progressively pinpointing the traits of the February 15 events. In chapter 9, we begin by asking the general question of whether people were mobilized via open (e.g., media) or closed (e.g., organizations) mobilization channels. In chapter 10, we elaborate on the organizational track by charting the associational microlevel networks that initially generated the protest. We further explore the looser and informal mobilization track in chapter 11, by assessing the role the Internet played in bridging diverse issue networks. Finally, in chapter 12 we disregard the structural aspect of the mobilization puzzle and turn to the cultural aspect by examining the framing of the Iraq issue by the media, by movement spokespersons or organizers, and the "ordinary" demonstrators.

Ultimately, this book focuses on an extraordinary series of demonstrations staged on one single day and serving one single purpose: preventing an imminent war on Iraq. As many of the aspects of the protests were identical or similar in the countries in our sample—action form, aim, slogans, organizers, timing—we can usefully compare the demonstrations and detect differences among the protests and the protesters in the eight countries. Guiding this inquiry, we draw on a loosely structured set of theoretical propositions—boiling down to the fact that context matters for the features of individual demonstrators—that do not form a strict theoretical model but that rather serve as a heuristic guide for the individual chapters. In summary, we believe that these context dimensions enable us to make sense of what happened on February 15, 2003, and, more generally, shed light on how protest events interact with their environment.

Note

1. As the London and Glasgow samples emerged to be similar—the political context was identical—we systematically collapsed data on the protesters in London and Glasgow. Unless specifically mentioned, we consistently utilize a collapsed UK dataset in this volume. The three U.S. demonstrations, for obvious reasons, have been pooled.

Works Cited

Barnes, Samuel, and Max Kaase. 1979. *Political Action: Mass Participation in Five Western Democracies.* London: SAGE Publications.

Diani, Mario, and Doug McAdam, eds. 2003. *Social Movements and Networks: Relational Approaches to Collective Action.* Oxford: Oxford University Press.

Favre, Philippe, Olivier Fillieule, and Nonna Mayer. 1997. "La fin d'une étrange lacune de la sociologie des mobilisations: L'étude par sondage des manifestants: Fondements théoriques et solutions techniques." *Revue Française de Science Politique* 47: 3–28.

Fillieule, Olivier. 1997. *Stratégies de la rue: Les manifestations en France.* Paris: Presses de Sciences Po.

———. 1998. "'Plus ça change, moins ça change': Demonstrations in France during the Nineteen-Eighties." In *Acts of Dissent. New Developments in the Study of Protest,* ed. Dieter Rucht, Ruud Koopmans, and Friedhelm Neidhardt, 199–226. Berlin: Sigma.

Gamson, William. 1992. *Talking Politics.* Cambridge: Cambridge University Press.

Gurr, Ted Robert. 1970. *Why Men Rebel.* Princeton, N.J.: Princeton University Press.

Jasper, James M., and Jane Poulsen. 1995. "Recruiting Strangers and Friends: Moral Shocks and Social Networks in Animal Rights and Anti-Nuclear Protests." *Social Problems* 42: 493–512.

Kitschelt, Herbert. 1986. "Political Opportunity Structures and Political Protest: Anti-nuclear Movements in Four Democracies." *British Journal of Political Science* 16: 57–85.

Klandermans, Bert, and Dirk Oegema. 1987. "Potentials, Networks, Motivations and Barriers: Steps towards Participation in Social Movements." *American Sociological Review* 52: 519–31.

Kriesi, Hanspeter. 2004. "Political Context and Opportunity." In *The Blackwell Companion to Social Movements,* ed. David A. Snow, Sarah A. Soule, and Hanspeter Kriesi, 67–90. Oxford: Blackwell.

McCarthy, John D., and Mayer N. Zald. 1977. "Resource Mobilization and Social Movements: A Partial Theory." *American Journal of Sociology* 82: 1212–41.

Norris, Pippa, Stefaan Walgrave, and Peter Van Aelst. 2005. "Who Demonstrates? Anti-State Rebels or Conventional Participants? Or Everyone?" *Comparative Politics* 2: 251–75.

Rochon, Thomas R. 1988. *Mobilizing for Peace: The Antinuclear Movements in Western Europe.* London: Adamantine.

Rosenstone, Steven J., and John Mark Hansen. 1993. *Mobilization, Participation and Democracy in America.* New York: Macmillan.

Rucht, Dieter, and Mundo Yang. 2004. "Wer demonstrierte gegen Hartz IV?" *Forschungsjournal Neue Soziale Bewegungen* 17: 21–27.

Snow, Robert D., E. Burke Rochford, Steven K. Worden, and Robert D. Benford. 1986. "Frame Alignment Processes, Micromobilization and Movement Participation." *American Sociological Review* 51: 464–82.

Tarrow, Sidney. 1998. *Power in Movement—Social Movements and Contentious Politics.* Cambridge: Cambridge University Press.

Tilly, Charles. 1994. "Social Movements as Historically Specific Clusters of Political Performances." *Berkeley Journal of Sociology* 38: 1–30.

Van Aelst, Peter, and Stefaan Walgrave. 2001. "Who Is That (Wo)man in the Street? From the Normalisation of Protest to the Normalisation of the Protester." *European Journal of Political Research* 39: 461–86.

Verba, Sidney, Kay Schlozman, and Henry Brady. 1995. *Voice and Equality: Civic Voluntarism in American Politics.* Cambridge, Mass.: Harvard University Press.

Waddington, David. 1988. *Flashpoints of Public Disorder.* London: Methuen.

1

February 15, 2003:
The World Says No to War

Joris Verhulst

A Historic Day of Worldwide Antiwar Action

On February 15, 2003, various slogans—"Not in my name!" "No war on Iraq!" "Don't attack Iraq!" "No blood for oil!" "The world says no to war!"— were the unifying mantras that echoed on the streets of more than six hundred cities throughout the world, on the marching cadence of ten to fifteen million protesters. Diehard activists shared the streets with citizens of all kinds: students, teenagers, young couples with children, but also housewives, doctors, university professors, and senior citizens (Simonson 2003). February 15 was the day the world stood up against an imminent United States–led invasion of Iraq in a simultaneous flood of protest demonstrations. Taken together, these were the largest and most momentous transnational antiwar protests in human history (Epstein 2003, 109), and all on one single day. Some of the protests were small and only local marches, in which a few neighbors sided with each other; others were national protest demonstrations of exceptional size and showed unparalleled internal diversity. But in all of them, the participants showed their aversion of the possibility of war. In the United States, the February 15 protests were the largest antiwar demonstrations since those against the war in Vietnam; in Europe they largely surpassed the 1991 Gulf War protests. In many countries, they even outshone the early 1980s demonstrations against the deployment of NATO cruise and Pershing II missiles in Europe, which were then considered to have "dwarfed all previous protest movements in Western Europe in the post-war period" and were believed to have engendered a "wave of political protest unprecedented" (Rochon 1988, xvi, 3). Apart from the West, protests were organized in countries across all other continents (e.g., Lebanon, Syria, and Israel; Japan, Malaysia, Thailand, and South Korea; South Africa, Tunisia, and many more), though in most cases turnouts were not half as spectacular. The largest non-Western demonstration was probably the one in Syria, where some hundred thousand people hit the streets; probably the smallest one took place in Antarctica, where a group of scientists held a rally at their observation station. The only region in the world where peace voices were silent was mainland China. Altogether, friend and foe, especially in the Western world, were surprised by the number of protests and protesters and by the diversity of the people at these demonstrations. Social movement scholars and other observers were startled by the transnational coordination: at first sight the different protesters were driven by the same ideological beliefs, in a surge of demonstrations that was alike concerning protest trigger, issue, and target. And the protests' timing and action repertoire were similar as well and, with only a single exception—in Athens and Thessaloniki in Greece—peaceful. A few days after the demonstrations, many commentators, following the *New York Times*'s Patrick Tyler (2003), referred to them as the expression of a new "superpower." Since February 15 there was talk of "two superpowers on the planet: the United States and World public opinion" (Cortright 2004, xi).

This chapter describes the history, the political context, the setup and coordination as well as the mobilization levels of the February 15 protest day. The worldwide coordinated character of the protest makes scrutinizing the organizational backbone most relevant: it's natural to ask, how were so many people at a time mobilized in these protests when the international peace movements appeared to have reached a low since the mobilizations against the Gulf War in 1991? How did their transnational coordination take place? The chapter also accounts for the size of the protest by detailing how many protests took place in how many countries.

War Talk: September 11, the Axis of Evil, and the Bombing of Baghdad

The Gulf region has a turbulent history, and the roots of the 2003 Iraq conflict can be traced back for many years (see Figure 1.1 for a summary timeline). The Iran-Iraq war had swept the region between 1973 and 1988. After a mere two years' breathing space, the Iraqi regime invaded the Emirate of Kuwait for annexation, claiming that this oil-rich region was a former Iraqi province. By mid-January 1991, the international community, led by the United States and backed by the United Nations, launched the military operation "Desert Storm" to set Kuwait free. This military confrontation would last no longer than forty days. Iraqi oil exports were put under a severe embargo and restricted by the "oil for food" programs; Iraq also had to allow

UN inspectors to search for weapons of mass destruction. For the next ten years, a U.S.-led military base kept control over the region and of the Iraqi no-fly zones in which it would sporadically carry out bombardments.

On November 31, 1998, U.S. president Clinton signed the Iraq Liberation Act. Because of several military maneuvers by the Iraqi army, and because the Iraqi regime had ceased all cooperation with the International Atomic Energy Agency and UN weapon inspectors, the U.S. Congress wrote the act to "support a transition to democracy in Iraq" through and after the "replacement of the Saddam Hussein regime" (U.S. Congress 1998). The act was made concrete through "Operation Desert Fox," led by then-president Clinton in mid-December 1998, which was intended to "decrease the Iraqi capacity to manufacture massive weapons of mass destruction" and essentially to "overthrow the Iraqi regime." The plans to get rid of Saddam Hussein were thus not intrinsically born in the Bush administration, as would later be regularly assumed, but can be traced to actions years earlier.

On September 11, 2001, several airplanes crashed into the New York World Trade Center towers and the Pentagon, resulting in the death of thousands of U.S. civilians. Although these attacks were attributed to (and later claimed by) Osama bin Laden, the American government also connected them to Saddam Hussein and his Iraqi regime. On October 7, 2001, a U.S.-led coalition army invaded Afghanistan for the search for Osama Bin Laden and to bring down the Taliban oppression. This war officially ended by mid-November 2001. In his State of the Union address of January 29, 2002, U.S. president George W. Bush used the expression "Axis of Evil." He pointed to three other countries that were presumed to be sponsoring terrorist development and activities and needed to be monitored with the utmost vigilance. North Korea, Iran and Iraq. The threat they posed was depicted as imminent and immediate: "Time is not on our side," Bush said. "I will not wait on events, while dangers gather. I will not stand by as perils draw closer and closer" (Bush 2002). The day after the one-year September 11 commemoration events, in a dossier titled "A Decade of Lies and Deceit," Bush addressed a request to the UN Security Council for the authorization of the removal of Iraq's president Saddam Hussein. Barely two weeks after that, UK prime minister Tony Blair presented a report—then suspected as and later proven to be exaggerated—on the Iraqi arsenal of chemical and biological weapons and Saddam Hussein's ability to launch such weapons within forty-five minutes. By the end of September 2002, the U.S. and British forces had resumed the first bombing of the Iraqi no-fly zones.

In October 2002, U.S. Congress adopted a resolution authorizing an attack on Iraq. The war preparations went full-speed ahead. Meanwhile, the

Date	Politics timeline	Protest timeline
December 1998	Operation Desert Fox, led by U.S. president Clinton.	
September 11, 2001	Terrorist attacks on World Trade Center and Pentagon.	
October 7, 2001	Invasion of Afghanistan.	
January 29, 2002	U.S. president Bush launches expression "Axis of Evil," pointing at North Korea, Iran, and Iraq as threats to world peace.	
September 12, 2002	U.S. address "A Decade of Lies and Deceit" to United Nations for removal of Saddam Hussein.	
September 24, 2002	UK prime minister Tony Blair presents report on Iraqi weapon arsenal.	
September 26, 2002	First bombings in Iraq no-fly zone. Condemned by Russia.	
October 2, 2002	U.S. Congress adopts resolution authorizing attack on Iraq.	European Social Forum preparatory meeting in Barcelona.
October 5–6, 2002		
October 16, 2002	Saddam Hussein reelected with 100 percent majority.	
October 17, 2002	Start of UN Security Council debate on Iraq.	
October 25, 2002		United for Peace and Justice Umbrella Organization is founded.
October 26, 2002		First antiwar protests with transnational traits, in United States and Europe. Set up by ANSWER Coalition.
November 7–10, 2002		European Social Forum in Florence. Official antiwar call issued. First major European antiwar demonstration.
November 8, 2002	UN Security Council unanimously approves Resolution 1441.	
November 16, 2002	First armed skirmishes between U.S. and UK and Iraqi troops. First civilian casualties.	
December 7, 2002	Iraq delivers 13,000-page document on weapon arsenal.	

Date	Politics timeline	Protest timeline
December 15, 2002		European Social Forum interim meeting in Copenhagen. Antiwar call reissued. Foundation of Platform against War on Iraq.
January 18, 2003		Second ANSWER Coalition U.S. protests coincide with small protests in Europe.
January 23–27, 2003		World Social Forum in Porto Allegre. Special workshop for planning February 15 protests.
January 27, 2003	Chief UN inspector Blix demands more Iraqi cooperation	
January 30, 2003	Joint statement by eight European country leaders to support war.	
February 5, 2003	U.S. secretary of state Powell presents evidence of Iraqi arsenal of weapons of mass destruction to UN Security Council.	
February 10, 2003	Belgium, France, and Germany make firm NATO stance against war.	
February 14, 2003	Blix mentions positive attitude by Iraq and says Iraq can be disarmed within months.	
February 15, 2003		Ten to fifteen million take to the streets against an imminent war in Iraq, in the largest worldwide coordinated protest event in history.
February 24, 2003	United States and United Kingdom apply for new UN resolution to justify attack of Iraq.	
March 5, 2003	Antiwar statement by Germany and Russia.	
March 7, 2003	United States, United Kingdom, and Spain give Iraq ultimatum: March 17.	
March 18, 2003	Iraq rejects ultimatum.	
March 20, 2003	Start of United States-led invasion of Iraq.	

Figure 1.1. Political and protest timeline leading to February 15 and the Iraq War

UN Security Council started debating a new Iraqi resolution. They agreed on the fact that Iraq had undertaken "obvious," "severe," "flagrant," and "unacceptable" violations of the previous Gulf War–ending resolution on the national disarmament of weapons of mass destruction (Wouters and Naert 2003). The UN Security Council demanded the Iraqi government give the UN weapon inspectors free rein so they could provide an "actual, accurate and exhaustive" list of all available weapons of mass destruction, and to immediately remove all of these from Iraq. If Iraq did not acquiesce, it would have to face "serious consequences resulting from its ongoing violations" (ibid.). At the explicit request of China, Russia, and France, three permanent members of the UN Security Council, this phrase "serious consequences" replaced the provision the United States had proposed earlier, in which the nation proclaimed that it would use military force if Iraq violated any of the UN demands. Still concerned that this more moderate expression could clear the way for unilateral American invasion of Iraq, the three countries were very explicit: the resolution was by no means an authorization to use violence in any cases of new violations; rather, in such cases, the UN Security Council would immediately assemble to discuss further measures. After eleven days of deliberation, UN Resolution 1441 was unanimously approved on November 8, 2002. Iraq accepted it within five days, and five days later the first inspectors set foot on Iraqi soil. In the shadow of these official measures, the first armed skirmishes were already taking place between the U.S.-UK and Iraqi troops.

On December 7, 2002, in response to the UN resolution deadline, the Iraqi government delivered a thirteen-thousand-page document on its weapons arsenal. Late in January 2003, chief UN weapons inspector Hans Blix declared before the Security Council that the Iraqi cooperation could be augmented. On January 30, the leaders of eight European countries issued a war-supporting statement to newspapers around the world:

> The Iraqi regime and its weapons of mass destruction represent a clear threat to world security. This danger has been explicitly recognised by the U.N. All of us are bound by Security Council Resolution 1441, which was adopted unanimously. . . . In doing so, we sent a clear, firm and unequivocal message that we would rid the world of the danger posed by Saddam Hussein's weapons of mass destruction. We must remain united in insisting that his regime be disarmed. . . . The combination of weapons of mass destruction and terrorism is a threat of incalculable consequences. It is one at which all of us should feel concerned. Resolution 1441 is Saddam Hussein's last chance to disarm using peaceful means.

The eight countries justified their cooperation and urged others to join them, referring to shared values proper to all countries in the Western world; shared fears and threats, based on the September 11 terrorist attacks; an historic debt toward the United States that has liberated the world from communism and Nazism; the fear for weapons of mass destruction, and the international justification of an attack on Iraq through the UN Security council.

Six days later, on February 5, 2003, U.S. secretary of state Colin Powell presented new alleged evidence to the UN Security Council about Iraq's disposal of weapons of mass destruction and of the link between Iraq and al-Qaeda. Five days after this speech, France and Belgium, with Germany's support, ratified their antiwar stance by using their NATO veto against what they considered the premature protection of Turkey. The alliance expected that Turkey would become involved in the war if Iraq was attacked and wanted to start preparing for this. France and Belgium, though, believed a diplomatic solution was still possible for the Iraq crisis and, according to Belgian minister of foreign affairs Louis Michel, complying with a NATO decision to prepare for war in Turkey would make them "get stuck in war logic, and the message will be given that it is too late for diplomatic initiatives" (Beirlant 2003). France, Belgium, and Germany wanted to at least await the new weapon inspectors' report to be presented in the UN Security Council on Friday, February 14. This day, on the eve of the February 15 protests, Hans Blix presented a much more mixed evaluation than he had previously, stating that Iraq had undertaken several positive cooperative steps and that a total disarmament of weapons of mass destruction would be possible within a few months.

In spite of the increasing Iraqi cooperation and in the face of the immense popular protest around the globe on February 15, governments from the United States, the United Kingdom, and Spain handed in a new motion for resolution in the UN Security Council on February 24, arguing that Iraq had not seized its final opportunity for disarmament and that military confrontation was needed and justified. However, China, France, and Russia did not support the new resolution, and the latter two countries were even prepared to veto it. The resolution could not get approval without a two-thirds majority, for which none of the five permanent members could have used its veto. But the war machinery was already in motion. The United States set up a search for a "moral majority": when nine of the fifteen Security Council members supported the proposal, it would be backed by a broad consensus within the Council, thus morally justifying war. Once again, the United States and its allies were turned down, leading the United States to abandon the path of a new UN resolution. On March 17, the United States,

Spain, and the United Kingdom agreed that Resolution 1441 provided sufficient justification for an armed intervention. On March 20, 2003, supported by the "Coalition of the Willing" the United States made the starting shot for the attack on Iraq.[1]

Peace Talk: Organizing against War in Iraq

By the time war was becoming unavoidable, peace activists and organizations started joining their forces to set up large, worldwide mobilizations. The enormous success of these actions would surprise not only commentators and politicians but, in no small amount, the activists and organizers themselves:

> It was clear by this time [late January 2003] that our movement had steadily gained momentum. Despite our successes however, of which we were all extremely proud, not even the most optimistic activists were prepared for what we saw on February 15. It was a day that we will never forget. In a worldwide show of unity and solidarity with the Iraqi people, we took to the streets in the millions, demanding an end to the Bush administration's war plans . . . that this administration is hell-bent for a war. The build-up in the Gulf during these days of demonstrations has been unceasing. I still expect that war to come, and soon. Nonetheless, I find myself amazed by the variegated mass of humanity that turned out yesterday. It felt wonderful. A mass truly, but each part of it, each individually made sign and human gesture of it, spoke to its deeply spontaneous nature. (Engelhardt 2003)

The gradual buildup toward an Iraq war was paralleled by growing antiwar sentiments in all parts of the world and by a gradual organization of and mobilization for protest against the idea of an upcoming war. Throughout the entire inception of war, dissident voices were heard. One might ask how these protests fit in the war race. Bearing in mind the astonishment of politicians, commentators, and organizers about the scale of the protests, the key question is: Where did these protests come from, and how were they set up?

Following an initial agreement made in a preparatory meeting in Barcelona in early October 2002, the idea to set up an international day of demonstrations against an impending war was first publicly voiced at the first European Social Forum in Florence, Italy, in November 2002. As this was a European meeting, the idea originally remained confined to Europe. In Florence, approximately forty thousand individuals and some six hundred organizations were present: trade unions as well as environmental, global justice, and peace organizations, among others. The forum was a four-day event set up for the "democratic debate of ideas, formulation of proposals, free exchange of experiences, and planning of effective action among entities and movements of civil society that are engaged in building a planetary society centered on the human being" (Simonson 2003). The Florence European Social Forum issued a joint antiwar call to "all citizens of Europe" to "start organizing enormous anti-war demonstrations in every capital on February 15."

Anti-war call

To all citizens of Europe

Together we can stop this war! We, the European social movements are fighting for social rights and social justice, for democracy and against all forms of oppression.

We stand for a world of diversity, freedom and mutual respect.

We believe this war, whether it has UN backing or not, will be a catastrophe for the people of Iraq—already suffering because of the embargo and the Saddam Hussein regime—and for people across the Middle East. It should be opposed by everyone who believes in democratic, political solutions to international conflicts because it will be a war with the potential to lead to global disaster.

There is a massive opposition to war in every country of Europe. Hundreds of thousands have already mobilized for peace.

We call on the movements and citizens of Europe to start continent-wide resistance to war, and

1. organising massive opposition to an attack on Iraq starting now
2. if war starts, to protest and organise actions immediately and call for national demonstrations the next Saturday
3. to start organising enormous anti-war demonstrations in every capital on February 15.

We can stop this war (European Social Forum 2002a)

The forum not only launched a call for future demonstrations, it also staged one of the first large antiwar demonstrations. On November 9, 2002, in the heart of Florence, between five hundred thousand and 1 million people (according to police estimates) took to the streets to oppose war (Simonson 2003). This was the first large European protest against war on Iraq and a significant precursor of what would follow. Chris Nineham from the UK Stop the War Coalition said of the European Social Forum and its antiwar position:

At the last preparatory meeting in Barcelona, we agreed that the main slogan of the demonstration in Florence would be "Don't Attack Iraq" and that the meeting would issue a call for cross-continent anti-war action. These were controversial decisions. They risked putting the forum on collision course with governments and social democrat organizations across Europe. But they were decisively correct. When word got out that the demonstration at Florence would focus on stopping the war, the European Social Forum became a magnet to activists. 1,300 people signed up to come from Barcelona alone in the three weeks before the forum. People were deeply relieved that such a mainstream project conceived on such a grand scale was to take a principle stand on the big issue. It was a stand that had eluded most politicians, and it showed that the European Social Forum was going to be something different, something honest, something that would make a difference. (Nineham 2002)

But the European Social Forum was not the first to set up internationally coordinated protests against war: between the Barcelona preparatory meeting and the Florence Social Forum, on October 26, 2002, the first internationally coinciding protests against an eventual war took place. These were the initial signs of the transnational efforts made by the antiwar campaign. Large manifestations in the United States with some two hundred thousand people hitting the streets were paralleled by more modest protests in Europe: twenty thousand in Berlin, ten thousand in Amsterdam, thirty thousand in Madrid. This first protest wave was coordinated by the U.S.-based International ANSWER (Act Now to Stop War and End Racism) Coalition, rooted in the left-wing Workers World Party (Cortright 2004, 5). ANSWER unites a broad spectrum of players in civil society, "including traditional peace groups, students, global justice and anti-racist activists, and mainstream labor, environmental, civil rights and women's organizations" (Simonson 2003, 7). Meanwhile, other organizations in the United States had also started discussing the coordination of future events. A new umbrella organization, United for Peace and Justice, was formed to take up the coordination role. It was established before the October 26, 2002, protests and consisted of more than fifty organizations: traditional peace organizations; Internet-based political action groups (e.g., MoveOn.org); global justice groups (e.g., Global Exchange) and major constituency organizations (e.g., National Organization for Women) (Cortright 2004, 14). This new umbrella organization would become the moderate pillar of the U.S. peace movement, and the catalyst for the February 15 protests on U.S. soil.

In Europe, one month after the European Social Forum in Florence, an interim preparatory meeting took place in Copenhagen in December 2002. Present were delegates from peace movements from all over Europe: Denmark, Greece, Macedonia, France, the United Kingdom, Germany, Sweden, Norway, Belgium, Italy, and Switzerland. These were joined by a delegation from the Philippine peace movement and one from the U.S. network United for Peace and Justice. In retrospect, it's clear that this is where the first steps toward the future transatlantic cooperation were made (Brabander 2004). Here, the original antiwar call was further elaborated, and a platform against war on Iraq was founded.

Platform against war on Iraq

Statement of the meeting to coordinate European-wide action against war on Iraq

As agreed at the assembly of the social movements in Florence in November, activists from 11 European countries, the USA and the Philippines have come together in Copenhagen to coordinate European-wide action against war on Iraq.

We endorse the anti-war call launched at the assembly in Florence. We believe that a war on Iraq, with or without UN support, would be a disaster for the people of the Middle East and beyond.

It is clear there is majority opposition to war in almost every country in Europe and across the world. That is why this war cannot be fought in our name. This is also why we believe it is vital to build the broadest possible anti-war alliances everywhere around the demand No War on Iraq.

Our meeting showed that the movement against the war is gaining strength.

All the countries represented have called action on 15 February.

We reinforce the decision to protest in every country immediately after war starts, to hold national protests the following Saturday and to organize coordinated mass national demonstrations in capital cities on February 15.

To this end we have decided to continue our coordination at a European level, to set up a European-wide anti-war website, and to have a common banner on each of our demonstrations demanding No War on Iraq. We are committed to spreading anti-war coordination both inside and beyond Europe, and to holding another enlarged meeting after the February 15 demo. We will continue to campaign until this war is stopped.

We urge the movements in countries not represented at our meeting to join in our initiatives. We urge every organization that opposes this war to work for a massive mobilization on February 15. Together we can stop the war. (European Social Forum 2002b)

Subsequent to the Copenhagen meeting, an intensive e-mail network was set up, connecting all European peace movements. The Europe-wide antiwar Web site that the Copenhagen text refers to did not get off the ground; instead all national umbrella organizations and coalitions set up their own sites, but they linked to one another and to one of the above-mentioned U.S. organizations listing all worldwide demonstrations, and/or to the UK Stop the War Coalition. The idea of a common banner was a success: all over Europe as well as the rest of the world, the same "Stop the War" logo would be used (albeit in different colors and different styles) on movements' communication outlets, websites, demonstration leaflets, and banners.

On January 18, 2003, a second wave of transnational protests took place, its center again in the United States. These demonstrations were for the second time set up by the ANSWER Coalition, and they coincided with the birthday of Martin Luther King Jr., who had been murdered thirty-five years earlier. In Washington, D.C., half a million protesters marched; in San Francisco a hundred and fifty thousand took the streets. Smaller protests were organized in Belgium, the United Kingdom, Spain, Italy, the Netherlands, Germany, and many other countries around the world (Simonson 2003).

Between January 23 and 27, 2003, the European Social Forum antiwar call was further disseminated on the third World Social Forum in Porto Allegre, Brazil. The World Social Forum Secretariat had set up a workshop exclusively devoted to planning the February 15 international day of protest. With some five thousand organizations present from every corner of the globe, the call was spread throughout the world. The ANSWER Coalition was present as well. It, along with two other U.S. antiwar coalitions—Win without War and Not in My Name—would strongly support the February 15 event but would leave the role of main U.S. organizer to United for Peace and Justice, as the latter group had attended the Copenhagen meeting. This was not surprising, since organizing the February 15 actions did not begin until mid-January, and turnout still was unpredictable.

February 15, 2003, was the first time in peace movement history that so many organizations from all corners of the world joined forces on a single action day. Earlier attempts by the peace movement to merge in a transatlantic effort, more specifically in the struggle for nuclear disarmament in the 1980s and 1990s, had failed, "partly because of the external constraints and opportunities defined by different national political debates and contexts, . . . and important differences between the U.S. and European peace groups" (Cortright and Pagnucco 1997, 159).

The February 15 mobilizations benefited from two relatively new and entwined mechanisms, the dynamics of the social fora and the use of worldwide electronic communication technologies. The European and World Social Forums and the different respective preparatory meetings were the main driving forces of the transnational coordination and mobilization. World-wide, national peace organizations, increasingly alarmed by both the 9/11 terrorist attacks and the aggressive reaction on part of the U.S. government, had since early 2002 all been active on a national level against the invasion of Afghanistan and the idea of war with Iraq. These national organizations now had the opportunity to meet each other at the different social forums intrinsically linked with the transnational global justice movement. These forums served as the operating base for the setup of February 15. Various organizations belonging to the global justice movements started their own (trans)national mobilizing campaigns and used these different occasions to update each other on their national efforts as well as strengthen bonds with their colleagues from other countries.

These important face-to-face meetings were complemented by a second major mechanism favoring the massiveness of the February 15 protests, namely the intensive use of the Internet and e-mail circuits. All national peace movements and coalitions were linked to each other by joint mailing lists and cross-referencing each other on the Web. On an international scale, the exact same thing took place, allowing the different movements to act very fast. In some countries, like the United States and Belgium, the effective mobilization efforts actually got off the ground only by mid-January and reached full force only after February 5, when Colin Powell presented the alleged U.S. evidence of Iraq's possession of weapons of mass destruction (Brabander 2004). Through these new channels, established lines of movement interactions and diffusion were supplemented with new ties, such as brokerage (Tarrow and McAdam 2003). The mechanisms of diffusion and brokerage made it possible to agree on one international day of protest, using the same slogans and banners and thus uniting all the people in the different streets into one global protest. That the transnational character of the protests was clear *before* the protests took place might have been appealing for the mobilizing campaign and might have functioned as a self-fulfilling prophecy, mobilizing people who wanted to take part in this global day of peace action.

Action: February 15, 2003, the World Moving for Peace

As you watch the TV pictures of the march, ponder this: if there are five hundred thousand on that march, that is still less than the number of people whose deaths Saddam has been responsible for. If there are one million, that is still less than the number of people who died in the wars he started.

The February 15 protests were remarkable for their size. Although many observers, scholars, and politicians intuitively regarded them as an isolated event coming out of the blue, we can now state that this was not the case at all. In the months preceding February 15, many other events were staged to challenge the prospect of war, and many efforts were undertaken to prepare this impressive transnational manifestation. Beside their overall magnitude, the February 15 mobilizations varied across countries. Several cities were flooded by an unseen mass of protesters, whereas other protests were rather modest and not exceptional at all. Let us take a look at the mobilization levels in different countries and, in particular, at the turnout in the eight countries under study here.

Table 1.1 shows February 15 mobilizations in different countries; listed are the national organizing groups and coalitions, turnouts, and the national mobilization levels as compared to the national populations. The list is far from complete: some accounts claim that mobilizations took place in six hundred cities, from the Danish city of Aalborg to the Spanish Zaragoza. This is only a non-exhaustive list of the largest demonstrations in some selected countries, to put the protests in the eight countries studied in this book into perspective. Many smaller and more local marches are not represented in the table, which could pose a problem in the interpretation of the U.S. turnout number, since there were activities in almost all U.S. states.[2]

Taking a close look at the turnout numbers, one is immediately struck by the differences. In Italy, for example, an incredible one in twenty citizens took to the streets—ten times more than in the Netherlands. Here are but a few examples of variation in turnouts.

The highest mobilization levels were found in Spain and Italy, where one in seventeen and one in twenty inhabitants joined the February 15 protests, setting participation records. In fact, the demonstration in Barcelona has been chronicled in the Guinness Book of World Records as the largest antiwar rally in human history (Guinness Book of World Records 2004). These countries' governments were the most conspicuously in favor of the war in continental Europe.

Italy and Spain are followed by Australia and Ireland: in both of these countries, about one in forty people took to the streets. In Australia, the protest could be considered an event against the official national support for war. In Dublin, this was not at all the case: since the Irish government did not endorse war without UN backing, the Irish protest can be seen as an expression of disapproval of the position of the British government as well as a statement of support of Ireland's government. Closing the top five ranking is the United Kingdom, where 1.7 percent of the population was displaying its disapproval of war. Other massive protests occurred in Greece (1.2 percent), which did not officially support war and even had organized a summit to reconcile the differences of opinion among the European states. Portugal, which officially supported the war and Norway, which opposed it, attained mobilization levels of 1 percent and 1.3 percent.

In many countries, the February 15 protests reached unprecedented proportions when compared to previous protests. Yet in others, previous record levels were not met. In Belgium, for example, seventy thousand took to the streets, versus the roughly three hundred thousand in 1983 that had protested the placing of the cruise and Pershing II missiles. In the Netherlands, the difference was even larger: on February 15, about 0.4 percent of the population took to the streets; the number had been ten times greater in 1983. In Germany, half a million protesters showed up, where there had been twice as many, in several protests combined, in 1983 (Rochon 1988, 5–7). The relatively low turnouts in Belgium and Germany, is not surprising, since the government opposed an imminent war and, thus, the stakes involved were lower. In the Netherlands, the official government position was pro-war, but the government was resigning at the time of the protests. The overall relatively small numbers in the United States are probably mainly due to the rally-around-the-flag effect. Many troops were already encamped in the Gulf, which led many Americans to place support for their own troops above their disapproval of war. Also, several marches in the United States, like the one in New York City, did not have approval of city officials, rendering them less legitimate than others and possibly dangerous.

The February protests will also be remembered for their truly transnational character. In spite of all the differences among them on the national level, it is beyond doubt that, taken altogether, they were exceptional: never before had such a large-scale, global, carefully planned and coordinated day of action taken place. It is this worldwide coordination that truly shows the uniqueness of the event and distinguishes it from other worldwide simultaneous mobilizations around one unanimous theme—for example, the annually recurring worldwide May 1 demonstrations and the International Women's Day events (March 8).

To conclude, the February 15 protests were unquestionably unique. They were exceptional for their size, shared themes and shared timing, and similar action repertoires.[3] They were, in the eyes of many, the foretelling of a new superpower. Jürgen Habermas and Jacques Derrida (2003) declared that the February 15 demonstrations would "go into history books as a signal for the birth of a European Public." But what about their participants? Were they the same protesters in different countries? Or did country-specific opportunity structures, societal contexts and/or historical strengths, and peace-movement development cause national differences regarding who took to which streets? In other words: did these protests that shared so many

Table 1.1. February 15 Protests: Country, city, organizers, turnouts and mobilization level

Country	City	Organizers[a]	Turnout numbers	Country population (millions)	Turnout (percentage of population)
Australia	Five state capitals		300,000	19.7	2.5
	Sidney		200,000		
Austria	Vienna		25,000	8.2	0.3
Belgium	Brussels	Anti Oorlogsplatform Irak and Stop USA	75,000	10.3	0.7
Canada	Toronto		[b]±50,000	32.2	0.4
	Montreal		100,000		
Denmark	Copenhagen		45,000	5.4	0.8
Finland	Helsinki		15,000	5.2	0.2
France	Paris		±350,000	60.2	0.5
Germany	Berlin	Netzwerk Friedenskooperation	500,000	82.4	0.7
	Stuttgart		50,000		
Greece	Athens		200,000	10.6	1.2
Hungary	Budapest		20,000	10.1	0.2
Ireland	Dublin		100,000	3.9	2.6
Italy	Rome	Fermiamo la Guerra all'Iraq	3,000,000	58.0	5
Japan	Tokyo		25,000	127.2	0.02
Netherlands	Amsterdam	Platform tegen de Nieuwe Oorlog	70,000	16.2	0.4
Norway	Oslo		60,000	4.6	1.3
Poland	Warsaw		10,000	38.6	0.03

Table 1.1. (continued)

Country	City	Organizers[c]	Turnout numbers	Country population (millions)	Turnout (percentage of population)
Portugal	Lisbon		100,000	10.5	1.0
Spain	Madrid	No a la Guerra	800,000	40.2	5.7
	Barcelona	No a la Guerra	1,300,000		
	Seville	No a la Guerra	200,000		
Sweden	Stockholm		±40,000	9.0	0.7
	Gothenburg		25,000		
Switzerland	Bern	Pas en Notre Nom	45,000	7.4	0.6
United Kingdom	London	Stop the War Coalition	1,000,000	60.1	1.7
	Glasgow	Scottish Coalition for Justice not War	50,000		
United States	Seattle	United for Peace and Justice	50,000	290.4	0.8
	New York	United for Peace and Justice	500,000		
	Los Angeles	United for Peace and Justice	200,000		
	San Francisco		250,000		
	Rest of United States		1,500,000		

Notes: [a]Organizers given for eight covered countries only.

[b]Numbers with a "±" symbol are average estimates between strongly diverging measurements.

characteristics mobilize the same people in all countries? These are the core questions of this entire volume.

Notes

1. This "coalition of the willing," whose members were willing to actively or passively support the forcible removal of the Iraqi regime, included Afghanistan, Albania, Angola, Australia, Azerbaijan, Bulgaria, Colombia, Costa Rica, the Czech Republic, Denmark, the Dominican Republic, El Salvador, Eritrea, Estonia, Ethiopia, Georgia, Honduras, Hungary, Iceland, Italy, Japan, Kuwait, Latvia, Lithuania, the Republic of Macedonia, the Marshall Islands, Micronesia, Mongolia, the Netherlands, Nicaragua, Palau, Panama, the Philippines, Poland, Portugal, Romania, Rwanda, Singapore, Slovakia, the Solomon Islands, South Korea, Spain, Tonga, Turkey, Uganda, the Ukraine, the United Kingdom, the United States, and Uzbekistan. According to a White House press release of March 21, 2003, "contributions from Coalition member nations range from: direct military participation, logistical and intelligence support, specialized chemical/biological response teams, over-flight rights, humanitarian and reconstruction aid, to political support." To further support its case, the White House also stated: "The population of Coalition countries is approximately 1.23 billion people; Coalition countries have a combined GDP of approximately $22 trillion; Every major race, religion, ethnicity in the world is represented; The Coalition includes nations from every continent on the globe" (White House, 2003).

2. For a comprehensive list of participating cities, see Chrisafis et al. 2003, Simonson 2003, Cortright 2004, and many newspaper accounts. In cases where different numbers are ascribed to the same demonstration, the most recurring, the most official, or the median number is taken.

3. Since 2003, antiwar protests have been organized worldwide each year around March 20, the date of the invasion of Iraq. Yet, as of this publication, turnout numbers have only been a fraction of those recorded on February 15, 2003.

Works Cited

Beirlant, Bart. 2003. "Brussel en Parijs blokkeren Navo-beslissing in Irak." *De Standaard,* February 12.

Brabander, Ludo de. 2004. Interview by Joris Verhulst, January, Brussels.

Bush, George. 2002. State of the Union address. January 29, Washington D.C.

Chrisafis, Angelique, David Fickling, John Henley, John Hooper, Giles Tremlett, Sophie Arie, and Chris McGreal. 2003. "Millions Worldwide Rally for Peace: Huge Turnout at Six Hundred Marches from Berlin to Baghdad." *Guardian,* February 17, 2003. http://www.guardian.co.uk/world/2003/feb/17/politics.

Cortright, David. 2004. *A Peaceful Superpower. The Movement against War in Iraq.* Goshen, Ind.: Fourth Freedom Forum.

Cortright, David, and Ron Pagnucco. 1997. "Limits to Transnationalism: The 1980s Freeze Campaign." In *Transnational Social Movements and Global Politics—Solidarity Beyond the State*, ed. Jackie Smith, Charles Chatfield, and Ron Pagnucco, 159–74. Syracuse, N.Y.: Syracuse University Press.

Engelhardt, Tom. 2003. "The March That Wasn't to Be." *TomDispatch*, February 16. http://www.tomdispatch.compost/410/the_march_that_wasn_t_to_be.

Epstein, Barbara. 2003. "Notes on the Antiwar Movement." *Monthly Review* 55: 109–16

European Social Forum. 2002a. "Anti-War Call." November 12. European Social Forum, Florence.

———. 2002b. "Platform against War on Iraq: Statement of the Meeting to Coordinate European-Wide Action against War on Iraq." December 15. European Social Forum, Copenhagen.

Guinness Book of World Records. 2004. "Largest Anti-War Rally." http://www.guinnessworldrecords.com/contentpages/record.asp?records id =54365.

Habermas, Jürgen, and Jacques Derrida. 2003. "Nach dem Krieg: Die Wiedergeburt Europas." *Frankfurter Allgemeine Zeitung*, May 31, 33–34.

Nineham, Chris. 2002. "The European Social Forum in Florence: Lessons of Success." *Znet*. December 12. http://www.zmag.org/content/showarticle.cfm?SectionID=1&ItemID=2758.

Rochon, Thomas R. 1988. *Mobilising for Peace: The Antinuclear Movements in Western Europe*. London: Adamantine.

Simonson, Karin. 2003. "The Anti-War Movement: Waging Peace on the Brink of War." Paper prepared for the Programme on NGOs and Civil Society, Centre for Applied Studies in International Negotiation, Geneva.

Tarrow, Sidney, and Doug McAdam. 2003. "Scale Shift in Transnational Contention." Paper presented at the conference on Transnational Processes and Social Movements. Bellagio, Italy. July 22–26.

Tyler, Patrick E. 2003. "Threats and Responses: News Analysis. A New Power in the Streets." *New York Times*, February 16, 2003. http://www.nytimes.com/2003/02/17/world/threats-and-responses-news-analysis-a-new-power-in-the-streets.html?pagewanted=1.

U.S. Congress. 1998. Public Law 105–388, An Act to Establish a Program to Support a Transition to Democracy in Iraq, October 31. http://news.findlaw.com/hdocs/docs/iraq/libact 103198.pdf.

White House. 2003. "Coalition Members." Press release. http://www.whitehouse.govnews/releases/ 2003/03/20030327–10.html.

Wouters, Jan, and Frederik Naert. 2003. "De oorlog tegen Irak schendt het Internationaal recht." *De Financieel-Economische Tijd*, March 22. https://www.law.kuleuven.be/iir/nl/onderzoek/opinies/FNJWirakFET.pdf.

2

Political Opportunity Structures and Progressive Movement Sectors

Michelle Beyeler and Dieter Rucht

It is widely argued that social movements are influenced by stable structural features of the political systems in which they are embedded. This is our starting point. We are interested in these nation-specific structures that, via a set of intermediary variables, ultimately may have an impact on the size, forms, and other properties of the antiwar protests that are at the center of this book. While it may be impossible to find a direct link between general political structures and specific protest incidents, we can at best explore a potential causal bridge between these general political structures and the structures of a large social movement sector or even specific kinds of movements. These, in turn, are expected to influence issue-specific protest campaigns or protest events. In this chapter, we shed light on structural features of political systems and their possible influence on social movement sectors in the eight countries under study.

The structural context of specific protests can be conceptualized at two levels. First, every protest is a manifestation of an extended mobilization structure that, in the case of antiwar protests, has developed over a long period. Such a mobilization structure encompasses two layers, that of the directly involved movement and that of a set of affinity movements. The directly involved movement, commonly referred to as the peace movement, is not at the center of this chapter (but see chapter 4). Rather, here we will focus on the broader set of movements (of which the peace movement is only one element), which are sympathetic to and potentially supportive of the cause of peace. Typically, large antiwar protests recruit from a cluster of movements and, to some extent, even attract people who are not affiliated with any social movement network but share the core protesters' worldviews and values. Such a cluster of movements can be referred to as a social movement family (della Porta and Rucht 1995, 230). Peace movements, notably in the societies we are investigating, draw on a mobilization potential whose core for the most part consists of progressive and leftist groups. Accordingly, one element we are interested in is the size and character of the progressive left in the countries under study, hereafter labeled the "progressive movement sector."

This movement sector, in turn, is influenced by general political structures, the second level of the structural context of the antiwar protests. Even in this era of internationalization and globalization, social movements and their activities are still profoundly marked by nation-specific factors, such as a regime type. We will turn first to the description of the nation-specific political context and then to the corresponding movement sectors in an attempt to explore the question of how the former might influence the progressive movement sector.

Political Structures as a Context for Protest Activities

The activities of protest groups and social movements are influenced in several ways by a number of environmental factors, among which, for good reasons, so-called political opportunity structures have by far attracted the most attention (Tarrow 1983; 1998; Kitschelt 1986; Kriesi 1995; 2004). The concept of political opportunity structures is not undisputed. Some scholars criticize it on more principal grounds (Goodwin and Jasper 1999); others acknowledge its value but emphasize additional dimensions beyond those included in it (Goldstone 2004). Yet most scholars agree that this concept comprises a set of factors that potentially and actually shape movement activity. Among these are formal institutional structures, informal procedures in relation to a given challenge, and the configuration of power as regards a given challenger (Kriesi 1995), or, according to McAdam's comprehensive account: "1. the relative openness or closure of the institutionalized political system, 2. the stability or instability of that wide set of elite alignments that typically undergird a polity, 3. the presence or absence of elite allies, 4. the state's capacity and propensity for repression" (1996, 27).

The concept of political opportunity structures was mainly used as a set of independent variables at the national level to explain, commonly in a cross-national comparative perspective, general features of social movements, for example, the movements' strengths or prevailing strategies.[1] Over time, the concept has been refined and amplified. For instance, dimensions beyond those of the political opportunity structure have been considered: Brand (1985) has pointed to the importance of deeply rooted societal cleavages,

Rucht (1996) has suggested a more encompassing concept of a societal context structure, and Koopmans and Statham (2000) and Ferree et al. (2002) have stressed the importance of discursive opportunities as independent factors shaping movement activity. Several social movement scholars have emphasized the role of both movement-specific and situational factors (Gamson and Meyer 1996; Rucht 1998; see also chapter 3), while still others have proposed the idea of transnational opportunities that, at least for certain kinds of movements, come into play (Marks and McAdam 1999). The range of dependent variables has also been extended, including both strength and strategy as well as outcomes of social movements (Kitschelt 1986; Rucht 1999; Kolb 2007). Given this extension of the concept, it is not surprising that this trend of concept stretching has raised critical comments on the part of some observers, pointing to the "danger of becoming a sponge that soaks up virtually every aspect of the social movement environment—political institutions and culture, crisis of various sorts, political alliances, and policy shifts" (Gamson and Meyer 1996, 275). Whatever the limits and flaws of the political opportunity structure concept may be—all assumptions derived from it remain at the macro level of general movement structures and refer neither to individuals engaged in protest activities nor to specific protest events.

Because we are mainly interested in cross-national differences of movement sectors as a background for specific antiwar protests that predominantly had a nationwide recruitment base, neither the subnational nor the transnational background is relevant. Accordingly, we concentrate on national structures. Second, we deliberately focus on political opportunities, which, with regard to the progressive movement sector in general and the peace movement in particular, are crucial. After all, engaging in armament or warfare is primarily a political matter of which governments and/or parliaments are the decision-making bodies. Accordingly, antiwar movements are genuine political movements, as opposed to other kinds, which are more oriented toward social or cultural issues.

Drawing basically on versions of the classical political opportunity structure approach, we will discuss two crucial dimensions in the eight countries under study: formal access to the decision-making system and the configuration of the left-wing power structures, that is, the strength of its parties and trade unions in particular. We believe that it is useful to take a closer look at the institutional context in which social movement sectors develop and particular protests, such as those of February 15, occur. The description of these contexts will contribute to a better understanding of the similarities and differences of the protests exposed in the main sections of this volume.

Formal Access to the Decision-Making System

Social movement scholars have rarely attempted to operationalize political opportunity structures for more than three or four countries (but see Kolb 2007). Once we aim at comparing a larger set of cases, we have to turn to highly aggregated indicators that only hint at the relative positions of the different systems. Kriesi (2004, 71) suggests summarizing the degree of institutional accessibility of the political system by drawing on Lijphart's (1999) distinction between majoritarian and consensus democracies. This concept of comparison estimates the degree to which power is centralized (as in majoritarian democracies) or dispersed among different actors or institutions (as in consensus democracies). Centralization of power has consequences for all political actors, including protest groups. In political systems where the locus of power is highly centralized and political parties are very strong, the ruling party or party coalition has much discretion when it comes to making decisions. In such systems, the role of oppositional political parties, dissenting interest groups, and challenger movements is to raise their voices in opposition to the government's plans or decisions. However, these oppositional voices are irrelevant unless they entail a reasonable likelihood of making a difference in future elections. Such systems can be classified as "closed." By contrast, we count systems as "open" when governments are composed of large party coalitions and/or many parties exist, when power is decentralized because of a strong federalist structure and when oppositional political parties and dissenting interest groups rely on directly influencing the policy-making process, for example, via referenda or appeals to courts.

Lijphart also includes corporatism into his concept of consensus democracy. Corporatism, however, has a differential effect on various types of societal groups. While providing access points for few and preferably hierarchically structured societal actors (mainly the top representatives of capital and labor), corporatism excludes a wide range of other actors who have little or no voice in political decision-making. Due to these inconsistent effects on social movements (of which trade unions can be part), we exclude corporatism from our estimate of openness and closedness of the political system. Instead, we focus on four items that, in summary, will provide us with a rough idea about the degree of openness or closedness of the decision-making systems in the eight countries, namely the number of effective parties in parliament, an index of federalism, an index of judicial review (all indexes taken from Lijphart 1999, 312–13, based on the period from 1972 to 1996),[2] and an index on the use of nationwide referenda. This latter variable has been inspired by Huber, Ragin, and Stephens (1997). We used a scale from 1 (never) to 5 (frequent).

Table 2.1 depicts the range of the respective countries in accordance with these criteria. The last column presents a simple additive index of the four variables.[3]

According to the additive index displayed in the far-right column, Great Britain stands out as the most closed political system or, using another terminology, the country where power is centralized the most. Only two major parties, each with a high degree of party discipline, are able to win national elections. Together with the few channels of access to the decision-making system, this creates a high degree of independence from the general public and special interest groups on part the of the officeholders. On the other end of the spectrum, Switzerland, for a variety of reasons, can be considered a prototype of a very open polity. A weak central government; a fragmented party system, with only loosely integrated national parties; a non-professional parliament; and low partisan discipline in parliamentary votes foster a political system very responsive to interest groups and social movements.

Within these two extremes, the other countries in our sample take intermediary positions, with the United States and Germany tending more toward the open pole and the Netherlands and Spain toward the closed. The political systems of the remaining countries tend to be very closed for actors beyond the political parties or (corporatist) interest groups. In these countries, the parties clearly dominate the decision-making processes. With regard to economic and social policies, strong economic interest groups are webbed into the decision-making process through either corporatist or informal arrangements, sometimes even clientelistic ones.

What does this mean for the social movement sector? The more sophisticated literature on political opportunity structures has postulated a curvilinear relationship between the degree of openness/closedness of the political

Table 2.1. Variation in the openness of political systems

	Federalism[a]	Number of effective parties[a]	Index of judicial review[a]	Frequent national referenda[b]	Additive index
United States	5	2.4	4	2	13.4
United Kingdom	1	2.2	1	1	5.2
Spain	3	2.8	3	1	9.8
Italy	1.5	5.2	3	2	11.7
Netherlands	3	4.7	1	1	9.7
Switzerland	5	5.6	1	5	16.6
Belgium	3.2	5.5	2	1	11.7
Germany	5	2.8	4	1	12.8

Note: [a]Indexes taken from Lijphart (1999, 312–13), based on the period from 1972 to 1996.
[b]Inspired by Huber, Ragin, and Stephens (1997).

system and the strength of the movement sector (Eisinger 1973, 28; Meyer 2004). Accordingly, we expected the strongest movement sectors in the countries ranging in the middle ground. As a corollary, weaker movement sectors were expected in both Switzerland (very open), and Great Britain (very closed). The comparative work of Kriesi et al. (1995) suggests that movement mobilization was indeed weaker in Switzerland than in France and the Netherlands from 1975 to 1989. The argument on curvilinearity would lead us to expect strong protests in Germany, which, according to the findings of Kriesi et al., was indeed the case in the 1970s and 1980s. It will be interesting to see whether our data will provide further support for the hypothesis on curvilinearity.

The structure of a decision-making system primarily hints at the degree movements have direct formal access to the government. Direct access, however, is only one part of the greater picture. To raise their issues and pass them through the decision-making system, social movements frequently rely on allies within the decision-making bodies. Particularly in those polities that offer few direct channels of influence, alliances with actors that do have formal access to the decision-making bodies are highly relevant. Therefore, the second aspect of the political opportunity structure that we consider is the configuration of political actors that matter for challengers, that is, the alliance and conflict structure (see Rucht 2004) in the eight countries. Given our interest in antiwar protests, we focus specifically on the configuration and relative strength of the institutionalized left, which traditionally has been an ally of peace movements.

Configuration and Relative Strength of the Institutionalized Left

From the literature and various surveys conducted in the past, we know that peace protests tend to predominantly recruit from left-wing groups. Some of these, most notably peace groups, provide the natural constituency for peace protests. Others, in particular left parties and trade unions, may contribute significantly to peace protests because of their sizeable membership. This reliance on left parties and trade unions was particularly salient in the peace movements in Belgium and the Netherlands in the 1980s (for the Netherlands, see Klandermans 1994; for Belgium, see Stouthuysen 1992 and Walgrave 1994). More generally, however, left parties and unions perhaps are vital not as recruitment pools but as allies of genuine peace groups in putting the peace issue on the public agenda and/or in influencing decision-making processes. After all, the media does not consider peace groups, at least in their early phases of mobilization, to be main players, whereas it cannot ignore left parties, especially when represented in parliament, and trade unions. By taking available data into account, we will attempt to present rough indicators for the relative strength of these two kinds of groups as well as their framework and position within the overall power structure.

Left Parties

A crude impression of the strength of left-wing parties (Communist, Social-ist, Social Democratic, and Labor parties) can be obtained by looking at the degree to which they have been represented in the national government (Table 2.2). Since we are interested in structural features rather than in short-term effects related to specific political constellations, we use averages of approximately the last fifteen years. According to this indicator, the left has been strongest in Spain (average 55.3 percent), followed by Belgium (45 percent). On the other end of the spectrum are the Netherlands and Germany with 28.6 and 24.5 percent, respectively. It is only in the polities with majoritarian voting systems (the United Kingdom, Germany, and Spain) where these parties were able to govern on their own (see column 3).

Based on the numbers of cabinet seats in the period from 1985 to 2002, progressive movements in Spain and Belgium stood the best chance of find-ing influential allies within the party system, whereas the opposite holds for Switzerland, Germany, and possibly the United States, where the Democratic Party cannot be classified as "left." But likelihood may not necessarily turn into manifest support: consider that some moderate left parties, in par-ticular social democrats, tend to be close to the center or compromise with a coalition partner from the center or even the right, therefore tending to

Table 2.2. Configuration and strength of left parties (1985–2002)

	Left seats in governments		Competing leftist parties	
	Average	Maximum[a]	Communist Party[b]	Green Party[b]
United States[c]	–	–	–	–
United Kingdom	33.3	100.0	–	–
Spain	55.3	100.0	10.5	–
Italy	30.7	49.9	27.9	2.7
Netherlands	31.7	50.0	–	7.3
Switzerland	28.6	28.6	–	6.1
Belgium	45.0	58.8	–	7.4
Germany	24.5	100.0	5.1	8.3

Source: Our own calculations, based on data compiled in Armingeon et al. (2004).

Notes: [a]The average of the Left parties' strength in government is measured by averaging the number of cabinet seats held by leftist parties as a percentage of total cabinet posts, 1985–2002.

[b]Maximum share of seats acquired during this period.

[c]The Democratic Party in the United States was not classified as left.

develop a conflicting relationship with radical leftist groups. A moderate left party in government is likely to attract strong criticism from the radical parliamentary and/or extra-parliamentary left. Even a (moderate) left-wing government may not necessarily be a blessing for the progressive movement, and at the same time, a decidedly conservative government may unwillingly contribute to strengthening forces on the left that, to challenge the government, tend to ally despite ideological differences. This, for example, was true for Italy in the government led by Berlusconi. More generally, research based on protest event data has shown that the overall volume of protest is greater under right governments than left (Koopmans and Rucht 1995). Given these differential potential effects of governmental constellations, we cannot draw strong conclusions regarding the effects on social movements.

According to the political opportunity structure literature, the "division of the left" is another determining aspect of the configuration of power on the left, and it has implications for the progressive movement sector. In those systems where social democrats compete with a strong Communist party, Kriesi (1995, 181) expects little action space for new social movements, as the social democrats traditionally had to subordinate their support of new social movement mobilization to their struggle for hegemony of the left. In our country sample, this applies to Spain and Italy. Communist parties were particularly influential in Italy, where the Partito Comunista Italiano nearly received 30 percent of the votes as late as in the mid-1980s (see Table 2.2, column 4). In Germany, (former) Communists only regained some of their political relevance after reunion. Therefore, we should not expect a strong effect on the strength of new social movements, which developed in large part before the political constellation changed. Also the presence of strong Green parties—which tend to be left-leaning and frequently serve as mouthpieces for progressive movements—indicates that the social democrats have to compete with other parties for left-wing votes. Unlike strong Communist parties, the presence of significant Green parties in the political system will not reduce the prospects for new social movements. On the contrary, these parties often originated from these movements and can be regarded as their strong allies. Green parties attracted sizeable numbers of votes in Germany, Belgium, Switzerland, and the Netherlands, but many fewer in Italy.

Trade Unions

Apart from some political parties, the trade unions are also significant actors in the left spectrum. When it comes to the respective infrastructure, we consider union density, calculated as the proportion of union members in the total of paid employees (see Table 2.3). Union membership indicates its organizational strength and, related, financial and personal resources. More members seem to imply more potential power; however, even a large membership may not be an asset in conflicts between unions and their opponents, as long as the unions are compliant and willing to compromise. Consider, for example, the trade unions in Germany: they are traditionally strong, but, since World War II, they have been reluctant to engage in bitter fights. Thus, we will utilize strike statistics as a second measure that, unlike union membership, does indicate actual engagement in protest.

An important characteristic regarding organized labor concerns the degree to which trade unions get formal, institutionalized access to the political system. While pluralist systems do not grant trade unions such privileged access, corporatist systems do. As the "Corporatism" column in Table 2.3 shows, there are considerable differences regarding the system of interest group mediation in the eight countries. In corporatist systems, the labor conflict has been pacified and transformed into an institutionalized mode of conflict resolution.

Union density also varies considerably. It is by far the highest in Belgium, with Great Britain and Italy following suit, and clearly lowest in the United States. As a matter of fact, in the 1980s and 1990s peace movements in Belgium enjoyed considerable support from trade unions. More generally, however, high union density does not necessarily translate into readiness for action. As it can be seen in Table 2.3, it tends to be accompanied by low strike activity. This is the case in the Netherlands, Switzerland, Germany, and,

Table 2.3. Indicators of the power configurations in the organization of labor

	Corporatism[a]	Union density[b]	Strike level[c]
United States	2.125	15	51
United Kingdom	2.000	39	50
Spain	2.000	11	294
Italy	3.000	39	136
Netherlands	4.125	25	14
Switzerland	4.000	24	2
Belgium	3.750	54	27
Germany	4.375	31	7

Source: Our own calculations, based on ILO data compiled in Armingeon et al. (2004).

Notes: [a]The indicator for corporatism is representative for the 1990s (Siaroff 1999).

[b]Trade union density in 1990 (OECD 2004).

[c]The strike level is measured by the average of working days lost per thousand employees between 1985 and 2000.

to some degree, Belgium. In the first three countries, additionally, the presence of strong independent central banks unwilling to accommodate high wage demands further contributed to silencing trade unions. Among those countries with pluralist interest group systems, labor activity is especially high in Spain and Italy, where governments and monetary authorities have frequently accommodated demands for higher wages, thereby encouraging further labor conflicts. Readiness for engagement in labor conflicts tends to be associated with a more general readiness for political action, so we may expect unions to support other leftist movement causes, particularly in Italy and Spain.

In compiling and consolidating the variety of information on the structure of the political context, we cannot arrive at straightforward conclusions. Different factors are at work, and we cannot expect these to consistently influence the progressive movement sector in one direction. Regarding the strength of this sector, the hypothesis of the curvilinear effect of the political opportunity structure, measured as distribution of power, leads us to expect a relatively weak progressive movement sector in Switzerland and possibly the United States, and, though for different reasons, in Great Britain as well. The situation of the institutionalized left suggests a weak support for progressive movements in Germany and Switzerland, but strong support in Spain and Italy concerning left parties in national government. Also, the high level of strike activity in Spain and Italy may indicate the unions' readiness to support progressive movements. Considering organized labor measured as union density, the unions appear to be the strongest potential partner for progressive movements in Belgium and the United Kingdom, while the opposite holds for the United States and Spain. In general, these results leave us with two relatively consistent assumptions only: First, for Switzerland and, to a lesser extent, for the United States, we expect unfavorable conditions for the progressive movement sector, whereas the opposite can be expected for Spain and Italy. Second, as to the composition of the progressive movement sector, the configuration of left power structures leads us to expect a dominance of the Old Left in Spain and, to a smaller degree, Italy. By contrast, we expect new social movements to be stronger in the Netherlands, Switzerland, Germany, and possibly Belgium, where the labor conflict has largely been pacified and the new social movement sector also enjoys support from strong Green parties.

In the next section, we look both for indications of the strength of the progressive movement sector as a whole and as for specific movements or types of organizations. We deliberately include the left parties and the unions, which we have so far considered a context variable for genuine social movements but can also be regarded as a constitutive part of the expansively defined progressive movement sector.

The Strength and Shape of Progressive Movement Sectors in Eight Countries

The best measurement for the strength of social movements is perhaps their effective mobilization as reflected in protest activities. These activities can be registered in protest event analysis data based on newspaper reports or police archives. Unfortunately, such data are not available for the eight countries under study.[4] Therefore, we have to rely on survey data that give us at least an approximate estimate on the mobilization potential that could be tapped by the organizers of the February 15 protests. Though far from being ideal for our purpose, the World Values Survey (WVS) can be used to infer indications of the strength of the progressive movement sectors in our eight countries. In population surveys, the number of respondents active in different social movement organizations is relatively small. To have a reasonable number of cases at our disposal, we use the integrated data file covering all four waves of the survey, from 1981 to 2004 (WVS 2006). Based on this data, we obtain a rough picture of the size of the mobilization potential of progressive groups in the eight countries.

We deliberately focus on the broader progressive movement sector because, as indicated, peace (or antiwar) protests typically recruit people far beyond the small core of committed hardcore peace activists. Mostly dependent on contingent political decisions, such as introducing new weapons or engaging in warfare, peace activities fluctuate considerably over time, being almost completely absent in some periods while in others attracting large numbers (Rochon 1988; Cooper 1996). In other words, there tends to be a large gap between the organizational weakness of the more or less permanently existing peace groups and the high potential or actual mobilization with regard to peace issues. Consider that in the period of the imminent war against Iraq, in some countries more than four-fifths of the populations were opposing the war (see chapter 3 of this book), thus providing a huge pool for recruitment that only could be activated to a low degree for the February 15 protests. Moreover, earlier research has shown that those who actually participate in peace activities are by no means representative of the overall population. Rather, to a large extent, they are politically aware citizens who are or have been active in a variety of groups not necessarily focusing on matters of war and peace. As Marullo and Meyer rightly stated, peace movements' successful mobilizations "rely on the co-optation of substantial resources from other movements typically not involved in peace politics" (2004, 644; see also chapter 4 of this book) Antiwar campaigns generally can count on the support of, and recruitment via, a wide range of different groups engaged in women's rights, environmentalism, third-world concerns, and other issues commonly attributed to new social movements. In addition, trade unions and leftist parties tend to participate readily in antiwar campaigns.

Left-Wing Orientation and Readiness of Protest Demonstration

As mentioned, the strength and other characteristics of the institutionalized left in the eight countries studied differ. These variations are also reflected in the percentage of people attracted by the clearly left political spectrum as measured by their self-positioning on a left-right scale.[5] The greatest share of people leaning to the far left can be found in Spain and Italy, the two polities where Communist parties have political weight and trade unions are highly militant. Given this constellation, it comes as no surprise that more of these respondents position themselves on the far left side of the political spectrum than, for instance, do those in the United States or the United Kingdom, where leftist parties are clearly marginalized in institutional politics. In particular the United States, where parties seldom mobilize on clear-cut left-right issues, stands out for its comparatively low level of citizens with a definite left-wing orientation.

Although we expect the peace movement to recruit demonstrators primarily from left-leaning people, we cannot simply assume that all people on the left are ready to take part in demonstrations. Therefore, we try to get a better estimate of the actual potential for political demonstrations by considering those respondents who did participate (or who at least were ready to participate) in a legal demonstration. For this purpose, we use the item "attending lawful demonstrations," combining the categories "have done" and "might do." We assume that this is the measure that comes closest to assessing the mobilization potential for the kind of protest of which the antiwar demonstration on February 15 is just one example. Figure 2.1 puts the demonstration potential in relation to the openness of the political system. The graph on the left suggests that the openness or closedness of the political system is related to the mobilization potential of left-oriented people. The readiness of these people to demonstrate is highest in Germany and Italy, countries with a semi-open system, and lowest in Great Britain, with its highly closed polity. In this respect, the picture corresponds to the assumption of a curvilinear relationship. Yet the left-wingers in the highly open Swiss system also have a great propensity to take part in demonstrations, while this is not the case for those living in the other country with an open system, the United States.

Figure 2.1 also shows peoples' readiness to participate in street demonstrations, regardless of their position on the left-right scale (see the graph on

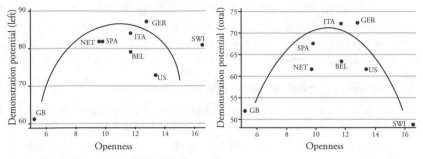

Source: World Value Surveys, 1981–2004.
Note: Openness of the political system is measured by the additive index presented in Table 2.1.
Demonstration potential is measured as a percentage of respondents who have participated or
might participate in a street demonstration. Those on the left are the respondents who placed
themselves on the values 1 to 3 on the left-right scale of 1 (far left) to 10 (far right).

Figure 2.1: Variation in the openness of political systems

the right side). Switzerland has the lowest participation rate; in this respect,
the data support the curvilinear hypothesis. Hence, the overall picture is mixed:
while our assumption that the protest potential in our eight countries is related to openness of the political system is supported, other factors seem to
be at work as well.

What accounts for the differences between the two graphs in Figure 2.1?
Overall, remarkable cross-country differences are apparent in the degree to
which protest is primarily an instrument of the left. In Switzerland and the
Netherlands, in particular, there is a clear bias toward the far left with regard
to the acceptance of protest. In the United States, Italy, and Germany, though,
many conservatives also participate in demonstrations.[6] These differences
cannot be deduced systematically from variation in the political opportunity
structures. However, the greater reluctance to take part in demonstrations
in Switzerland can be explained in that the Swiss civil society organizations
have more institutionalized channels to put their demands on the political
agenda as well as directly influence political decisions by referenda. Such an
open political system is likely to be accompanied by a low level of political
mobilization outside institutionalized decision-making processes.

Involvement in Progressive Groups

In order to assess the strength of the progressive movement sector, we have
to take into account the degree of citizens' actual involvement in political
groups. Before we turn to group involvement of left-wing activists, we present overall involvement rates in different groups (Table 2.4). The upper half
of the table shows the percentage of respondents who declare themselves

Table 2.4. Involvement in political groups and social movement organizations (percent of respondents belonging to a group and/or doing unpaid work)

	Union	Party	Ecology[a]	Women	Peace	NSMO[b]	N
United States	13.8	22.2	10.1	11.8	3.2	17.6	5,364
Great Britain	14.4	4.3	6.6	3.9	2.7	11.0	3,651
Spain	5.1	3.1	2.2	1.3	1.0	4.5	8,859
Italy	6.6	5.2	3.6	0.5	1.4	5.5	5,366
Netherlands	18.9	8.9	27.3	6.0	3.1	34.2	3,241
Switzerland[c]	11.2	12.7	10.4	–	–	–	1,400
Belgium	15.0	5.6	9.7	9.3	2.1	19.3	5,849
Germany	21.1	6.8	5.0	5.4	1.3	10.2	6,778
Averages[d]	13.3	8.6	9.4	5.5	2.1	14.6	

Source: World Value Surveys 1981–2004.

Notes: [a]The ecology category includes all respondents who belong to one or several groups concerned with conservation, environment, ecology, and animal rights.

[b]The NSMO (new social movement organization) category includes all respondents who belong to one or several groups concerned with peace, women's issues, ecology, and human rights.

[c]For Switzerland, we used "inactive/active membership" as a proxy for "belong to a group / do unpaid work."

[d]Averages were calculated without the Swiss data.

involved in trade unions, in a political party, or in different types of social movement groups, including the peace movement. As we can see, there are quite remarkable differences, both across groups and across countries. High levels of involvement in trade unions can be observed in the Netherlands and Germany, while involvement in political parties is particular high in the United States and in Switzerland. Regarding the movements' thematic fields, groups working on ecology attract more people than those focusing on women and peace. Involvement in peace groups is highest in the United States and the Netherlands, and lowest in Italy and Germany. Considering the larger set of new social movement organizations, the degree of involvement is particularly high in the Netherlands (followed by Belgium and the United States), but amazingly low in Italy and Spain.

We argue that the peace groups primarily mobilize among a left-wing constituency. Table 2.5 presents the percentage of leftists active in different kinds of groups. Based on this indicator, we may identify different patterns of mobilization structures in our eight countries. In Spain and Italy, where the labor conflict has not yet been settled (see Table 2.3), voluntary work in new social movement organizations is relatively rare, particularly when compared to in the United States and Belgium. However, involvement of Spanish and Italian left-wingers is not high in trade unions or parties either.

Table 2.5. Left-wing activists in different groups, including overlapping membership (percentages)

	Union	Party	NSMO[a]	NSMO[a] and Union	NSMO[a] and Party	N
United States	1.9	6.6	11.1	0.4	2.3	513
United Kingdom	2.2	3.4	7.3	0.7	1.2	413
Spain	4.1	3.3	4.3	0.8	0.8	1561
Italy	4.9	6.6	4.5	0.3	0.9	1086
Netherlands	2.3	3.1	7.3	0.3	1.6	577
Switzerland[b]	10.6	10.6	–	–	–	161
Belgium	4.2	4.3	9.8	1.2	2.0	600
Germany	6.9	7.2	6.6	0.3	1.4	970
Averages[b]	3.8	4.9	7.3	0.6	1.5	

Source: World Value Surveys 1981–2004.

Notes: The data include percentages of active group members, that is, those who "do unpaid work," based on all respondents who clearly have a left-wing orientation—who position themselves on points 1 to 3 of the ten-point left-right-scale (see also notes to Figure 2.1 and Table 2.4).

[a]New social movement organization.

[b]The data on Switzerland are not directly comparable to the other data because of differences in the questions asked. Thus, we used "inactive/active membership" as a proxy to "belong to a group / do unpaid work." We calculated averages without the Swiss data.

Thus far, we have not considered multiple memberships or overlapping activity in different groups. We generally assume that mobilization structures are especially strong and effective in countries with a high level of permeability of, or overlap between, different social movement organizations. Significant overlaps are an indicator for opportunities to engage in joint action. While such links are extremely helpful for fostering mobilization, they do not have to be strong, as Granovetter (1973) showed on more general grounds. As argued above, this is particularly true for antiwar protests, which, due to the small membership of peace groups, heavily rely on recruitment from other political groups or social movements. We expect that antiwar mobilization is achieved more effectively in countries with a high degree of unity among the different movements of the left. As a rough measure for the extent of unity or fragmentation of the progressive movement sector, we look at the degree to which leftist people who are actively involved in new social movement organizations are also active in either trade unions or political parties. To correctly interpret this data, we have to take into account that the overlap is partially driven by the size of the activity rates in the different groups. Furthermore, we should also take into account that these estimates are calculated from a relatively low number of respondents. The link between new social movement organizations and trade unions is by far strongest in Belgium, followed by Spain and the United Kingdom. The British case is particularly interesting because of the relatively low overall number of trade union activists. In Germany, however, where unionization is relatively high, the overlap is small. Also in the Netherlands and Italy, the two sectors appear rather disconnected; in the Netherlands, however, the parties and new social movement organizations tend to be significantly linked. Even stronger links between them exist in the United States and Belgium.

Conclusion

Our aim here is to describe the nation-specific political opportunity structures and the corresponding progressive movement sectors in the eight countries under study. We relied on quantitative data; drawing on it, we explored relationships between the opportunity structure and the movement sectors relevant for protest mobilization. Using the premise of the political opportunity structure approach, we hypothesized a curvilinear relationship, that is, that both relatively closed and relatively open political systems offer less favorable conditions for the progressive movement sector than do semiopen systems. Regarding especially left-wing parties and trade unions—as a potential alliance partner and mobilization pool for movement activities—we expected a weak established left to be unfavorable to the progressive movements.

Furthermore, we expected to find a stronger position of new social movements within the progressive movement sector in countries with pacified labor movements and relevant Green parties.

In the first step of our analysis, we have selected and operationalized two basic dimensions of the general political environment: the openness of the political structures and the strength of the established left. Regarding the first, we found that the United Kingdom is the least open system and Switzerland and the United States are the most open. According to the hypothesis of curvilinearity, our data would suggest the least favorable structural conditions for progressive movement sectors in these three countries. Regarding the second dimension, we found strong left parties in Spain and Belgium and a strong Communist Party in Italy. Hence, we would expect strong progressive movement sectors in these countries. Yet significant Green parties in Germany, Belgium, Switzerland, and the Netherlands also tend to be allies for progressive movements. As far as organized labor is concerned, we found union density the highest in Belgium and the lowest in the United States and Spain. Yet perhaps more important, by far the highest levels of strike activity exist in Spain and Italy. Moreover, we found a large proportion of leftists in Spain and Italy. Summarizing these findings, our structural data would suggest progressive movement sectors weak in the United States and Britain, and presumably strong in Italy and Spain.

In the second step of our analysis, we measured the strength and characteristics of the progressive movement sector by looking at participation in demonstrations, membership in groups, and activity in groups based on WVS data. Considering the various measurements, we could not establish a clear and consistent ranking order in terms of the strength of the progressive movement sector in the eight countries. When it comes to the strength of new social movement organizations in particular, the Netherlands, Belgium, and the United States rank high, while the Old Left seems to be strong in Spain and Italy, countries where the class conflict is still viable.

What do these findings mean in light of our hypotheses? Unfortunately, we could not arrive at entirely conclusive results. On the one hand, at least in our sample, we were unable to establish a clear link between the degree of openness of the political systems and the overall strength of the progressive movement sector. Thus, we could not confirm our hypothesis; however, we found the degree of openness to be indeed related to the strength of the demonstration potential (not to be equated with actual participation in demonstrations). Very open and very closed political systems contribute to lower overall potential participation rates in demonstrations. If we do, however, only look at the demonstration potential among the left-wingers, the picture is less clear again. Only regarding the composition of the progressive movement sector can we confirm the expectations to a certain extent.

Why were we unable to consistently explain cross-national variations in the strength of progressive movement sectors by political structures? One reason may be that political structures consist of many dimensions whose ranges and relative weights, let alone interaction effects, are unclear regarding the impacts of these political structures on social movements. Furthermore, the progressive movement sectors are certainly influenced by additional factors as well, for example, political cultures—that is, factors that we could not grasp in our analysis. In addition to relatively inert political context structures, more flexible and volatile structures may come into play in a given country, whether, for example, a right or a left government is in charge, the government is open to reforms, or countermovements are present.

Although we found variation regarding the independent variables, in particular the degree of openness among the eight political systems we compared, this variation likely is too small to generate significant and robust results. The countries studied here are liberal democracies with similar basic structures. It was not a deliberate choice to rely on a "most similar systems design" (see Przeworski and Teune 1970) in this book, but this is what we essentially have, as long as we disregard differences in more specific institutions such as electoral systems. We would probably identify clearer relationships if we were to investigate a set of countries with greater variation of political systems, for example, if we had included authoritarian regimes. In this case, it may well be that both very closed (authoritarian, repressive systems) and very open/responsive systems (such as those in Scandinavian countries) would more clearly support the validity of the argument on curvilinearity.

Regardless of such a possibility, we have no reason to assume a direct link between the stable national political opportunity structure and specific events, such as the February 15 protests. While we maintain that such general structures account for ample and general properties of movement sectors, it may be more rewarding to search for domain-specific opportunities that influence corresponding social movements. Why, for example, should contextual factors that influence the strength of the gay movement or the farmers' movement matter for the strength of the peace movement? In addition, when looking at particular policy domains, we can assume that the corresponding movements are shaped by more contingent factors, such as the specific governmental position on the matter of conflict or precipitating incidents, for example, a nuclear accident that may spur anti-nuclear protest. We agree with the assumption that "shifts in political opportunity structures

. . . are too broad to tell us much about the development or success of specific movements" (Goldstone 2004, 356; see also Rucht 1998).

Nevertheless, certain basic political context factors may well have some impact on specific protest campaigns, though these are plausibly strongly mediated by additional factors. For example, the general ideological line of the national government may influence the composition of the protesters. Accordingly, a conservative government favoring the war in Iraq is likely to foster a broad and inclusive leftist antiwar coalition, while a leftist government taking the same position is likely to be confronted with a less broad alliance of protesters, because some groups critical toward the war are supportive of the government at large. Such considerations will be the focus of the remaining chapters in this volume, which specifically concern the antiwar protests and their participants.

Notes

1. Note that in the context of protest studies, the first empirical attempt to apply the concept of political opportunities did not refer to nation-states but to the "*structure of political opportunities* of a community" to explain the intensity of protest in forty-three cities in the United States (Eisinger 1973, 11).

2. This index takes into account two aspects of judicial review: first, whether the courts (or a specific constitutional court) have the power to invalidate parliamentary laws, and second, the degrees of activism in the assertion of this power by the courts. (These degrees include: no judicial review, weak judicial review [formal right of courts, but judges use it with caution and moderation], medium-strength judicial review, and strong judicial review [Lijphart 1999, 225–28]).

3. The maximum values of the four variables are not identical; therefore, not every variable carries exactly the same weight. We ignore this fact because the differences are minor.

4. Earlier research covering four Western European countries has shown significant variation in the volume and composition of progressive protest (see Kriesi et al. 1995). This research, for example, suggested that unconventional protest activity of labor and other left groups was high in France and the Netherlands but low in Germany and Switzerland. In Germany, nearly three quarters of them could be attributed to the new social movements, whereas the corresponding proportion in France was only 36 percent (ibid., 20). Also, relative to the size of the population, participation in new social movement protests was much higher in Germany than in France. However, participation in labor protests, again controlled for the size of the population, was much higher in France than in Germany, the Netherlands, and Switzerland (ibid., 22). It remains to be seen whether this picture, based on newspaper coverage from 1975 to 1989, also holds for more recent periods.

5. We classify as clearly left-wing those respondents who position themselves on the values 1 to 3 on the ten-point scale from 1 ("far left") to 10 ("far right.") Based on estimations from the World Value Survey 1981–2004, these are the percentages of left-wingers in our eight countries: Spain 29.3 (N = 10070), Italy 26.3 (N = 5366), the Netherlands 19.7 (N = 3241), Germany 18.2 (N = 8804), Belgium 14.3 percent (N = 5849), Switzerland 15.1 (N = 2612), Great Britain 13.3 (N = 4744), and the United States 10.6 (N = 6906).

6. According to the World Value Survey 1981–2004 data, 72.5 percent of those on the right in Germany participated or might participate in a demonstration. In the United States, that figure in is 61.7 percent, and in Italy it is and 62.9 percent. However, figures are low in Switzerland and the Netherlands (33.7 and 38 percent).

Works Cited

Armingeon, Klaus, Philipp Leimgruber, Michelle Beyeler, and Sarah Menegale. 2004. *Comparative Political Data Set 1960–2001.* Berne: Institute of Political Science, University of Berne.

Brand, Karl-Werner. 1985. "Vergleichendes Resümee." In *Neue soziale Bewegungen in Westeuropa und den USA,* ed. Karl-Werner Brand, 306–34. Frankfurt a.M.: Campus.

Cooper, Alice Holmes. 1996. *Paradoxes of Peace: German Peace Movements since 1945.* Ann Arbor: University of Michigan Press.

della Porta, Donatella, and Dieter Rucht. 1995. "Left-Libertarian Movements in Context: A Comparison of Italy and West Germany, 1965–1990." In *The Politics of Social Protest: Comparative Perspectives on States and Social Movements,* ed. Bert Klandermans and Craig Jenkins, 229–72. Minneapolis: University of Minnesota Press.

Eisinger, Peter K. 1973. "The Conditions of Protest Behavior in American Cities." *American Political Science Review* 67: 11–28.

Ferree, Myra Marx, William A. Gamson, Jürgen Gerhards, and Dieter Rucht. 2002. *Shaping Abortion Discourse: Democracy and the Public Sphere in Germany and the United States.* Cambridge: Cambridge University Press.

Gamson, William A., and David Meyer. 1996. "Framing Political Opportunity." In *Opportunities, Mobilizing Structures, and Framing: Comparative Applications of Contemporary Movement Theory,* ed. Doug McAdam, John D. McCarthy, and Mayer N. Zald, 275–90. Cambridge: Cambridge University Press.

Goldstone, Jack A. 2004. "More Social Movements or Fewer? Beyond Political Opportunity Structures to Relational Fields." *Theory and Society* 33: 333–365.

Goodwin, Jeff, and James M. Jasper, 1999. "Caught in a Winding, Snarling Vine: The Structural Bias of Political Process Theory." *Sociological Forum* 14: 27–54.

Granovetter, Mark. 1973: "The Strength of Weak Ties." *American Journal of Sociology* 18: 1360–80.

Huber, Evelyne, Charles Ragin, and John D. Stephens. 1997. "Comparative Welfare States Data Set." Northwestern University and University of North Carolina.

Kitschelt, Herbert. 1986. "Political Opportunity Structures and Political Protest: Anti-Nuclear Movements in Four Democracies." *British Journal of Political Science* 16: 57–85.

Klandermans, Bert. 1994. "Transient Identities? Membership Patterns in the Dutch Peace Movement." In *New Social Movements: From Ideology to Identity*, ed. Enrique Larana, Hank Johnston, and Joseph R. Gusfield, 168–84. Philadelphia: Temple University Press.

Kolb, Felix. 2007. *Protest and Opportunities: The Political Outcomes of Social Movements*. New York: Campus.

Koopmans, Ruud, and Dieter Rucht. 1995. "Movement Mobilization under Right and Left Governments: A Look at Four West European Countries." Discussion Paper FS III, 95–106. Wissenschaftszentrum Berlin für Sozialforschung.

Koopmans, Ruud, and Paul Statham. 2000. "Migration and Ethnic Relations as a Field of Political Contention: An Opportunity Structure Approach." In *Challenging Immigration and Ethnic Relations Politics: Comparative European Perspectives*, ed. Ruud Koopmans and Paul Statham, 13–56. Oxford: Oxford University Press.

Kriesi, Hanspeter. 1995. "The Political Opportunity Structure of New Social Movements: Its Impact on Their Mobilization." In *The Politics of Social Protest: Comparative Perspectives on States and Social Movements*, ed. J. Craig Jenkins and Bert Klandermans, 167–98. Minneapolis: University of Minnesota Press.

———. 2004. Political Context and Opportunity. In *The Blackwell Companion to Social Movements*, ed. David Snow, Sarah A. Soule, and Hanspeter Kriesi, 67–90. Oxford: Blackwell.

Kriesi, Hanspeter, Ruud Koopmans, Jan Willem Duyvendak, and Marco G. Giugni. 1995. *New Social Movements in Western Europe: A Comparative Analysis*. Minneapolis: University of Minnesota Press.

Lijphart, Arend. 1999. *Patterns of Democracy: Government Forms and Performance in Thirty-six Countries*. New Haven, Conn: Yale University Press.

Marks, Gary, and Doug McAdam. 1999. "On the Relationship of Political Opportunities to the Form of Collective Action: The Case of the European Union." In *Social Movements in a Globalizing World*, ed. Donatella della Porta, Hanspeter Kriesi, and Dieter Rucht, 97–111. London: Macmillan.

Marullo, Sam, and David S. Meyer. 2004. "Antiwar and Peace Movements." In *The Blackwell Companion to Social Movements*, ed. David A. Snow, Sarah A. Soule, and Hanspeter Kriesi, 641–65. Oxford: Blackwell.

McAdam, Doug. 1996. "Conceptual Origins, Current Problems, Future Directions." In *Opportunities, Mobilizing Structures, and Framing: Comparative Applications of Contemporary Movement Theory,* ed. Doug McAdam, John McCarthy, and Mayer N. Zald, 23–40. Cambridge: Cambridge University Press.

Meyer, David S. 2004. "Conceptualizing Political Opportunity." *Social Forces* 82: 1457–92.

OECD. 2004. *OECD Economic Outlook.* Paris: OECD.

Przeworski, Adam, and Henry Teune. 1970. *The Logic of Comparative Social Inquiry.* New York: Wiley.

Rochon, Thomas R. 1988. *Mobilizing for Peace: The Antinuclear Movements in Western Europe.* Princeton, N.J.: Princeton University Press.

Rucht, Dieter. 1996. "The Impact of National Contexts on Social Movement Structures: A Cross-Movement and Cross-National Comparison." In *Opportunities, Mobilizing Structures, and Framing: Comparative Applications of Contemporary Movement Theory,* ed. Doug McAdam, John McCarthy, and Mayer N. Zald, 185–204. Cambridge: Cambridge University Press.

———. 1998. "Komplexe Phänomene—komplexe Erklärungen: Die politische Gelegenheitsstrukturen neuer sozialer Bewegungen." In *Paradigmen der Bewegungsforschung,* ed. Kai-Uwe Hellmann and Ruud Koopmans, 109–27. Opladen, Germany: Westdeutscher Verlag.

———. 1999. "The Impact of Environmental Movements in Western Societies." In *How Social Movements Matter,* ed. Marco Guigni, Doug McAdam, and Charles Tilly, 331–61. Minneapolis: University of Minnesota Press.

———. 2004. "Movement Allies, Adversaries, and Third Parties." In *The Blackwell Companion to Social Movements,* ed. David A. Snow, Sarah A. Soule, and Hanspeter Kriesi, 197–216. Oxford: Blackwell.

Siaroff, Alan. 1999. "Corporatism in Twenty-four Industrial Democracies: Meaning and Measurement." *European Journal of Political Research* 36: 175–205.

Stouthuysen, Patrick. 1992. *In de ban van de Bom: De politisering van het Belgisch veiligheidsbeleid, 1945–1985.* Brussels: VUB Press.

Tarrow, Sidney. 1983. *Struggling to Reform: Social Movements and Policy Change during Cycles of Protest.* Western Societies Program, Occasional Paper No. 15, Center for International Studies, Cornell University, Ithaca. N.Y.

———. 1998. *Power in Movement: Social Movements and Contentious Politics.* New York: Cambridge University Press.

Walgrave, Stefaan. 1994. "Nieuwe sociale bewegingen." In *Vlaanderen: Een sociologische verkenning.* Leuven, Belgium: SOI.

WVS, European Values Study Group and World Values Survey Association. 2006. *European and World Values Surveys Four-Wave Integrated Data File, 1981–2004.* v. 20060423.

3

Politics, Public Opinion, and the Media:
The Issues and Context behind the Demonstrations

Joris Verhulst and Stefaan Walgrave

February 15 was organized by a closely collaborating transnational network of social movements. Demonstrations in all eight countries studied in this volume shared the same action repertoires, frames, and goals (see chapter 1). Yet, each country's protest was organized by specific national movements against the backdrop of specific national opportunities. It goes without saying that mobilizing against war in the United States, for example, was different than mobilizing in Germany. The protests were rooted in, or at least affected by, different national political and societal contexts. The UK government supported the war and sent troops to help the Americans get rid of Saddam Hussein, and the Belgian government strongly opposed the war—the position of the government in each country must have had consequences for its protest movement. Since the political and societal context in each of these nations was substantially different, we expect the demonstrators in each to be different too and to bear the traces of their respective milieus. In chapter 2 we analyzed the general, non-issue-specific structural similarities and differences among the eight countries in terms of access for challengers and strength of the progressive social movement sector. The approaches to social movements among these core elements of the political opportunity structure remained unrelated to the Iraq conflict. Since we are studying a single protest event and not a social movement, and since we are interested here in the individual features of the demonstrators and not in the levels of mobilization in the different countries, we need to complement the classic opportunity structure elements with more specific contextual factors. We accept that protesters' engagement is determined not only by large overall structures but also by specific political and societal contexts. As relevant context factors, we take into account politics, media, and public opinion. As Neidhardt and Rucht (1991) state, political elites, mass media, and public opinion are among the most important reference groups for social movements and protest.[1] Mutually influencing each other, political elites form the power center most movements are trying to influence; the media can marginalize movements or they can be an important ally affecting public opinion, and public opinion support can boost a movement's mobilization and subsequent political impact.

By focusing in this chapter on politics, media, and public opinion, we underscore our claim that protests such as the worldwide February 15 demonstrations cannot be fully understood within the general context of a certain society with its inclination to nurture or discourage protest in general. The protested issue itself matters, as do the stance of government and opposition on the issue; the way the media handles it; and the resonance of political positions and media coverage in the public. In other words, apart from the long-term, general political opportunity structure, the specificity of the February 15 events calls for a more specific political context.

Why do politics, media, and public opinion matter? Protest can, on the one hand, be marginal, rowing against mainstream opinion and behavior in society; on the other hand, it can also sail on dominant opinion and practice in a given society. In the first instance, protesters are a minority fighting a conflictual issue with a clear domestic target; in the second, protesters are representatives of a majority struggling for a valence issue mostly without domestic target, since (almost) everybody seems to agree. We expect this diverging context, apart from affecting the size of the mobilization, to dramatically affect the kind of people showing up to vent their discontent. In a nutshell, our general argument runs as follows: if protesters stand up against dominant opinion and practice in a given society, they will differ from the population at large in terms of sociodemographic profile (higher education), political attitudes (more political interest, stronger ideological stance), and political behavior (more protest participation, more associational membership). Protesting groups that go against the mainstream are often "strong." The opposite applies to valence issue mobilization, in which we expect "weak" groups also to be represented and, thus, a more representative sample of the population will take the streets.

Government and Opposition on the War

Obviously, the official positions regarding the war differed dramatically among the eight countries, which include the most war-favoring countries, like the

United States and the United Kingdom, and some of those most fiercely against the war, Germany and Belgium. Yet, not only government's official stance matters. The opposition counts too: it may support government or fight it. In some of the studied countries, moreover, government was internally divided; in others, the opposition parties were internally split. In short, the alignment of government and opposition regarding the war is an important context variable. For example, if the Left opposes war, against a right-wing government that backs it, we expect mobilization against the war to take the form of antigovernment protest, predominantly populated by left-leaning persons and groups. Let us sketch in some more detail the government-opposition configuration in the eight countries. Figure 3.1 summarizes our argument and places the countries on a single pro-war to contra-war continuum.

The most prominent war-initiating country was, of course, the United States: framed by the "war on terror" in the post-9/11 era, the U.S. government was eager to invade Iraq with the threefold objective of diminishing the Iraqi threat to engage in terrorist acts or acts of war in the region and dispossessing the country of all resources to do so; bringing about a regime change, leading to better life conditions for the Iraqi people; and effectuating the first step in the democratization of the Middle East. The U.S. government—led by Republican president George W. Bush, backed by a neo-conservative administration consisting of Vice President Dick Cheney, Defense Secretary Donald Rumsfeld, and his deputy Paul Wolfowitz—was supported by almost all Republican congress members. The Democratic opposition, conversely, was internally divided on the issue. On October 10, 2002,

	Government	Government parties	Opposition parties
War-initiating countries			
United States	pro	right/conservative (pro)	center left (pro)
United Kingdom	pro	center left (divided)	conservative (pro) and liberal (contra)
War-supporting countries			
Spain	pro	right/conservative (pro)	center and far left (contra)
Italy	pro	right/conservative (pro)	center and far left (contra)
Netherlands	pro	right/conservative (pro)	center and far left (contra)
War-opposing countries			
Switzerland	contra	center left (contra)	left (Greens) (contra)
Belgium	contra	center left/liberal (contra)	right/conservative (contra)
Germany	contra	center left (contra)	right/conservative (contra)

Figure 3.1. Position of government and opposition parties regarding Iraq War

Congress approved a resolution authorizing the American president to "use the armed forces of the United States as he determines to be necessary and appropriate . . . against the continuing threat posed by Iraq." The resolution was backed by 296 members of the House and opposed by 133. Of the Democrats, 126 voted against it, while 81 of them supported it, whereas only 6 of 212 Republicans voted against the bill. In the Senate, the pro-contra ratio was even more in favor of war: only one of the forty-nine Republican senators voted against, and twenty-one of the fifty Democratic senators supported the war resolution, among them future Democratic presidential candidate John Kerry. Although war support seemed overwhelming, African American, Latino, and female legislators voted in majority against the war (Cortright 2004, 8–11). In short: the government was firmly pro-war and the opposition did not really challenge government.

The United States' most staunch ally and war defender, especially active in developing public arguments in favor of war, was the United Kingdom, represented by its Labour prime minister Tony Blair. The United Kingdom would remain the only Western European country with a left-wing government to endorse the war. In this perspective, Labour's internal struggle is far from surprising: on February 27, 2002, 121 of 408—nearly one in three—Labour members of Parliament voted against war. This was the biggest revolt ever within a UK government party. The Tories supported Blair, but the Liberal Democrats fully opposed war, with 52 of their 54 members rejecting it. UK government, hence, was painfully divided on the issue: war supporters found support among Conservatives, whereas Labour Party dissidents were backed by the Liberal Democrats.

Spain and Italy were among the most overtly war-supporting countries. The Spanish government, in particular, seemed to follow U.S.-UK war policy. Spain, in fact, sent (noncombat) troops, whereas Italy's support would be limited to opening bases and airspaces to the coalition (though not for direct military attacks). An almost equally large left-wing opposition challenged the Iraq policy of Spanish conservative Partido Popular prime minister Aznar. The Italian case was very similar, with Prime Minister Silvio Berlusconi of Forza Italia and his right-wing government coalition fully backing war and a strong and united left-wing opposition ferociously against it. In both countries, the political polarization around the Iraq issue was huge.

Prime Minister Jan Peter Balkenende of the Netherlands and his right-wing government with Christian-democrats and liberals also supported the idea of war: the Dutch government agreed to send (noncombat) troops to the region. The social democrats and greens resolutely opposed to this involvement. The situation in the Netherlands was a bit peculiar, though, because

Balkenende I had resigned from office. Three weeks before February 15, general elections had been held, but the new government, which would be called Balkenende II, would not be formed until May 26. At the time of the February 15 demonstrations, government negotiations were just starting; thus, the Dutch government could not as clearly be situated in the pro-war camp as its Italian and Spanish counterparts.

In Germany, chancellor and chairman of the German social democrats Gerhard Schröder had been openly opposing a possible war during his fall 2002 election campaign. This stance had helped him and his green coalition partner to get a new term. Later, however, the Schröder government would become somewhat more temperate in its condemnation of war, granting the U.S. troops clearance to use German airspace for matériel and troop transport and not even ruling out a possible UN Security Council vote in favor of war. This slightly more flexible attitude led Angelika Beer, the newly elected leader of the government-participating Green Party, to condemn this clearance, arguing that it would be a breach of the German constitution. In summary, the German government was not really divided about potential participation in a possible war; there were, however, minor frictions on the degree of non-participation they should adopt. Both parties agreed that Germany would not take part in any military action against Iraq, not even when this would be endorsed by the UN. Meanwhile, opposition leader Angela Merkel (Christian-democrat) had also turned her party's stance from one of compliance with the United States to a cautious and moderate antiwar position. Thus, in Germany both government and opposition ultimately rejected an upcoming war.

In Belgium, all political parties simply (tacitly) agreed on the national government's antiwar stance. In Belgium, although led by center-right (liberal) Prime Minister Guy Verhofstadt seconded by center-right (liberal) Foreign Minister Louis Michel, government fiercely and loudly opposed war. The country even temporarily blocked a NATO decision about potential support for Turkey, in case that country would have become engaged in the war. All opposition parties, from greens to Christian-democrats, opposed war as well.

In Switzerland too, all parties rebuffed the possibility of war on Iraq. But in line with the country's long-standing neutrality tradition, Switzerland opposed war only silently. The only exception was the Green Party, which wanted the Swiss government to breach its silent opposition and make a clear and manifest statement against war.

Figure 3.1 summarizes our findings; it shows that the number of different government-opposition configurations is limited. In the officially war-opposing countries Switzerland, Belgium, and Germany, governments and the challenging parties all rejected war; antiwar was a valence issue. In Spain,

Italy, and the Netherlands, countries that supported the war but did not participate in it, right-wing government was in favor of war but the left-wing opposition vehemently opposed it. In these countries, the conflict corresponded with the traditional government-opposition clash. In the United States and the United Kingdom, the governments were, of course, pro-war, but the opposition was divided: U.S. Democrats were split, while UK conservatives supported Blair and UK liberals rejected war. The most complex configuration doubtlessly was found in Britain with the leading party, the Labour Party—the only European left-wing party in power to support the war—bitterly divided on the issue. Taking all this into account, we ordered the eight nations from most war seeking to most war-opposing. Although the Netherlands and Spain superficially had the same political configuration, it is clear that the Spanish government went much further in defending the war than the Dutch did. We will use this favoring-opposing order of countries throughout the book.

Mass Media and the War

Mass media are significant political actors; they intermediate between politics and the population, and their coverage affects both public opinion and political actors' behavior. Especially when it comes to international affairs, conflicts, and war, mass media are often the sole information channel people can rely on. Therefore, international war and conflict are interesting cases for those studying the relations among the elite, mass media, and public opinion. The 1991 Gulf War, especially, received ample scholarly attention (Bennett and Paletz 1994; Taylor 1992; Wolfsfeld 1997). By and large, the argument goes that the American government effectively succeeded in steering and manipulating the news flow to legitimize its military actions in the Gulf (Hachten and Hachten 2000). The more general idea is that political elites determine media coverage, be it completely and monolithically (Herman and Chomsky 1988) or only to a limited extent and in combination with other actors (Bennett 1990). Either way, the media take cues from political elites, and their independence is limited, especially in war times (Entman and Page 1994). Entman conceptualized this top-down process as "cascading activation" (Entman 2003). The ruling administration feeds other political elites; these affect the media and their news stories, which affect public opinion. Entman acknowledges that a feedback mechanism exists and that lower-level frames affect higher levels but this is not the rule.

The 2003 Iraq conflict increased attention to the interaction between media coverage and war. One key difference between the 2003 conflict and the 1991 Gulf War is that there were very few officially war-opposing voices to be heard in 1991. In 2003, many national governments opposed it and tried to sell their point of view to national and world public opinion. A real battle over the facts and their interpretation took place on the international media scene, with the UN Security Council as a primary stage. As a consequence, and corresponding with the elite-dominance hypothesis, we expect substantive differences in war coverage across nations in 2003, with the national media following their governments.

A few 2003 Iraq War studies were recently published focusing on the American media (Calabrese 2005; Entman 2004; Lule 2004; Rutherford 2004). One study concluded that the American media, as expected, supported the bellicose president and hardly fostered any war-opposing sources (Rendall and Broughel 2003). Comparative studies about the media coverage of the 2003 Iraq War are rare (Berenger 2004). Hooghe and Stolle (2005), analyzing a week of TV news coverage in nine different nations in the run-up to the war, counterintuitively found that differences between countries were limited. Only the American and, to a certain extent, French TV stations had diverging, more war-supporting or war-opposing coverage; in other war-supporting nations (the United Kingdom, for example) the TV news coverage was no different from that in war-opposing countries (Germany, Belgium). The authors, hence, reject the idea that TV news tends to follow the national government's position. Their analysis, though, is confined to only one week's media and a limited number of news items per country. Moreover, coverage in TV news may be much more mainstream and homogeneous than in newspapers.

Regarding the war in Iraq in 2003, the question is threefold. First, did the media emphasize the salience of the Iraq issue? Second, did mass media support or oppose war on Iraq? And third, how did the mass media regard the protests against war? The third question will be covered in chapter 12, and the first two are largely addressed in this section. Governments in the eight nations diverged fundamentally in their stances on Iraq, and the opposition parties in the different countries had differing opinions. Consequently, we expect the national mass media to bear the traces of these political differences. Are political intercountry differences reflected in media differences?

It is clear that the Iraq issue was extremely prominent in all mass media in all countries in the period preceding the February 15 protests. People's attention was aroused, and media coverage of the imminent war was extensive. Previous peace demonstration waves, like the protest against the deployment of cruise missiles in Europe in the early 1980s, had drawn much less media attention. Although foreign politics is not the primary issue in most countries' media, the Iraq crisis was omnipresent. In a comparative analysis of two major newspapers in each of four countries—France, Germany, Italy, and the United Kingdom—Kritzinger (2003) contrasted the amount of attention devoted to the Iraq conflict with the amount of coverage of the 1999 Kosovo crisis, both for the January–March period. Despite the fact that the Kosovo crisis was happening geographically much closer to the countries under study, differences in coverage are striking. In one newspaper, the Iraq crisis got at least forty times the attention as the Kosovo crisis had four years earlier, and in most newspapers Iraq was five times more written about than Kosovo.

In terms of the framing of the imminent war, we engaged in an original media analysis in the eight nations under study. In each country, we content-analyzed three newspapers: the major left-leaning broadsheet, the major right-leaning broadsheet, and the most popular national (or local) newspaper. Each paper was scrutinized for Iraq conflict articles for two months—between January 21, 2003, that is, three weeks preceding the February 15 protests, and March 21, 2003, the day after the invasion of Iraq started (see appendix B for more information).

A first step to assess the media's position on the war is to chart the discussion about the justness of the war. Were only arguments in favor of the war mentioned, only arguments that dismissed a potential war on Iraq, or was coverage fairly neutral? Table 3.1 contains the results of this exercise per country. First, it shows that the discussion about war and its justification was at the heart of the media coverage in the run-up to the war. In well over half of all (potential) Iraq War articles, at least one motive for or against war was mentioned. Media did not just report about war preparation, its cost, new weaponry, the respective strategies, the likely course, and the consequences. Overall, the press devoted a large amount of its coverage to the question of why this war was necessary or unnecessary. We would need systematic comparative data about previous conflicts to substantiate this—for example, late-stage coverage of the Vietnam War, which was also largely devoted to war's justification—but it appears that this obsession with war's justification or disqualification was exceptional. People who followed the media in the run-up to the war on Iraq were, thus, constantly confronted with arguments about the war and incited to take sides in the debate between supporters and opponents.

Yet, clearly, there are some striking differences among the countries. The debate about the reasons for war was not equally strong in all countries. In Spain, the United States, and the United Kingdom, as well as in Belgium and Germany, the articles mentioning one or more reasons for or against war outnumbered the ones that did not bring up any of these. One possible explanation could be the link with the national governments' stances on war:

Table 3.1. Media mentionings of reasons for going and not going to war (percent)

	US	UK	SP	IT	NL	SW	BE	GE	Total
No reasons mentioned	34.4	30.3	34.9	53.5	61.7	85.4	43.4	20.0	44.8
Only reasons pro-war	16.5	24.2	20.4	18.0	11.7	3.1	14.6	15.3	15.8
Only reasons antiwar	12.5	15.6	25.1	21.1	16.7	9.6	21.6	20.2	18.1
Reasons pro- and antiwar	36.7	29.9	19.6	7.4	9.9	1.9	20.4	44.4	21.2
Inclination of coverage (arguments in articles)	+4.0	+8.6	4.7	-3.1	-5.0	-6.5	-7.0	-4.9	-2.3
Article pro-war inclination	5.3	10.9	7.0	4.1	2.2	0.0	0.8	2.8	4.1
Article antiwar inclination	1.9	5.7	14.5	9.1	8.9	1.6	7.4	6.9	7.3
Inclination of coverage (coder judgment)	+3.4	+5.2	-7.5	-5.0	-6.7	-1.6	-6.6	-4.1	-3.2
N	425	488	387	635	639	322	514	509	3,927

Note: For more information on data collection, see appendix B, this volume.

the first three countries were most involved in the build-up toward war, and the two latter were the most fierce war opposers in our sample. In Italy, the Netherlands, and Switzerland, this was exactly the other way round: here, official war support or opposition was less explicit, possibly leading the media to engage in more descriptive coverage of the eventuality of war.

A third general observation is that newspapers in all countries highlighted both sides' arguments in the debate. In none of the countries did one of the sides get all the credit. Even in the United States and United Kingdom, the balance was fairly equal, with a comparable number of articles mentioning no reasons at all, and articles mentioning arguments from both sides of the pro-contra war debate. At first sight, hence, the media coverage in the news-papers was fairly balanced, although we did not analyze how the arguments were presented. Still we find interesting country differences. It is, of course, difficult to weigh the arguments quantitatively against each other, but the table shows that there were considerable differences among the countries. Sub-tracting the percentage of positive arguments from the negative ones, we can rank-order the countries' media from supporting to opposing war. It comes as no surprise that the U.S. and UK press were most prone to war, with the former having a +4.0 and the latter a +8.6 percent difference between pro- and contra-war arguments. Newspapers in the United States and the United Kingdom seem to have been inclined to follow their political leaders in en-dorsing the war. In all other countries this difference is negative: the majority of the press in continental Europe seemed to have been on the same antiwar wavelength. Governments' antiwar stances were supported in the three war-opposing nations (Belgium, Germany, and Switzerland). Yet, strangely, in the three war-supporting countries (Italy, Spain, and the Netherlands), the press was been even more inclined to counter the official governments' pro-war arguments and to emphasize cases against war.

Finally, we asked our encoders to subjectively evaluate whether, accord-ing to their personal judgments, the article explicitly displayed a pro- or contra-war position. Each judgment, however, was only taken into account when they could substantiate it by indicating a (part of a) sentence that made clear their choice. Whereas the figures in the upper part of the table are more an indication of how the debate about (not) going to war was held, here we try to measure actual, explicit, and thus intended, media bias opposing or in favor of war. The results of this evaluation exercise are shown at the bottom of Table 3.1.

First, more than 10 percent of the articles analyzed displayed a bias for or against war. When we look at the spread of biased articles over the coun-tries, we see a very similar pattern as in the previous analysis. Though in most countries, many articles favoring or articles disapproving war were found, the differences are clear. The British press featured the most overtly war-endorsing articles, followed by the Spanish and U.S. Explicit antiwar articles, however, were most found in Italy, the Netherlands, Belgium, and Germany. Clearly, the Swiss press seems to have largely been joining that country's ever-neutral status. In none of the countries were both types of articles balanced. Overall, the press sided either with war endorsers or with war opposers. When we subtract the number of pro-war articles and the number openly opposing war, very similar results to those of the previous analyses appear: the UK press was most biased toward endorsing the war (+5.2 percent). The U.S. (+3.4 percent) and the UK media are the only ones to have positive balances between pro- and antiwar articles; in all remaining European countries, it is clearly negative.

Overall, the national newspapers produced a fairly balanced picture of the run-up toward war. Since the international debate about going or not going to war was very vivid, national media devoted a large amount their coverage to it. Yet, in both war-initiating countries, the United States and the United Kingdom, pro-war arguments clearly were more salient; and when the media in these countries explicitly took sides, they most often did so in favor of war, which was exactly the opposite for all other European countries in our sample. We conclude that there seems a causal link between official government positions and the press coverage of (upcoming) war. But this link is weak, and it is conditional. In war-leading nations the media seemed to follow the government, but in the countries where government only verbally endorsed the war, the press opposed the government viewpoint. In other words: only when national governments took strong and rigid positions were they followed by the press. Maybe the way national public opinion saw the eventuality of war was a determining factor for the direction of press coverage.

Public Opinion and the War

Most new social movements neither have strong organizational resources nor are the beneficiaries of long-established loyalties that help them overcome periods of invisibility. The public's opinion on an issue determines the movement's mobilization potential. Although the relationship between what Klandermans (1984) called consensus mobilization and actual turnout is not linear, because of diverging action mobilization capacities, a favorable public opinion can boost protest turnout. Also, public opinion support is relevant in terms of the protest's impact. Supportive public opinion is paramount especially for countries waging war. Did the public in the eight nations favor war or not?

Between January 21 and 27, 2003, just before the February 15 protests, European Omnibus Survey (EOS) Gallup Europe (2003) conducted a comparative opinion poll in thirty European countries, covering 15,080 people aged fifteen years and older.[2] The poll contains extensive evidence regarding European public opinion about the potential war. We look first at the war's salience among European populations and then at war support.

Salience was measured somewhat awkwardly. The respondents were confronted with six pending international problems and were asked which of these most urgently needed to be solved. Apart from the imminent war on Iraq, the respondents could choose among the Israeli-Palestinian conflict, Indian-Pakistani tensions, international terrorism, the Chechnyan war, and the North Korean nuclear crisis. Hence, issue saliency was not measured via the traditional open "Most Important Problem" question. But since we are interested in differences between countries and not in absolute levels, this is not too problematic.[3] In Figure 3.2 the white bars illustrate the responses of the EU states, with Switzerland added.

In all sixteen nations, except for Spain, public opinion considered a war

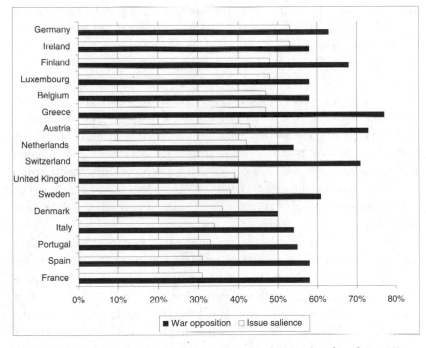

Figure 3.2. Percentages of European nations' populations that found Iraq War the most important issue and that opposed it

in Iraq as the single most important international problem. Yet, there are large intercountry differences. Our eight countries nicely cover the whole range of opinions. The German population was most (53 percent) concerned with the Iraq War, followed by the Belgian (47 percent). The Dutch, Swiss and British populations each scored around 40 percent, while both the people of Spain and Italy seemed to have cared considerably less about Iraq (both around 30 percent); the Spanish people, especially, did not perceive the possibility of war as the most important international problem. Probably because of their domestic terrorism problems, Spaniards mention international terrorism as top priority (35 percent). Italians also had severe domestic terrorism in the past and, likely consequently, attributed great priority to terrorism (27 percent) but also to solving the Israeli-Palestinian conflict (19 percent). Both the Italians and Spaniards considered the risk of terrorism in their own country significantly higher than did the residents of the other European countries, and both considered the United States as best capable of effectively fighting international terrorism.

Issue salience is only half the story. The Gallup Poll also elicited people's opinion on several statements regarding the Iraq conflict. We combined seven statements about Iraq into one simple war opposition scale.[4] The results are shown in the dark bars in Figure 3.2. Again, our eight countries span the whole spectrum of public opinion vis-à-vis the war. UK citizens, clearly, are by far the least opposed to war; on average, only 40 percent of them agreed with antiwar propositions. Of all European countries, public opinion in the United Kingdom is most divided. In the Netherlands, Italy, Spain, and Belgium (large) majorities oppose war. The most war-rejecting populations are found in Germany and Switzerland. Only Greece and Austria, countries not covered in this book, beat the Swiss in antiwar feelings. Saliency and opinion direction seem only weakly related. A country like Spain, for example, scores particularly low on saliency but contains a fair amount of war opposers. The correlation between saliency and war opposition is positive, but modest (r = 0.36).

Let us further specify the precise content of public opinion in the eight nations, since the above scale draws only a raw picture. We focus on four specific propositions: that Iraq poses a threat to world peace; that the respondents' country can take part in a war when justified by a UN resolution; that oil is the main motivation for the United States to invade Iraq; and that the United States should intervene militarily in Iraq, even unilaterally. We choose these because we presented the participants in the February 15 protests with exactly the same statements and, later, we will compare public opinion with that of the demonstrators. Figure 3.3 contains the results for the seven European nations in our sample.

Most European populations agreed that Iraq was a threat for world peace; this first diagnostic statement is not really causing much discord among Europeans. The same applies to their account of the third element, the United States' motivation to invade Iraq: a large majority concurs that a self-interest driven search for oil is the main incentive. A large majority, as well had the same response to the fourth proposition, rejecting the possibility of the United States' unilateral invasion of Iraq without UN backing, which is what eventually happened. The real divisive issue is the second one, the justification of (their own country's partaking in) a potential invasion via the UN Security Council. Here, opinions differ strongly. In the United Kingdom, an overwhelming majority would approve war backed by such a resolution, while in Switzerland even a Security Council endorsement would not convince a majority of Swiss of the justness of war. No wonder Blair's UK government did everything within its power to get UN backing. This divisive statement goes to the heart of the debate about the war in Europe, especially the unilateral and even illegal character of a possible Iraq war.

For the main purpose of this book—explaining why demonstrators in eight nations differ—divergences among countries are most interesting. Again, the UK population endorses war the most by far, followed by the Dutch and Italian populaces, who moderately favor the war. German and Belgian people are more skeptical about invading Iraq, while Swiss and Spanish citizens seem absolutely opposed to it. Put otherwise: while the United Kingdom's Tony Blair was more or less successful in at least sparking doubts about Iraq in the minds of the British people and while Italian prime minister Silvio Berlusconi was less convincing, Spanish prime minister José Maria Aznar completely failed to convince his population of the need to invade Iraq. Of course, the fact that a majority of Britons would have supported war with UN backing does not imply that they supported the actual war, which was being waged without UN support; UN approval was crucial for British public opinion. The fourth statement clearly shows that a majority of British citizens did not support the actual war. And Swiss, Belgian, and German public opinion contested war, in line with their governments' positions.

Unfortunately, the EOS Gallup Poll is confined to Europe and contains no evidence on U.S. public opinion. Where would the U.S. public stand? U.S. polling evidence is widely available but not always comparable with European surveys. We choose to focus on a poll conducted by the same polling company around the same time as the European EOS Gallup Poll.[5] At this time, 56 percent of Americans would give the weapons inspectors more

	UK	SP	IT	NL	SW	BE	GE
"Iraq represents a threat to world peace." (disagree)	23	35	28	33	43	37	34
"Oil is the main motivation for which the United States wants to intervene militarily in Iraq." (agree)	60	79	73	74	75	72	72
"Do you consider that it would be justified or not that our country participates in a military intervention in Iraq if the UN Security Council decides on a military intervention in Iraq?" (unjustified)	15	43	33	29	66	40	52
"The United States should intervene militarily even if the United Nations does not give its formal agreement." (disagree)	68	77	79	80	86	78	87
N	507	502	500	515	500	501	500

Figure 3.3. Percent agreement or disagreement among opinion with statements on the war on Iraq.

time to conduct their inspections, versus 41 percent who believed that Iraq had already had enough time to prove that there were no such weapons. Relatedly, 39 percent of the surveyed answered that the United States should invade Iraq as soon as the Bush administration decided on it; 56 percent of the people could not favor an invasion without a new UN vote authorizing military action. This last figure is particularly relevant, since it can directly be compared with the European data. In Europe, between 68 and 87 percent rejected war without UN backing, while "only" 56 percent did in the United States. On the question "Which comes closer to your view? UN weapons inspectors alone can eliminate the threat Iraq poses to other nations. Or, military action is needed along with weapons inspections to eliminate the threat Iraq poses to other nations," 71 percent of the people agreed with the latter proposition. Evidence from other polls at that time largely underpins the far more war-supportive attitude of the U.S. people before the war: approval rate for the way the Bush administration handled the Iraq conflict was high, military action "to remove Saddam Hussein from power" was favored by a large majority, and more than half of the Americans said they would support war even if it was not approved by the Security Council, and more than 90 percent considered Iraq a threat to the United States. By and large, it is safe to consider U.S. public opinion the most supportive of war of all the countries under study. A majority of the U.S. people believed in the necessity for military intervention. Of the governments in all war-supporting countries, the Bush administration was doubtlessly most successful in convincing its people of the need for war. However, this does not mean that the U.S. public was not divided about the issue: a considerable minority of U.S. citizens did oppose the war.

Conclusion

Political context, media coverage, and public opinion—the three relevant dimensions of societal context possibly determining the features of protesters in our eight countries—are not independent from one another. The direction of the possible causal chain connecting these three is not straightforward, yet we tend to believe that the government's initial stance on Iraq and the political opposition's reaction to this position are essential factors influencing the kind of media coverage and (subsequent) public opinion. Governments set the agenda of the media. And, as—at least in the West—war on Iraq is an unobtrusive issue not experienced directly by the people but only intermediated by the media, we believe the media influence public opinion. At the same time, the commercial forces most mass media are subject to also make them to cater to their public. Whatever the causal path, politics, media, and

	Politics	Media	Public opinion
United States	pro	pro	pro
United Kingdom	pro	pro	pro
Spain	pro	contra	contra
Italy	pro	contra	contra
Netherlands	pro	contra	contra
Switzerland	contra	contra	contra
Belgium	contra	contra	contra
Germany	contra	contra	contra

*Figure 3.4. Summary of position of political actors, media, and public opinion
regarding the Iraq War*

public opinion are associated. Figure 3.4 summarizes our findings. It presents
a very rough simplification of reality: government stance and public opinion are complex phenomena, and summarizing them in a single pro- or antiwar continuum cannot but oversimplify reality to some extent. The same goes
to a possibly even larger extent for national media, certainly when one takes
into account that they contain viewpoints from both broadsheets and tabloids
and both left- and right-leaning news outlets. Nonetheless, the scale in the
figure is very useful, as will be demonstrated later in this volume.

Figure 3.4 shows that the United States and United Kingdom on the
one hand, and the officially war-opposing countries on the other, had a very
clear and homogeneous position vis-à-vis the war: politics, media, and public
opinion fostered and supported war in both countries. The opposite applied
to Germany, Belgium, and Switzerland: all three agreed on their disapproval
of war. In Spain, Italy, and the Netherlands, a far more mixed pattern appears,
with the national government's war-supporting position being challenged by
both media and public opinion in all three countries. National leaders clearly
lacked media support to convince their citizens of their Iraq policy.

Notes

1. For reasons of convention we will use the term "public opinion" for the aggregate of individual opinions usually measured in surveys. We are aware that these
opinions are mostly not publicly expressed and do not target the public as media and
protesters do and that, in the strict sense, these aggregated opinions are not "public
opinion."

2. All public opinion data in this chapter are derived from this study, unless
mentioned otherwise.

3. The exact wording of the statement was "The potential war in Iraq should be
solved as first top priority." Agree (percent).

4. The scale was simply the mean (in percentage) of the aggregation of the war-opposing answers on the following statements: (1) Iraq represents a threat to world peace (disagree); (2) Oil is the main motivation for which the United States wants to intervene militarily in Iraq (agree); (3) The United States should intervene militarily in Iraq even if the United Nations does not give its formal agreement (disagree); Do you consider that it would be absolutely justified, rather justified, rather unjustified, or absolutely unjustified that our country participates in a military intervention in Iraq? (4) If the Iraqi regime does not cooperate with UN inspectors (unjustified)? (5) If the UN inspectors discover weapons of mass destruction in Iraq (unjustified)? (6) If the United States intervenes militarily in Iraq without a preliminary decision of the United Nations (unjustified)?

5. It concerns a CNN / *USA Today* / Gallup poll, which asked a sample of a thousand adults nationwide about their opinions on several Iraq-related propositions. The poll was conducted on January 23–25, 2003. Evidence can be read at http://www.pollingreport.com/iraq17.htm (we accessed the Web site December 7, 2009).

Works Cited

Bennett, Lance. 1990. "Toward a Theory of Press-State Relations." *Journal of Communication* 2: 103–25.

Bennett, Lance, and David Paletz, ed. 1994. *Taken by Storm: The Media, Public Opinion, and U.S. Foreign Policy.* Chicago: University of Chicago Press.

Berenger, Ralph. 2004. *Global Media Go to War: Role of News and Entertainment Media during the 2003 Iraq War.* Spokane, Wash.: Marquette.

Calabrese, Andrew. 2005. "Casus Belli: U.S. Media and the Justification of the Iraq War." *Television and News Media* 6: 153–75.

Cortright, David. 2004. *A Peaceful Superpower: The Movement against War in Iraq.* Goshen, Ind.: Fourth Freedom Forum.

Entman, Robert M. 2003. "Cascading Activation: Contesting the White House's Frame after 9/11." *Political Communication* 20: 415–32.

———. 2004. *Projections of Power: Framing News, Public Opinion, and U.S. Foreign Policy.* Chicago: University of Chicago Press.

Entman, Robert M., and Benjamin I. Page. 1994. "The News before the Storm: The Iraq War Debate and the Limits of Media Independence." In *Taken by Storm: The Media, Public Opinion, and U.S. Foreign Policy,* ed. Lance Bennett and David Paletz, 82–104. Chicago: University of Chicago Press.

EOS Gallup Europe. 2003. International Crisis Survey, January 2003. http://www.eosgallup europe.com/int_survey/index.html.

Hachten, William, and Marva Hachten. 2000. "Reporting the Gulf War." In *Media Power in Politics,* ed. Doris A. Graber, 317–25. Washington D.C.: CQ Press

Herman, Edward, and Noam Chomsky. 1988. *Manufacturing Consent.* New York: Pantheon.

Hooghe, Marc, and Dietlind Stolle. 2005. "Kroniek van een aangekondigde oorlog: Een vergelijkend onderzoek naar de verslaggeving in de aanloop naar de oorlog in Irak." In *Nieuws op televisie: Televisiejournaals als venster op de wereld,* ed. Marc Hooghe, Knut De Swert, and Stefaan Walgrave, 175–93. Leuven, Belgium: Acco.

Klandermans, Bert. 1984. "Mobilization and Participation: Social-psychological Expansions of Resource Mobilization Theory." *American Sociological Review* 49: 583–600.

Kritzinger, Sylvia. 2003. "Public Opinion in the Iraq Crisis: Explaining Developments in the UK, France, Italy and Germany." *European Political Science* 3: 30–34.

Lule, Jack. 2004. "War and Its Metaphors: News Language and the Prelude to War in Iraq, 2003." *Journalism Studies* 5: 179–90.

Neidhardt, Friedhelm, and Dieter Rucht. 1991. "The State of the Art and Some Perspectives for Further Research." In *Research on Social Movements,* ed. Dieter Rucht, 421–61. Frankfurt a.M.: Campus Westview.

Rendall, Steve, and Tara Broughel. 2003. "Amplifying Officials, Squelching Dissent: FAIR Study Finds Democracy Poorly Served by War Coverage." *FAIR: Fairness and Accuracy in Reporting.* http://www.fair.org/index.php?page=1145.

Rutherford, Paul. 2004. *Weapons of Mass Persuasion: Marketing the War against Iraq.* Toronto: University of Toronto Press.

Taylor, Philip. 1992. *War and the Media: Propaganda and Persuasion in the Gulf War.* Manchester, UK: Manchester University Press.

Wolfsfeld, Gadi. 1997. *Media and Political Conflict: News from the Middle East.* Cambridge: Cambridge University Press.

4

Legacies from the Past:
Eight Cycles of Peace Protest

Bert Klandermans

Although the protest against the war in Iraq can be studied in its own right, it is also a link in a much longer chain of protest events regarding issues of peace and war. Large protest movements proceed in cycles; periods of mobilization and demobilization alternate. That no mass mobilization takes place does not necessarily mean a movement has disappeared, because between periods of mobilization, movements might continue to exist in abeyance (Taylor 1989), and such abeyance structures appear important in later periods of mobilization (see Downton and Wehr 1998; Everts and Walraven 1984; and Kleidman 1993 for examples regarding the peace movement).

The dynamics underlying such cyclical developments are in part built into the very features of the movement. Obviously, peace movements respond to issues of peace and war in national and international contexts. Therefore, the peace movements in all eight countries of our study share a history of comparable mobilizations. Indeed, each has a tradition that goes back a long way and on occasion has been shown to have a strong mobilizing capacity. Perhaps more than any other, peace movements have reacted to international developments, be they nuclear armament, immanent wars, or tensions between states, for example. This explains why the various national movements have gone through similar cycles. At the same time, although the cyclical patterns are comparable, the amplitudes can be very different: there can be very big demonstrations in one country, while another sees only marginal ones. National circumstances are, of course, responsible for this variation.

In this chapter I will try to show how the interplay of general and country-specific movement characteristics, international relations, and national politics account for similar, yet different, dynamics of mobilization. In doing so, I will concentrate on the last two protest waves—that against the deployment of cruise missiles and that against the First War in Iraq.[1]

The Movement against Cruise Missiles

The movements against cruise missiles in Europe and the movement for a nuclear freeze in the United States developed against a background of a relatively stable geopolitical situation that underwent an increased polarization and remained largely unchanged over the course of the movement's life (Klandermans 1991b). The Reagan years were characterized by marked tension between the superpowers, which were infused with new ideological zeal. Reagan's rhetoric of the "Evil Empire" accompanied a massive escalation in U.S. defense expenditures and assumed a conception of security that made nuclear war seem possible in the European theater. This resulted in a general perception of threat that fueled the European peace movements (Rochon 1988). Moreover, that each national government had to decide on its territory's deployment brought the issue of nuclear armament home and constituted the basis for international alliances among national peace movements. The peace movement of the 1980s constituted one of the first occasions of significant interdependence among the social movement sectors of different European countries. Activists traveled extensively not only within countries but also between them, wherever the front of the struggle was perceived to be. None of the national movements could prevent its government from deciding to deploy cruise missiles, but this is not to say that the movements were failures. They did mobilize large proportions of the population, and they kept the cruise missiles on the political agenda for many years. The unspoken consensus on armament issues was definitely broken down.

The movement in the United States took a different direction. The call for a nuclear freeze succeeded in creating a broad coalition that mounted a formidable political force. The movement commanded enough resources and allies that it could successfully challenge the president's planned deployment of a new generation of missiles, the MX.

Despite the common grievance, the movements in the various countries differed sometimes considerably because of local circumstances. A brief overview of the movements in the countries where we conducted our research underlines this point.[2]

United States

In the United States the campaign against cruise missiles never really got off the ground, primarily because the trajectories of the peace movements in

Europe and the United States were rather different.[3] Indeed, at some point the goals that the European and U.S. movements had defined for themselves were almost incompatible. While in Europe the peace movement focused on cruise missiles, in the United States it centered on a nuclear freeze. Although the movements on both sides of the Atlantic felt obligated to support each other, providing this mutual reinforcement was fairly complicated. Essentially a proposal for bilateral disarmament, the freeze did not coincide very well with the more unilateral position of the movements against cruise missiles. Moreover, as far as specific weapons systems were concerned, political action against the MX was more likely to succeed than similar action against cruise missiles. To the average American, cruise missiles were a European problem rather than a U.S. one. Consequently, in the United States it was difficult to mobilize protest against cruise missiles, and little action was undertaken to prevent the deployment of the missiles in Europe, despite European requests for such active support.

This is not to say that the U.S. peace movement was inactive. On the contrary, the nuclear freeze movement was one of the major peace mobilizations of the twentieth century. It followed earlier mobilizations against atmospheric atomic testing and the war in Vietnam in the 1960s and 1970s respectively. On the withdrawal of the United States from Vietnam the peace movement dissipated, after an apparent victory, but also as in the earlier episode, the movement left behind an enlarged residue of peace movement organizations, trained activists, and sympathetic middle-class adherents who would be mobilized more rapidly during the next cycle of antiwar protest. This cycle exploded in 1980, as people unified behind the banner of the nuclear freeze (Marullo 1992).

At the start of the nuclear freeze the U.S. peace movement consisted of a wide range of groups and associations, ranging from moderate arms-control associations to radical pacifists. These diverse segments of the peace movement were largely invisible to the public and shared little with each other except their pursuit of peace. The call for a nuclear freeze changed that by providing a short-term goal that most groups accepted, a set of tactics familiar to most, and a recruitment message that greatly expanded the base of adherents (Kleidman 1993).

By 1984, however, the diversity of goals, strategies, and tactics of various segments of the movement had begun to reemerge, and new fissures developed. The range of problems confronting the movement, along with an increasingly less bellicose president and the warming of the U.S.-USSR relations, led to the withdrawal of resources from the movement and its further retrenchment and splintering.

United Kingdom

The British movement against cruise missiles had its roots in the Campaign for Nuclear Disarmament (CND). Founded in 1958, CND is one of the oldest peace movement organizations in Western Europe. Originally, CND directed its protest against Great Britain's own nuclear force. Before the movement against cruise missiles took hold, CND engaged in several protests against nuclear armament. These protests reached their peak in 1962, when a hundred and fifty thousand people participated in the annual Easter march. CND became the backbone of the movement against cruise missiles. From 1979 until 1983 this movement figured prominently on the British political stage, though the political opportunity structure during these years was not very favorable. Prime Minister Margaret Thatcher's government was extremely unreceptive to any of the movement's claims and, in fact, engaged in outright repression. However, the movement was successful in persuading the Labour Party to support unilateralism. After the government decided to deploy the cruise missiles in 1983, the peace movement and CND declined. Apart from Greenham Commons—the women's camp at the base where the missiles were deployed—no major actions were organized. Yet CND did not disappear; it survived, although in a less spectacular fashion.

CND's alliance system encompassed the unions, some of the churches, and some of the local governments. Coalitions, however, existed primarily at the local level. At the national level, churches were reluctant to enter into coalitions, and affiliations with the parties of the Left only underscored the government's claim that the movement was primarily a leftist affair. Although at its peak CND contained 1,100 local groups with 250,000 members, its organization was rather centralized compared to that of other peace movements. Activists and members were typically middle class. Fifty percent of the membership was employed in non-manual, professional jobs; the ranks of the CND included almost no blue-collar workers.

Spain

At the time of the cruise missile controversy, Spain was still to become a member of NATO, and therefore the Spanish peace movement did not engage in the struggle against cruise missiles.[4] The Spanish movement did launch, however, with its Portuguese counterpart a campaign for nuclear-free zones. In 1986 about four hundred town councils in Spain and Portugal had declared themselves nuclear-free zones (Carter 1992).

The major issues in those years were, however, specific to the Spanish situation, namely the presence of U.S. military bases in Spain, and Spain's entrance into NATO. In 1953, head of state Francisco Franco signed a treaty with the United States about military bases, and a new agreement was to be signed in 1982. In January 1981, the first big Spanish peace demonstration, aimed at the military base in Torejon, took place as twenty thousand people marched from Madrid to Torejon (Carter 1992).

A second issue the peace movement attempted to mobilize the public against was Spain's membership in NATO. In 1982, the then-conservative government took Spain into NATO. Afterward, the Spanish peace movement's central aim became bringing Spain out of the Alliance as soon as possible. When the Partido Socialista Obrero Español (PSOE; Spanish Socialist Workers Party) took over government, the country's moves toward military integration in NATO halted, but soon it became clear that the government was reluctant to withdraw from NATO. In 1986, Spain held a referendum, and to the great shock of the peace movement, not only did a large proportion of the electorate abstain from voting, only one quarter of those who did vote opted to leaving (Carter 1992).

Italy

Compared to other European movements against cruise missiles, the one in Italy was particularly weak and transient. It began later than the others, as an ad hoc body that met to organize a demonstration against cruise missiles to be held in Rome in 1981. The Italian government decided rather early (1983) to deploy cruise missiles at Comiso in Sicily, and most of the movement's protest activities took place after this decision, aiming at the base where missiles were to be located. A massive demonstration in Rome, in which five hundred thousand people participated, did not make the government change its mind. Shortly thereafter, the movement collapsed.

The movement against cruise missiles in Italy was a heterogeneous coalition of the Communist Party and the leftist parties and several nonpolitical organizations. In addition to the traditional sociopolitical organizations, groups of grassroots activists from such different backgrounds as the student, feminist, and environmental movements and Catholic lay organizations joined the campaign against cruise missiles. Together, the movements had a very loose structure, and attempts to institutionalize them invariably failed.

The little that is known about the popular support of the movement suggests that 25 to 40 percent of the Italian population sympathized with it. Compared to the other European peace movements, the Italian group was not very successful. Although it could mobilize massive demonstrations, it did not really have much impact on Italian politics.

The Netherlands

The movement in the Netherlands really acquired momentum with the petition against the neutron bomb in 1977. At the same time the Interdenominational Peace Council (IKV) began its campaign against nuclear arms. For more than four years it was uncertain whether a majority in the parliament supported nuclear deployment. By exploiting this situation, the movement was able to have the decision to deploy postponed several times. As a consequence, the Dutch movement lasted longer than any other European peace movement. As late as the end of 1985, it was still organizing a mass petition. Even though the government did decide in November 1985 to deploy cruise missiles, the 1987 signing of the INF treaty prevented implementation of this decision. Thus, the Netherlands was the only NATO country in which cruise missiles were never actually deployed. The movement succeeded in persuading the Social Democratic Party and the labor unions to join it, but despite the movement's strong position within the churches, it failed to persuade the Christian Democratic Party.

The movement developed an elaborate alliance system—leftist parties, unions, women's organizations, youth organizations, and others coalesced in so-called peace alliances at the national and local levels. The movement itself was fairly decentralized. Although it had national headquarters, its main strength was the local peace groups that did the actual mobilizing. The activists were typical of the participants in new social movements: young, middle-class professionals employed in social services.

After the government's decision to deploy cruise missiles, the movement declined rapidly. Although it could not prevent the government from deciding to deploy cruise missiles, the repeated postponements of the decision were considered a success. Public support of the movement was impressive: 35 to 40 percent of the population was unconditionally against deployment of cruise missiles; 30 percent opposed deployment upon specific conditions; and 25 percent was in favor of deployment (Oegema 1991). The movement has been able to mobilize massive participation in two demonstrations and a petition, but participants were primarily left-wing citizens. The movement succeeded in keeping nuclear armament on the political agenda for almost ten years.

Switzerland

The Swiss movement against cruise missiles—whose demands were not directed at any Swiss authority—was a result of international opportunities and the influence of mass peace protests in neighboring countries (Giugni

2004).[5] Kriesi et al. (1995) argue that the protests against cruise missiles in Switzerland to a large extent followed the early mobilization of the German peace movement. Like Germany, Switzerland had a history of strong mobilization for the Easter marches. The Swiss peace movement can be characterized by a strong focus on internal issues and an extensive use of direct democratic instruments to influence the political agenda. The most important peace movement organization during the first decades after World War II was the "Swiss peace council," founded in 1945. The protests against cruise missiles in Europe spread to Switzerland by the end of 1981. In December 1981, the Swiss peace council together with some other groups, such as Women against War, as well as trade unions and left-wing political parties, mobilized thirty thousand people for a large national demonstration against global nuclear armament. In 1982, thirty thousand participated in the traditional Easter march. In November 1983, a second national demonstration on the issue of global nuclear armament took place. With fifty thousand participants, this was one Switzerland's biggest-ever political gatherings.

The roles of the Swiss army defense industry, which were already a concern before the cruise missile protest wave in Europe, remained heavily on the agenda of the Swiss peace movement thereafter. The Swiss army became the most central target of the peace activists. One way of resistance was the refusal of military service, and the numbers of young men going to jail for their political convictions increased drastically. The most important means to bring these issues to the political agenda were, however, not protest and other unconventional forms of political participation but, rather, direct democratic instruments. Since 1969, there have been a number of popular votes on issues like arms trade, civil service, abolition of the Swiss army, and even the purchase of warplanes. While in the beginning, the Swiss peace council has been heavily engaged in this political work, it lost most of its importance for political mobilization of peace issues during the 1990s. During the 1980s, the Group for a Switzerland without an Army (GSoA), became the most visible peace movement organization in Switzerland.[6]

Belgium

Belgium had a strong movement against cruise missiles.[7] Indeed, it was the only country in which the movement continued to organize mass demonstrations after the government had decided to deploy cruise missiles. The Belgian peace movement differed from those in the other European countries by being completely rooted in the new social movements. More specifically, it was embedded in the network of environmental, women's, and third-world groups and centers crisscrossing the country. This network became the structural base of the peace movement. Although the new social movements provided the infrastructure for the peace movement, they could not turn it into a mass movement. Only when the peace movement entered a coalition with traditional political and social organizations—such as labor unions, political parties, and church organizations—did the true mass movement come into being. It maintained a rather loose structure of local groups and organizations coordinated by a national umbrella organization. The activists in the Belgian movement, too, were young, highly educated professionals employed in civil service or education. Popular support for the movement ranged from two-thirds to three-quarters of the population.

Despite the strong support, the movement was could not prevent the government from deploying cruise missiles, although it was strong enough to force the government to postpone its decision several times. Initially, the political opportunities had seemed favorable. Members of Parliament, including Christian Democrats, were divided on the issue, and the odds for a parliamentary strategy looked good. But at the crucial vote, thirty Christian Democratic members who had previously supported the movement stuck with the party line and voted in favor of deployment.

Germany

Like the British peace movement, the German movement has a long history, one that goes back to the early 1950s when Social Democrats, unions, Protestant church members, communists, students, and university professors protested West Germany's entry into NATO and its subsequent rearmament. A decade later, West German protesters, following CND, organized annual Easter marches that, at their peak in 1968, would attract more than 350,000 participants. In the 1980s, the movement against cruise missiles grew—the largest social movement West Germany had experienced since World War II. In this decade, a whole array of new groups, arising from the extra-parliamentary opposition, joined the movement. These groups, to a large extent, determined the nature of the new German peace movement. Starting as an ad hoc committee for the organization of large demonstrations in Bonn in 1981, the West German movement against cruise missiles developed later than parallel movements in other countries. Unlike the previous peace movements in West Germany, the movement against cruise missiles did not initially have the support of the Social Democratic Party (SPD) and the labor unions. Later, when the SPD was no longer in office, it changed its policy and became more sympathetic toward the peace movement. This shift, together with the relatively closed German political system, produced a movement rooted primarily in extra-parliamentary opposition. Most of the groups that played a central role in the campaign against cruise missiles had their origins in other movements—feminist, environmental, citizen, or youth. After 1983, when the government decided to deploy, the movement declined, although it did not disappear and continued to organize occasional protests.

The German peace movement had perhaps the most decentralized organization of all the ones in Europe. A steering committee was responsible for coordinating events and activities on the national level, but the groups represented in this committee took great pains to ensure that it did not become too powerful. For the most part, local peace groups were not related to any overarching organization and were eager to keep their autonomy. The movement was basically a grassroots organization with only a very loose superstructure, and the many different currents within it easily led to factionalism.

Public support of the peace movement was overwhelming. At its peak, it had the backing of more than 60 percent of the people, from every sector of the population (young and old, working and nonworking class, left and right, religious and nonreligious) (Cooper and Eichner 1991), while an estimated 2 to 4 million people were active within the movement.

Entr'acte

Soon the international situation changed radically. Soviet president Mikhail Gorbachev started a program of reforms, which over time led to substantial reduction of the nuclear arsenal of both superpowers. When Gorbachev began a foreign policy inspired by new values of openness and a search for dialogue with the West, perceptions of threat began to diminish, and former activists became increasingly difficult to mobilize. Established goals of the movements became less relevant and were actually achieved in the context of the East-West superpower summits, which to many symbolized the end of the cold war. Then came the events of 1989. One by one, Eastern European countries underwent radical political change that the Soviet Union did not hinder and even, as in the cases of East Germany and Bulgaria, actively promoted. These events created a new social and political reality in Europe that significantly affected the peace movement sector. Within a decade, dissolution of the Soviet bloc took place, effecting a further reduction of the sustained international tension that had characterized the cold war. Many peace activists point to the movement's delayed effect in achieving these changes in the security arrangements. Other analysts viewed the change as the consequence of an untenable economic situation in the eastern bloc.

In any event, after the collapse of the eastern bloc, the prospect for the peace movement changed substantially. The next international crisis developed in a radically different environment—one in which there is only one superpower and wars increasingly come to be presented as guided by moral motives (Ruzza 2004).

The Protests against the Gulf War

On August 2, 1990, Iraq invaded Kuwait. Washington, D.C., reacted by immediately blocking Iraq's assets and obtaining international approval for an arms embargo. Soon after, a multinational military contingent primarily composed of American, French, British, Egyptian, and Syrian troops was assembled. A few days after the congressional elections on November 6, President George Bush ordered a doubling of the 150,000 troops already present in the Gulf. On November 29, the United Nations voted to author-ize member states to "use all necessary means" to implement Resolution 660 if Iraq did not withdraw from Kuwait by January 15, 1991. On January 17, air strikes began. A February 23 deadline for a ground offensive passed, and a last-minute Soviet proposal for a negotiated solution of the conflict was not accepted by the coalition. A "hundred-hours" war crushed the Iraqi mil-itary and inflicted heavy Iraqi casualties, forcing that nation's withdrawal from Kuwait.

As Koopmans (1999) observed, no other war in the 1980s or 1990s led to such immediate and massive protest as the Gulf War. Particularly inter-esting was the growing importance of international diffusion of protest. What started with the movements against the cruise missiles further expanded in the protests against the Gulf War, that is, the internationalization of protest and of protest issues. The importance of protest diffusion is perhaps most clearly demonstrated by the phrase "No Blood for Oil," which became the peace movement's slogan across the globe. The build-up to the war was ac-companied by a short spell of intense protests between January 12 and 26 all over the world. Western European movements began to grow and mobilize (Brittain 1991). As the deadline approached, activities steadily increased in intensity and reached the high mobilization level of the early 1980s. But the levels of mobilization differed for the various countries; France, for example, which had hardly mobilized against cruise missiles, witnessed large demon-strations, while countries such as the Netherlands, where massive demonstra-tions against cruise missiles took place, had no protest of any significance. What follows is a brief overview of the anti–Gulf War protests in the eight countries where we conducted our study.

United States

Thousands of American citizens protested their country's military interven-tion. The first national demonstration in New York, on October 10, 1990, sponsored by the Coalition to Stop U.S. Intervention in the Middle East, was a modest one of between 10,000 and 20,000 people. But the protest soon escalated, and demonstrations reached much higher numbers: on January 19, 50,000 in Washington, D.C., and 100,000 in San Francisco; one week later, during the National Campaign for Peace in the Middle East, between 100,000 and 250,000 demonstrated in the capital city and 100,000 marched the streets on San Francisco. At the same time the protest became more disruptive. On January 19, a thousand people were arrested in San Francisco for civil disobedience actions; in the following three weeks no fewer than twenty-seven hundred were arrested.

United Kingdom

The Gulf War of 1991 led to a brief revival of the peace movement in Britain, but mobilization fell far short of the antinuclear protests of the early 1980s. One factor was the support of the war by the Labour Party, which had been the main political basis of the movement against cruise missiles. Only a handful of Labour dissidents opposed the Gulf War. With the Liberal Democrats backing the war effort as well, only fringe parties, such as the Greens and Plaid Cymru (Welsh Nationalists), and a range of far left groupings supported the peace movement. CND remained the dominant player, seeking to bring together a range of peace, church, and political groups in the Committee to Stop War in the Gulf, which formed in 1991. Another British initiative that gained some media attention was the Gulf Peace Team, formed in London in 1990, establishing a protest camp with eighty-six volunteers in Iraq near the Saudi border, all of whom were deported ten days after the war started. In Britain, various protest events did attract thousands of people, but support for the movement appeared limited to committed peace activists and backing fringe organizations. Once the war had ended, activities quickly dwindled.

Spain

The Spanish peace movement in the Gulf War era comprised two currents, one more pacifist, with a long and successful history of fights against compulsory military service and in support of conscientious objectors, and the other current consisting of the antiwar movement that engaged in campaigns against almost any then-current war. The major protest events in those days, however, were the demonstrations against the Gulf War. Between 1990 and 1991 at least sixty demonstrations against the war were held in Madrid alone, with about 230,000 total protesters.

Italy

The threat of U.S. intervention in Kuwait generated a new wave of protest in Italy. After Iraq invaded Kuwait, reinforced by the U.S. ultimatum for military intervention, large demonstrations took place (Giugni 2004). For example, on October 7, 1990, a hundred thousand people took part in a demonstration in Assisi, the starting point of the traditional peace marches. On January 12, and January 26, 1991, one hundred thousand and two hundred thousand people, respectively, demonstrated in Rome. Furthermore, a whole range of actions was held before and during the war. Obviously, the peace mobilization was motivated by the Italian army's involvement in the conflict. Even more so than the Gulf War, however, the military intervention in Kosovo rallied the Italian peace activists, who staged an impressive number of demonstrations.

The Netherlands

Surprisingly, at least in view of the massive mobilization against the cruise missiles, there were hardly any protests against the Gulf War in the Netherlands. While in Germany on February 17, some 120,000 people took part in various protests, in the Netherlands no more than 50 protested in The Hague in front of the parliament and 200 in Amsterdam's central square. Altogether, only an estimated 19,000 people took part in various demonstrations. There were several reasons for the low turnout. First, the Social Democrats were in government and in favor of military intervention, as were other major organizations, such as unions; only the small radical left parties opposed it. Second, the peace movement was internally divided. The large, church-based Interdenominational Peace Council seconded the Social Democrats, and again only the radical Left was against the war.

Switzerland

In January 1991, the Swiss peace movement staged several demonstrations against the Gulf War—the largest in Bern, which brought fifteen thousand participants in the streets. These demonstrations were part of an ongoing wave of protest organized by the peace movement regarding a variety of national and international issues. In 1993, a new wave of demonstrations targeted the war in Bosnia. In December of that year, a coalition of women's and peace organizations called for a Women against War protest day, which mobilized about thirteen thousand people in different Swiss cities. The aim of this action day was to draw attention to the sexual abuse of women in Bosnia. Although there were a number of demonstrations, compared to that of the early 1980s, the size of this antiwar mobilization was quite moderate. Also, the participation rates at the traditional Easter marches had diminished considerably.

Belgium

In Belgium the protests did not reach the levels they had in the 1980s either. The largest demonstration on January 13 brought no more than twenty thousand participants into the streets of Brussels. This was to a considerable extent due to discord in the peace movement. In 1990, two main umbrella organizations of the movement of the 1980s had merged into one organization, Vlaams Aktie Komite tegen Atoomwapens / Overleg Centrum voor Vrede (VAKA-OCV; Flemish Action Committee against Nuclear Arms / Consultation Centre for Peace). However, internal bickering about the distribution of power between the member organizations immediately led to a split, prompting several important peace organizations to break away. It took a much more critical stand toward the government, reproaching it for its lack of action. This viewpoint was a reaction to the formation of another, even more radical Maoist peace group. By the end of 1990, the peace organizations that had left VAKA-OCV rejoined the umbrella to establish an Initiative Group for Peace in the Middle East, which organized the January 13 demonstration. One week later, the same coalition organized another demonstration; again the Maoist peace group was present, which made the two largest labor unions withdraw from the coalition; soon the traditional-basis militants and the constituency of the traditional peace groups would drop out as well. By early February, the umbrella organization could only mobilize a few hundred in just a few local demonstrations.

Germany

The scale of protest in Germany came as a great surprise. Altogether, close to a million people took part in dozens of different protests and demonstrations. Within a few weeks, there were protests all over the country, despite the fact that after the major mobilization against cruise missiles in the early 1980s the peace movement seemed to have declined seriously, as suggested by the gradual decrease of participation in the yearly Easter marches. This was because the organizational network of the movement remained operational as the movement continued to protest various peace and war issues. Moreover, the political situation in Germany was relatively favorable: the Social Democrats were against the war, as were the unions. At the same time, a coalition of other new social movements supported the antiwar mobilization; the high schools were an important recruitment ground for these protests.

Conclusion

Peace movements existed in each of the countries where we conducted our research; however, their individual histories differed considerably. To be sure, in all countries, the movements were part of the same cycle: the protests against nuclear armament (especially cruise missiles) and against the Gulf War. Indeed, national movements responded to the same international phenomena. However, I observed significant differences between the countries in terms of the actual features of the campaign.

Figure 4.1 compares the two campaigns in the eight countries on two dimensions: the organization of the campaign and the level of mobilization. A difference between the two campaigns that catches the eye immediately concerns the mobilization levels; with Spain as the exception, mobilization levels were high in all countries during the cruise missile campaign, and I observed significant differences between countries during the anti–Gulf War campaign. Shifting coalitions are the second marked difference between the two. Whereas most of the cruise missile campaigns were organized by a coalition of new social movements, the traditional Left, and the churches, the latter two were absent in the anti–Gulf War campaign (with the exception of Germany). As far as the set-up of the campaigns is concerned, the cruise missile campaign was always both locally and nationally organized. However, in the anti–Gulf War campaign, there was much less local activity, especially in those countries where the mobilization levels were low. Finally, countries differ in terms of how mobilization levels vary between the two campaigns. On the one hand, I find countries such as the United States, Germany, and Italy with high mobilization levels during both campaigns. And Switzerland also reveals stable though lower mobilization levels over the two campaigns. On the other hand, however, there are countries such as the United Kingdom, the Netherlands, and Belgium, where mobilization levels during the anti–Gulf War campaign were much lower than they had been during the cruise missile campaign. The differences in the Netherlands are especially striking. Spain, finally, is the only country where the mobilization level in the anti–Gulf War campaign was far higher than it had been during the cruise missile campaigns; it's worth noting, however, that in those early days, the peace movement in Spain was still in its infancy.

The differences I observed between the two campaigns suggest that one cannot predict from a previous campaign whether the next will succeed or fail. In countries where I witnessed high mobilization levels and broad coalitions in one campaign, the movement failed to build viable coalitions and realized negligible protest activity in the other. Indeed, from the one cycle

	Cruise missiles		Anti–Gulf War	
	Organization	Mobilization	Organization	Mobilization
United States[a]	National and local campaigns against nuclear armament; nuclear freeze campaign	Large demonstrations in various cities; largest demonstration 1 million participants	National and local campaigns	Several large demonstrations; initially 10,000–20,000, later 100,000–250,000
United Kingdom	National and local campaigns; CND, new social movements and traditional left, churches	Large demonstrations with several hundreds of participants	National campaign; CND and far left	Marginal; largest demonstration only several thousand participants
Spain[a]	Peace movement in its infancy; campaigns on NATO and conscientious objection	Marginal; largest peace demonstrations 20,000 participants	National and local campaigns	Over sixty demonstrations; largest demonstration 230,000 participants
Italy	National campaigns; new social movements and traditional left, churches	Largest demonstration 500,000 participants	National and local campaigns;	Several large demonstrations of between 100,000 and 200,000 participants
Netherlands	National and local campaigns; new social movements and traditional left, churches	Large demonstrations of 400,000–500,000 participants; petition by 3.75 million people	National; only radical left	Marginal; demonstrations of only 50–200 participants
Switzerland	National and local campaigns; traditional left, churches	Several demonstrations; largest demonstration 50,000 participants	National and local campaigns; new social movements	Several demonstrations; 10,000–15,000 participants
Belgium	National and local campaigns; new social movements and traditional left, churches	Several demonstrations; 200,000–400,000 participants	National campaign; new social movements	Largest demonstration 20,000 participants
Germany	National and local campaigns; new social movements and traditional left, churches	Several large demonstrations of over 300,000 participants; overall 3–4 million people participated in some protest	National and local campaigns; new social movements and traditional left	Many demonstrations with 1 million participants in total

Note: [a]No cruise missiles were to be deployed in these countries.

Figure 4.1. A comparison of the two campaigns

of protest to the other, networks and coalitions had to be reanimated. A strong coalition in one cycle does not guarantee an equally strong coalition in the next, nor does a high mobilization level in one cycle guarantee high mobilization levels in the next. As Taylor (1989) maintains, movements go into abeyance when the tide turns and must be reactivated and remobilized for the next wave. Obviously, the conditions that prevail when and where this revival takes place determine the form of the new campaign. This implies that the characteristics not so much of the peace movement alone nor of the general political opportunity structure, but rather the time- and space-specific opportunities and the issue-specific context (see chapter 3) determine what coalitions can be built and what mobilization levels can be achieved. A complex interplay of general and country-specific factors accounts for the diverse appearance of the movement at various points in time and space. The unique opportunity offered by the demonstrations of February 15 is that they provide us with the possibility to disentangle the processes behind this diversity.

Notes

1. The movement against cruise missiles was a European matter; in that same period the movement in the United States concentrated on nuclear freeze. As we will see below, the two campaigns did not really collaborate.

2. Much of this section is based on Klandermans (1991a).

3. I am grateful to David Meyer for his help with the U.S. sections.

4. I am grateful to Ramon Adell for his help with the Spanish sections.

5. I am grateful to Michelle Beyeler for her help with the Swiss sections.

6. The GSoA was founded in 1982 to launch a popular initiative for the abolition of the army. Since then it has picked up a range of different issues and become a central player in mobilizing for peace demonstrations.

7. I am grateful to Stefaan Walgrave for his help with the Belgian sections.

Works Cited

Brittain, Victoria. 1991. *The Gulf between Us: The Gulf War and Beyond.* London: Virago.

Carter, April. 1992. *Peace Movements: International Protest and World Politics since 1945.* London: Longman.

Cooper, Alice, and Klaus Eichner. 1991. "The West German Peace Movement." In *Peace Movement in International Perspective. International Social Movement Research* 3, ed. Bert Klandermans, 149–74. Greenwich, Conn.: JAI Press.

Downton, James, Jr., and Paul Wehr. 1998. "Persistent Pacifism: How Activist Commitment Is Developed and Sustained." *Journal of Peace Research* 35: 531–50.

Everts, Philip P., and Guido Walraven. 1984. *Vredesbeweging*. Utrecht: Spectrum.

Giugni, Marco. 2004. *Social Protest and Policy Change: Ecology, Antinuclear, and Peace Movements in Comparative Perspective*. Lanham, Md.: Rowman & Littlefield.

Klandermans, Bert, ed. 1991a. "The Peace Movement and Social Movement Theory." In *Peace Movement in International Perspective. International Social Movement Research* 3, ed. Bert Klandermans, 1–42. Greenwich, Conn.: JAI Press.

———. 1991b. *Peace Movement in International Perspective. International Social Movement Research* 3. Greenwich, Conn.: JAI Press.

Kleidman, Robert. 1993. *Organizing for Peace: Neutrality, the Test Ban, and the Freeze*. Syracuse, N.Y.: Syracuse University Press.

Koopmans, Ruud. 1999. "Globalization or Still National Politics? A Comparison of Protests against the Gulf War in Germany, France, and the Netherlands." In *Social Movements in a Globalizing World*, ed. Donatella della Porta, Hanspeter Kriesi, and Dieter Rucht, 57–70. London: Macmillan.

Kriesi, Hanspeter, Ruud Koopmans, Jan Willem Duyvendak, and Marco G. Giugni. 1995. *New Social Movements in Western Europe: A Comparative Analysis*. Minneapolis: University of Minnesota Press.

Marullo, Sam. 1992. *Ending the Cold War at Home: From Militarism to a More Peaceful World Order*. New York: Free Press.

Oegema, Dirk. 1991. "The Peace Movement in the Netherlands." In *Peace Movement in International Perspective. International Social Movement Research* 3, ed. Bert Klandermans, 93–148. Greenwich, Conn.: JAI Press.

Rochon, Thomas R. 1988. *Mobilizing for Peace: The Antinuclear Movements in Western Europe*. Princeton, N.J.: Princeton University Press.

Ruzza, Carlo. 2004. "Peace Movements." In *Democracy and Protest: Popular Protest and New Social Movements*, ed. Gary Taylor and Malcolm Todd, 290–306. London: Merlin.

Taylor, Verta. 1989. "Social Movement Continuity: The Women's Movement in Abeyance." *American Sociological Review* 54: 761–75.

5

New Activists or Old Leftists?
The Demographics of Protesters

Stefaan Walgrave, Dieter Rucht, and Peter Van Aelst

This chapter analyzes the sociodemographic profile of the February 15 demonstrators. Who are they, in terms of age, sex, education, social class, and religion? Since this cannot be answered without a comparative yardstick, we can narrow down our quest to the specificities of the February 15 protesters when compared to other social groups. In more precise terms: Are the peace protesters typical new social movement supporters? Are they emblematic Old Left activists? Or do they, in contrast, mirror the population as a whole and, as such, represent an example of protest normalization? The comparative design of the book begs for an additional descriptive question: To what extent are the protesters' sociodemographic profiles different in the eight countries under study? The answer to this permits us to make headway with a causal question: How can we account for the differences in demonstrators' profiles in these countries? After all, these people demonstrated against the same issue on the same day, shouting the same slogans, carrying the same billboards, and relying on the same action repertoire.

The sociodemographic makeup of protest events may vary considerably. Sometimes, protesters are rather homogeneous. This is true, for example, when distinct social groups, such as farmers, defend their economic existence by means of protest. In other cases, protest groups express broad concerns that potentially affect large segments of the populace, if not humankind as a whole, for example, human-induced climate change or the risk of nuclear war. In these cases, we can expect the protesters to be recruited from different social backgrounds and to hold diverging ideological beliefs. As broad and heterogeneous as such protests may be—it is unlikely that they are representative of the population as a whole. From many surveys, we know that in the aggregate people who are politically active—and more specifically those who participate in protest actions—tend to be younger, better educated, and male (Norris 2002). Of course, the degree of deviation from the average population does vary greatly depending on the issue at stake. Also, the form of protest has an impact on recruitment. It is well known that in violent protests young men are strongly overrepresented. The organizers of protests, as well, may have a differential effect on recruitment patterns. We can expect that protesters following the call of broad alliances of diverse groups will be more heterogeneous when compared to those organized by radical groups from the political fringe. In addition, the location and timing of a protest action may have an impact on its social composition; for example, apart from strikes, workers rarely protest during the week, and elderly people do not tend to travel long distances to participate in protests. Finally, we can also expect that the tools and channels for mobilization affect the composition of the participants: calls via the Internet will not, or will only indirectly, reach those not hooked to the net (Internet users tend to be young and well educated). In sum, a set of structural and situational factors determine recruitment. General assumptions and predictions are likely to be inadequate concerning specific protest events.

First, in terms of the February 15 protest in 2003 against an imminent war in Iraq, we can reasonably hypothesize the sociodemographic profile of the protesters. Relative to other issues that directly pertain to specific social groups, this is a matter that affects people in moral terms without having immediate consequences in their daily lives. Hence, we expect protesters to be relatively heterogeneous regarding age, sex, education, social class, and religion. With regard to past peace protests, however, this general expectation must be differentiated. From many studies on peace movements and peace protests in the second half of the twentieth century, we know that participants tend to be male and younger and better educated than the rest of the population (Norris 2002). Chapter 4 in this volume focuses on two previous waves of peace protests and makes this point regarding the eight countries in this study; demonstrators against cruise missiles in Europe in the 1980s and protesters against the Gulf War in the 1990s were highly educated and typically middle class. As far as the period since the student revolt in the 1960s is concerned, peace protesters in Western countries in general share the specific features of what characterizes the activists and constituents of the so-called new social movements. Young, well-educated people from the human-service sector with liberal or leftist attitudes are strongly overrepresented among new social movement constituencies. Compared to the population as a whole, this activism is predominantly male-dominated. Women are better represented, though, compared to other kinds of political activism (e.g., within parties). Previous peace activism research, thus, leads us to expect that February 15 activists are rather heterogeneous, as we may have anticipated, but still be dominated by the "usual suspects."

Second, the story of February 15 is more complicated. Chapter 1 showed that the events were coordinated and staged by an international network of movement organizations, most of which originated within the so-called global social justice movements. It was on the European Social Forum meetings of these movements that the protest was set up and organized. Although the global justice movements are closely associated with the typical new social movement sector, they explicitly attempt to bridge these movements with the Old Left, that is, the labor movement and the traditional left-wing political parties with their working-class supporters (male, older, lower degree of education, active in traditional industrial sectors). In many countries, indeed, labor unions and traditional left-wing parties engage in the struggle for global justice; they are represented in the movement's central agencies and contribute substantially to the movements' mobilization potential (see chapter 8 concerning parties and chapter 10 concerning unions). Especially when it comes to peace activism, the Old Left shows a significant track record, at least in Western Europe; in the United States, the peace movement had weaker links with the Old Left. Chapter 4 elaborates this in more detail. Pre-1960s peace protesting in Western Europe was basically carried by the Old Left. Also, during the big marches against cruise missiles in the early 1980s, labor unions and left-wing parties did their part. As chapter 4 shows, in some of these countries it was the Old Left's mobilization machinery—wherever it was in the opposition—that contributed to the impressive peace protest wave of the 1980s. More than the environmental movement or the third-world movement—two other emblematic examples of the new social movements—in many countries the peace movement has been a coalition movement focused on mass mobilization and drawing support from a broad range of movement organizations. The movement's organizational backbone was most of the time diverse, with different organizations (temporarily) joining forces to further peace protest. In sum: contemporary and historical considerations lead us to expect that the February 15 protesters will not only consist of the typical new social movement constituency but might also be characterized by a strong presence of the Old Left. Both hypotheses boil down to the expectation that these protesters will not be representative of their respective populations but will consist of very specific segments of them.

However, in many countries, the political constellation regarding the war on Iraq—in particular that, as shown in chapter 3, in many countries opposition to the war was not confined to the Left but was dispersed throughout the political landscape—suggests the opposite hypothesis: February 15 brought a fairly representative sample of citizens to the streets. As we saw in chapter 1, many media accounts emphasized the protesters' high internal diversity and portrayed them as coming from a wide range of political and social backgrounds. This corresponds with the thesis of "normalization of protest" that has gained scholarly support since the late 1990s. It states that protest is becoming ubiquitous, just another strategy employed by citizens to defend their interests, and that there is an ongoing evolution of increasing diversity on the streets (Fuchs and Rucht 1994; Van Aelst and Walgrave 2001). The context in which the February 15 protest took place in many countries might indeed have been conducive to such normalization. First, this foreseeable war against the Iraqi regime was highly disputed among the leaders and populace in the Western world and beyond. That—according to various surveys—an overwhelming majority in most European countries opposed the war implied that the mobilization potential was not only large but also included people from different social strata and with different ideological leanings (chapter 3). While antiwar mobilizations during the second half of the twentieth century mobilized politically progressive groups, the mainstream was either undecided or tended to be on the other side. By contrast, the recruitment pool for this particular antiwar mobilization was extremely large and thus, almost by definition, very heterogeneous in terms of its sociodemographic profile. Moreover, that quite a few national governments were skeptical or even frontally opposed to war leads us to expect a large degree of heterogeneity among the protesters. In such a situation, protest was less likely to be perceived as outsiders challenging the establishment; both opponents and supporters of incumbent governments could be expected to participate.

Thus, three contradicting heuristic hypotheses can be established: first, February 15 was, in terms of the participants' sociodemographic profile, a typical new social movement event (young, better-educated people working in the human services sector); second, it was a typical Old Left event (older, less schooling, from industrial sectors); and third, it was neither of these but rather a case of large internal diversity, reflecting the normalization of protest.

The comparative design of the present study might lead us to conclude that all three hypotheses are true at the same time, though in different countries. The context in which the protests took place, in fact, differed extensively among countries. Chapter 3 showed that there were substantial differences among the eight nations in terms of the political stance of the incumbents and the opposition, in public opinion vis-à-vis the war, and in the way the war was covered in the mass media. Chapter 2 established that the countries under study differ not only regarding issue-specific aspects but, more fundamentally, in terms of their openness to challengers and protest and the strength of what was called the "progressive movement sector." For example, the degree of pacification of the labor issue varies across countries, and so does the strength of the new social movements. All these factors can be expected to affect the demonstrators' sociodemographic profile.

Who Are the February 15 Participants?

Bivariately analyzing the composition of the February 15 demonstrators, we see that men and women were present almost equally in the antiwar demonstrations (see Table 5.1). In most countries women were slightly in the majority. In Belgium, however, there was a striking overrepresentation of men. On the other side of the spectrum, in the United States, two-thirds of the protesters were female. In Italy, Germany, and, especially, Switzerland, the number of young demonstrators is much higher than the average. In these countries, about one-third of the participants were students. In Spain and in the United States, the youngest cohort is underrepresented: only one out of ten participants was a student. The U.S. demonstrations counted as many young people as they did those over sixty-five, which is quite unusual for a protest march. One thing is very clear for all of the countries we studied: the average antiwar protester is highly educated. In almost every case, the category of participants with a university degree is the largest. Again, Switzerland and the United States are the most extreme cases. Switzerland has a large number of demonstrators with lower educational degrees, many of these being young people yet to receive high school diplomas. The United States, however, had a spectacular 93 percent of demonstrators with higher education (non-university or university). The professional categories are more difficult to compare. The Spanish protesters differ from the other countries because far more of them are office and manual workers. The demonstrators overwhelmingly worked in health, education, care, and research, and, to a lesser extent, private services. Only a modest number of people worked in the industrial sector. Of course, these sociodemographics are correlated (not shown in table). Female protesters, for example, have slightly higher educations, are younger, and are more active in the service sector than men. It is not surprising that the younger people among the demonstrators, those who had not yet completed their studies, have a significantly lower degree of education than other protesters.

Table 5.1 reveals that in all countries every major group in society was represented to some extent. The February 15 protests unquestionably attracted

Table 5.1. Basic sociodemographic features of February 15 demonstrators in eight countries (percent)

		US	UK	Sp[a]	IT	NL	SW	BE	GE	Average
Sex	Male	37	46	48	50	45	49	57	47	47
	Female	63	54	52	50	55	51	43	53	53
Age	0–24	11	16	13	27	19	31	23	26	21
	25–44	35	38	48	46	36	39	38	36	39
	45–64	43	39	36	25	38	26	35	31	34
	65+	11	7	3	2	7	4	5	7	6
Education	None and primary	0	2	2	2	3	9	2	1	3
	Lower secondary	1	7	7	11	6	23	5	10	9
	Higher secondary	6	15	15	41	31	26	21	25	23
	Non-university higher	15	9	18	6	23	13	27	3	13
	University	78	67	58	40	37	30	46	61	52
Profession	Manual worker	6	8	31	9	5	7	4	4	8
	Office worker	16	12	40	21	38	32	47	27	27
	Professional, independent	34	37	1	12	10	10	6	9	16
	Manager	6	6	0	2	4	3	3	2	3
	Not working	15	13	12	1	16	13	17	18	14
	Student	12	20	10	32	21	35	22	32	24
	Other	10	4	6	14	7	1	2	7	7
Work sector	Industrial	17	12	–	18	11	17	12	13	15
	Private services	21	11	–	14	23	14	19	25	18
	Health, education, care, research	42	47	–	27	43	33	37	44	38
	Government	6	5	–	16	11	9	20	12	11
	Charity	12	11	–	6	10	8	10	4	9
	Other	2	14	–	19	0	19	2	2	9
N		666	1116	448	1002	528	629	503	769	5661

Note: [a]Spanish respondents were not asked about work sector.

people from all pockets of society and can, overall, be considered heterogeneous events. Yet the table also illustrates that the internal diversity of the protest differed from country to country. To account for these differences in internal diversity and to synthesize this diversity in one measure, we calculated fractionalization indexes (Table 5.2). A fractionalization index conveys the chance that two randomly drawn individuals fall in two different categories of a variable. The higher the index, the more diversity there is. Since the index is dependent on the number of categories of a variable, it cannot be used for comparisons between variables (with different categories) but merely between countries.

Table 5.2 shows notable differences among countries. The U.S. protesters, for example, are the least diverse concerning sex and education. Those from Spain are least diverse in terms of age, those from Belgium in terms of profession, and those from Switzerland are most likely to come from the same economic sector. Aggregated internal diversity, averaging the five fractionalization indexes for each country, is more or less similar across countries, though some differences exist. The U.S. and UK demonstrators seemed to have been the most homogeneous, leading to the lowest fractionalization indexes, while the Swiss and Dutch were substantially more diverse internally.

Only by comparing the sociodemographic characteristics of the protesters with those from the population in general can we assess whether the February protesters were a fair sample of their respective populations. In the United States, for example, protesters' educations may be higher simply because U.S. citizens in general are better educated than their European counterparts. We relied on demographic statistics published by the Organisation for Economic Co-operation and Development and the United Nations for sex, age, and education and calculated differences in proportional presence of the categories in Table 5.3.

Large proportions of men and women protested against war, with the United States featuring a majority of female and Belgium a majority of male protesters. In general, we find a slight overrepresentation of women, which corresponds with previous findings that women have since long started to catch up with their male counterparts in terms of protesting (Jennings and Van Deth 1990). All but the oldest age categories were overrepresented. Youth, however, is not more overrepresented than young adults and adults. Younger groups are most overrepresented in Italy and Switzerland, while older groups were most represented in the United States. Reasons for the globally enduring underrepresentation of older people on the streets are multiple: people in their seventies probably have less protest experience (generation effect) and have to overcome more physical barriers to join protest marches (age

Table 5.2. Fractionalization indexes for sociodemographic features of antiwar demonstrators in eight countries

	US	UK	SP	IT	NL	SW	BE	GE	Total
Sex	.412	.497	.500	.499	.495	.500	.49	.498	.498
Age	.668	.673	.653	.622	.685	.683	.678	.702	.685
Education	.365	.515	.656	.603	.710	.765	.669	.554	.651
Profession	.696	.691	.708	.749	.691	.729	.639	.678	.726
Work sector	.732	.718	–	.810	.728	.711	.762	.792	.772
Total (average)	.575	.619	.657	.629	.662	.678	.648	.645	.666
N	666	1116	448	1002	528	629	503	769	5661

Note: The formula to calculate fractionalization is $= 1 - \Sigma\, S^2_{ki}$. The index measures the probability that two randomly drawn individuals belong to different categories of a variable. Each term S_{ki} is the proportion of demonstrators with a certain feature.

Table 5.3. Over- and underrepresentation for sex, age, and education: Subtraction of share (percent) of protesters and share of population in the same category)

		US	UK	SP	IT	NL	SW	BE	GE	TOTAL
Sex	Male	-12	-3	-1	+1	-4	-1	+8	-2	-1.8
	Female	+12	+3	+1	-1	+4	+1	-8	+2	+1.8
Age	15–24	-7	+1	-5	+13	+4	+17	+8	+13	+5.5
	25–44	-4	+1	+11	+10	-3	+2	+2	-1	+2.3
	45–64	+16	+10	+10	-4	+9	-4	+6	+0	+5.4
	65+	-4	-12	-17	-19	-10	-15	-15	-12	-13.0
Education (25–64)	Lower secondary or lower	-12	-31	-53	-45	-28	+12	-36	-5	-24.8
	Higher secondary	-47	-28	+1	+10	-13	-42	-14	-44	-22.1
	Tertiary	+59	+59	+52	+36	+41	+29	+50	+49	+46.9
Total (average difference)[a]		19.69	16.11	15.69	14.28	12.61	12.72	16.36	13.72	13.21
N		666	1116	448	1002	528	629	503	769	5661

Note: [a]The average weighed difference was calculated as follows: the absolute differences per category were aggregated within each variable and divided by the number of categories of that variable. These weighed average differences were then averaged over the three variables.

Source: Sex and age population data are based on the Demographic Yearbook (2002) of the United Nations. The education data are based on OECD statistics for the population aged between 25 and 64.

effect). A comparison with the population in terms of education shows clearly that protesters in all countries had higher educations than the average citizens. Individuals with tertiary (university and non-university) education degrees were especially strongly overrepresented among the demonstrators. In terms of schooling, hence, the antiwar protesters are hardly representative, least so in the United States and the United Kingdom. Averaging demonstrators' representativity, we calculated average differences between the demonstration and corresponding population categories in every country: the lower this figure, the more demonstrators resemble their populations. Protesters in the United States, the United Kingdom, Italy, Spain, and Belgium were less representative of their respective populations at large than those in the Netherlands, Switzerland, and Germany.

In sum: people protesting imminent war were not representative of the populations of their countries. They were somewhat younger, slightly more female, and especially much better educated than the average citizen. This is hardly surprising: social movements defend certain interests and are rooted in corresponding population segments. Social movements that are able to mobilize true cross-section of the population have yet to be invented. Since movement support is not evenly present in all population segments, it is no revelation that neither is movement participation evenly present. A movement can only mobilize people who agree with its goals, and supporting the movement in word (attitudes) is something other than supporting it in deed (Klandermans 1984). Our next question then is this: Were the demonstrators at least exemplifying the war-opposing segments in their respective populations?

To compare antiwar activists with antiwar supporters in the respective populations, we need population data. We draw upon a population survey carried out by European Omnibus Survey (EOS) Gallup Europe between January 21 and 27, 2003, only a few weeks before the February 15 protests actually took place (EOS Gallup Europe 2003). All seven European countries covered in this book are included in the poll; the United States, unfortunately, is not. Chapter 3 presents the general results of this survey, suggesting massive antiwar sentiment among European citizens. In this chapter, however, we are only interested in the sociodemographic profile of these war resisters. To compare the population's antiwar segment's sociodemographics with the features of the movement activists, we must first determine movement support. What was the mobilization potential? What was the "official" stance of the peace movements? This is difficult to determine. Peace movement officials would probably reject war in any case. Since many EOS Gallup Poll questions were hypothetical and since some questions concerned motives for war and not the justness of war, we decided that opinions about U.S. intervention in Iraq without UN resolution best captured the stake and aim of the anti-war protest. We are aware that relying on one single question to delineate mobilization potential is a problem, as it artificially reduces the scope of the movement. In the seven European nations of this study, no less than 79 percent of the populace rejected war without UN approval. Consequently, we narrowed the movement's mobilization potential down to the people who *completely* disagreed with an intervention without UN backing and considered this still very large group of 54 percent as the mobilization potential of the movement. Who were those people?

The mobilization potential in the seven countries is characterized by a slight overrepresentation of women; a remarkably older composition, with the fifty-five and older group being the largest; having higher education although not being overeducated; relatively small shares of professionals and manual workers; especially high shares of non-professionally active citizens; and, finally, citizens with clearly left-leaning political stances. Thus, at first glance, the antiwar supporters look like the actual protest participants. Table 5.4 contains the differences between these groups based on the subtraction of their proportional presence. A negative figure means that this group is underrepresented among the actual protesters: this category was more present among the antiwar supporters than among actual movement participants. Hence, negative figures suggest a mobilization deficit: more people of this category supported the movement's claim than actually showed up at demonstrations. Positive figures mean the opposite, namely that relatively more activists than supporters were present.

The results in Table 5.4 must be interpreted with caution, since some EOS-Gallup categories did not completely match ours. In addition, the Gallup Poll samples were small and therefore prone to random errors. Only large differences merit our attention. The general picture is clear and confirms the literature about mobilization biases and political participation thresholds. Advanced age seems to be a very tough barrier for mobilization: in the oldest groups, it was not successful. Low education, too, is a formidable barrier; people with a higher degree of education are strongly overrepresented, and all other categories are underrepresented. Since the profession categories were recoded on a less reliable base and the differences do not seem that large, we must be extremely careful when interpreting these results in particular. The gender factor did not have much impact either. The most striking mobilization deficit, though is among right-leaning people. A considerable number of them supported the antiwar claim; yet they are very strongly underrepresented at the actual protest events. This suggests that mobilization for February 15 mostly targeted left-leaning people and that supporters from the Right

Table 5.4. Mobilization deficit: Comparison of protest potential and participants at the February 15 protests

		US[a]	UK	SP	IT	NL	SW	BE	GE	TOTAL
Sex	Male	—	-4	-3	+4	+0	-5	+11	-1	-1
	Female	—	+4	+3	-4	+0	+5	-11	+1	+1
Age	15–24	—	+5	-10	+4	+8	+19	+8	+15	+6
	25–39	—	+8	+11	+5	+1	+1	+1	+0	4+
	40–54	—	-2	+13	+6	-1	-9	+10	+5	+3
	55 and older	—	-12	-14	-20	-8	-11	-18	-20	-14
Education (years)	15 or fewer	—	-15	-16	-28	-3	+21	-3	-11	-7
	16–20	—	-44	-20	+5	-11	-21	-39	-46	-25
	21 or more	—	+59	+36	+24	+12	+1	+42	+57	+33
Profession	Self-employed	—	+39	-7	+6	-1	+3	+4	+6	+12
	Employee	—	-28	+17	-3	+8	-17	+12	-2	-5
	Manual worker	—	-4	+21	-3	-5	+0	-6	-7	-2
	None	—	-6	-31	+0	-2	+14	-9	+3	-4
Political position	Left	—	+24	+23	+43	+22	+34	+30	+25	+30
	Center	—	+2	-6	-13	+12	-21	+7	+9	-2
	Right	—	-27	-17	-28	-34	-13	-37	-34	-28
Total (average)			25.22	18.50	17.89	12.31	15.87	20.99	23.21	16.10
N		566	1116	448	1002	528	629	503	769	5661

Notes: "Protest potential" is defined as the segment of the population completely disagreeing with the statement "The U.S. should intervene militarily even if the United Nations does not give its formal agreement."

[a]No comparable data on U.S. public opinion was available.

were not reached and/or attracted. For a more in-depth analysis of the mobilization process of February 15, we refer to chapter 9.

People protesting against imminent war on Iraq may not have been representative of the entire protest potential, but they may have been typical for peace protesters in general. Therefore, we can compare their sociodemographic profiles with those of people active in previous peace protests. Unfortunately, past major and cross-national surveys on specific peace protests are not available. However, some population surveys have been carried out in various countries and at various times—surveys that included questions on participation in or support of peace movements. While most of these cannot be compared across countries because the wordings of the questions differ, four Eurobarometer surveys, conducted in 1982, 1984, 1986, and 1989 in Belgium, the Netherlands, Germany, Italy, and Britain, can be used for our purposes. Although these surveys serve as a reasonable basis for comparing peace activists in the 1980s and in the early twenty-first century, one methodological caveat should be underlined. In 2003, we surveyed protesters on the spot, regardless of whether they considered themselves part of a peace movement. In the Eurobarometers, people were not approached as participants in a specific peace protest but were asked questions, usually in their homes, about their relationship with the peace movement (along with several other movements). The survey asked whether people approved the "anti-war and anti-nuclear weapons movement" and whether they were members of or might join it. We classified those respondents as actual activists who approved strongly or somewhat and considered themselves members of such a movement. In addition, we classified as potential activists those who approved strongly or somewhat and said they might join the movement. We compared the sociodemographic characteristics of actual activists (usually low numbers) and potential activists (higher numbers) on a country-by-country basis, combining the four Eurobarometer surveys. Because the results for activists and potential activists were similar, we decided to put the two groups into one single category. Table 5.5 compares these 1980s potential and actual peace activists with 2003 actual peace activists.

The comparison yields substantial differences between the 1980s (potential and actual) and 2003 actual peace activists. Considering gender, there is no univocal pattern, but the divergences in education and age are flabbergasting. Most remarkable, especially in the United Kingdom and Belgium, is the great proportion of highly educated protesters in 2003 compared to the earlier peace activists. This tremendous difference cannot be explained sufficiently by the growing proportion of highly educated people in the intervening two decades. It is likely not coincidental that the distribution of age

Table 5.5. Sociodemographic characteristics of (potential) peace movement activists in the 1980s and actual antiwar protesters in 2003 (percent)

		Belgium		Netherlands		Germany		Italy		United Kingdom	
		1980s	2003	1980s	2003	1980s	2003	1980s	2003	1980s	2003
Sex	Male	54.7	57.0	44.8	45.0	48.5	47.0	52.0	50.0	48.2	46.0
	Female	45.3	43.0	55.2	55.0	51.5	53.0	48.0	50.0	51.8	54.0
Education	Low	21.5	4.0	21.4	6.0	38.9	1.4	53.5	3.5	32.4	3.8
	Middle	55.7	22.6	47.5	34.1	46.8	34.8	30.2	49.8	49.9	19.8
	High	22.8	73.4	31.1	59.9	14.3	63.7	16.0	46.6	17.7	76.4
Age	Young	39.2	22.8	23.9	18.8	31.5	25.7	36.3	26.6	35.3	15.7
	Middle	54.7	61.1	60.1	58.2	51.7	53.2	48.4	64.4	48.8	58.8
	Old	6.1	16.1	15.9	23.0	16.9	21.1	15.3	9.1	15.8	25.5
Left–right	Left	23.8	76.8	80.8	65.4	46.7	76.9	53.3	90.6	42.1	76.3
	Center	46.2	20.0	17.1	13.9	43.1	22.1	38.5	7.7	50.7	22.4
	Right	30.1	3.2	2.1	1.7	10.2	1.0	8.2	1.7	7.2	1.2

Source: Eurobarometer surveys 1982 (17), 1984 (21), 1986 (25), and 1989 (31a). The number of respondents varies by item. The combined number of respondents in the four Eurobarometer surveys is approximately 4,000 per country.

groups among the 1980 and 2003 peace activists differs strikingly; in all five countries, the proportion of young peace activists dropped considerably. Perhaps many peace activists of the 1980s, who then were predominantly coming from the young and middle generations, became reactivated in 2003— altering that year's age balance in favor of the middle and older groups. Our data support this interpretation to some extent; there is a linear and significant relationship between age and previous peace activism. The older February 15 protesters were much more likely to have participated in previous peace protests. Another explanation, of course, is that we compare very different groups from the 1980s and from 2003. Potential activism is something completely different than real activism.

Until now, we have only indirectly answered the central question underlying this chapter. We have not given a comprehensible answer to the question of how the February 15 demonstrators can be typified best: as the usual new social movement suspects, as the typical Old Left activists, or as a representative sample of the population? All analysis so far clearly shows that February 15 may have been internally diverse, but that demonstrators were not at all a fair sample of the population. Most analysis also suggests that February 15 was, above all, a classic new social movement event with a high proportion of women and an overrepresentation of relatively young, highly educated people working in the service economy. Although supported by the traditional Old Left in many countries, as chapter 3 shows, our antiwar demonstrators globally did not share the typical characteristics of the Old Left activists. Protesters who were male, older, less educated, and industrial workers were strongly underrepresented. Unfortunately, a direct comparison between other new social movement and Old Left protest activists based on surveys similar to the one this volume draws upon does not exist, since surveying people at demonstrations is relatively new. However, we have at our disposal a similar dataset containing participants in six other large demonstrations staged in Brussels, Belgium (Van Aelst and Walgrave 2001). The Belgian surveys covered most of the biggest demonstrations held in Brussels during the 1998–2001 period, which were staged by typical Old Left agencies, new social movements, and difficult-to-classify organizers. The profile of the Belgian February 15 demonstrators is clear: they are typical new social movement protesters, strongly resembling, for example, the antiracist and global justice demonstrators while systematically differing from all other demonstrators in the Belgian dataset. In particular, the similarity between the February 15 and antiracist activists corresponds strikingly. These Belgian data, thus, strongly suggest that February 15 was a typical new social movement event. Of course we cannot generalize this finding based on evidence for a single country. The evidence presented earlier, though, suggests that the Belgian February 15 demonstrators certainly were no outliers but resembled the antiwar protesters in the other seven countries. Though this is not conclusive proof, it corroborates our basic finding that February 15 was not, as massive and impressive as the event may have been, extraordinary in terms of the kinds of people who participated. Rather, demonstrators resembled the typical new social movement's constituents in advanced industrial democracies at the beginning of the twenty-first century.

How to Account for the Differences among Countries?

Having higher degrees of education, being younger and female, working more in the health, education, care, and research sectors, the February 15 demonstrators were not representative of their respective populations. As stated, they look like the typical new social movement supporter. This very general conclusion, however, has to be more nuanced when one turns to the demonstrators in the eight countries under study. Although they had much in common, we detected differences among countries. All demonstrated on the same day, for the same reason, making the same claim, but they did not share the same sociodemographic characteristics. Why? The whole range of comparisons pursued above shows that, ultimately, countries do make a difference. Variations among countries cannot be accounted for simply by differences in population compositions or dissimilarities among the war-opposing segments in their publics. We will rely here on two of the factors introduced in chapter 3: the eight countries' political constellations regarding the Iraq issue and public opinion vis-à-vis war. The phenomenon to be explained here is the degree of diversity of the demonstrators in the eight nations in contrast to the degree of their correspondence to the typical new social movement activist. Since diversity is easier to measure, we can reformulate our explanatory question as follows: Why was there more diversity among February 15 protesters in some countries than in others?

Tables 5.2 and 5.3 best capture the differences in diversity; they contain comparative fractionalization indexes and deviations of antiwar protesters compared to the entire population. Both tables roughly point in the same direction: the Netherlands, Switzerland, and Germany witnessed more internally diverse protest than the United Kingdom, Italy, and the United States, though there is no clear-cut dichotomy between these two groups of countries. Belgium and Spain show a less consistent pattern, with Tables 5.2 and 5.3 contradicting each other. The evidence, hence, suggests that the political stance of the government, anti- or pro-war, might have played a role in determining the protesters' profiles: in countries with governments explicitly and strongly supporting the Iraq War, turnout is less diverse and differs from the population as a whole. This makes sense: participating in antiwar protest in these circumstances might be considered as opposing the domestic government and challenging the incumbents, which might deter government supporters from participating even if they do not support the government on this particular issue.

Remarkably, the two most internally diverse countries were the most difficult to classify in our crude anti- or pro-war scheme: the Dutch government was only halfheartedly in favor of war—it had dissolved, and new government negotiations were underway—while the Swiss government was only weakly opposed. The Netherlands and Switzerland certainly witnessed the most heterogeneous crowds of all eight countries, given their highest fractionalization, which pointed to the most absolute diversity (Table 5.3), the lowest deviation showing large resemblances to the population as a whole (Table 5.3), and with the smallest mobilization deficit (Table 5.4). This is all the more striking since the level of protest in these countries was relatively small, as each had only modest turnouts, as chapter 1 reveals. This suggests that, apart from the simple pro-war/antiwar scheme, a complementary explanation might be valid: if governments do not express themselves clearly but take an intermediate position, participating or not participating in the demonstration can be considered neither challenging nor supporting government. Consequently, opposition and government parties could mobilize for the demonstration, bringing a highly diverse crowd to the streets.

How are people's attitudes linked to the government's stance and, subsequently, to diversity? Unity or discord among the population might play a role. Especially when a country actively participates in a war and bears the burden of war, people tend to be divided: patriotic feelings are in balance with antiwar attitudes. This might lead to polarization. In such a situation, it is not likely that a diverse constituency takes to the streets, because resistance and support for the war are not randomly spread over the population but concentrated in certain population segments. This certainly was the case in the United Kingdom and the United States. Chapter 3, indeed, makes it clear that—although largely opposing the war—UK public opinion was more divided and much more in favor of the war than all the other six European countries under study. U.S. public opinion supported the war but was divided as well. So government position determines the protesters' profiles directly by deterring or not deterring government's supporters, and indirectly by means of its polarizing effect on public opinion. This might be an explanation for the more homogeneous protesters' profiles in the United States and the United Kingdom.

Finally, the presence or absence of elite allies or the mobilizing role of oppositional parties (and civil society) challenging the incumbent war supporting party may also have a role in the population's relation to the government stance on the war. The question is whether the political opposition is willing and able to mobilize against the government's support of war. Ability depends on the strength of the party's own mobilization machinery, while willingness depends on the party's intent to link the antiwar issue with a more general criticism of the government. What happens if the opposition, in this case left-wing, goes ahead full force with mobilizing against war and, thus, against government? The issue becomes yet another battlefield between incumbents and challengers; it loses its capacity to unite people of different political and societal leanings and, as a result, the people showing up are not diverse but correspond to the constituency of the (left-wing) opposition. In other words: the war issue primarily becomes domestic politics, with the usual cleavage between government and opposition parties. Therefore, the Spanish population's relative nondiversity is due not to disagreement within the majority of the populace but the mobilizing role of the opposition and the resulting reinforced abstention of government supporters from protest. Note that in the United States, because its administration initiated the war and because the country would bear its costs in human lives, the Democrats—the challenging party—did not take the lead of the antiwar protest but rather decided to rally around the flag (see chapter 3).

In summary, we believe three factors to be crucial in explaining the diversity of the protest: government loyalty stopping some people from protest against the government they support, division among the populace, and the (in)capacity of intra- and extra parliamentary opposition to reach beyond its own constituency. If government loyalty is activated, public opinion is divided, and the oppositional forces are unable to bridge traditional cleavages, diversity will be lowest. Diversity is largest if government loyalty is only latent, public opinion is converging, and the opposition is not perceived as the driving force to mobilization. All three factors are ultimately caused by the initial position vis-à-vis the war taken by the incumbents. Governments could take four different positions regarding the war on three dimensions: clear or unclear position, supporting or the opposing war, supporting in words; supporting in deeds. Table 5.6 summarizes this logic.

The Netherlands and Switzerland belong to the first type, Germany and Belgium to the second, and Spain and Italy to the third, while the United States and the United Kingdom represent the fourth type. The United Kingdom is more difficult to classify, however, since there clearly was oppositional mobilization, though situated within the governing Labour Party.

Table 5.6. Government position and intermediary factors leading to different levels of protest diversity

Government position	Intermediary factors		= Diversity
(1) Unclear	Division in public opinion	–	
	Active government loyalty	–	High
	Mobilizing opposition	–	
(2) Clear: Opposing war	Division in public opinion	–	
	Active government loyalty	–	Moderate
	Mobilizing opposition	–	
(3) Clear: Supporting war with words	Division in public opinion	–	
	Active government loyalty	+	Low
	Mobilizing opposition	+	
(4) Clear: Supporting war with deeds	Division in public opinion	+	
	Active government loyalty	+	Low
	Mobilizing opposition	–	

Conclusion

We started with three heuristic hypotheses about the sociodemographic profile of the protesters on February 15. Are they largely diverse, thus coming close to representing the overall population? Do they resemble the Old Left constituency? Or are they emblematic of the new social movement adherents? Based on various ways of comparing the protesters with other groups, among which are potential peace activists and participants in other kinds of protests, we conclude that the new social movement pattern strongly prevails. Contrary to the newspaper reports cited in chapter 1 and the claims by many organizing groups, the demonstrators did not mirror the population at large. Still, we identified differences among countries that, as one could expect, can be attributed to the specific political context, for example, the position of the government toward the war and the reaction and composition of the oppositional forces in a given country. Thus, the very fact of the identical point of reference and the similarity of claims basically brought together the same kind of people in the countries under study, though national context modified their profile.

Works Cited

EOS Gallup Europe. 2003. International Crisis Survey, January 2003. http://www.eosgallup europe.com/int_survey/index.html.

Fuchs, Dieter, and Dieter Rucht. 1994. "Support for New Social Movements in Five Western European Countries." In *A New Europe? Social Change and Political Transformation,* ed. Chris Rootes and Howard Davis, 86–111. London: UCL Press.

Jennings, M. Kent, and Jan Van Deth. 1990. *Continuities in Political Action: A Longitudinal Study of Political Orientations in Three Western Democracies.* Berlin: Walter De Gruyter.

Klandermans, Bert. 1984. "Mobilization and Participation: Social-Psychological Expansions of Resource Mobilization Theory." *American Sociological Review* 49: 583–600.

Norris, Pippa. 2002. *Democratic Phoenix: Reinventing Political Activism.* Cambridge: Cambridge University Press.

Van Aelst, Peter, and Stefaan Walgrave. 2001. "Who Is That (Wo)man in the Street? From the Normalisation of Protest to the Normalisation of the Protester." *European Journal of Political Research* 39: 461–86.

6

Peace Demonstrations or Antigovernment Marches? The Political Attitudes of the Protesters

Bert Klandermans

Why did so many people bother to demonstrate? The obvious answer seems to be that they were opposed to the war in Iraq, but is this all there is to it? Was it solely opposition to the war, or was it also greater dissatisfaction in general that made people protest against their government?

Questions about dissatisfaction are the subject of grievance theory, which attempts to account for the grievances that motivate people to take part in protest. How did such grievances develop, and how are they embedded in the opinions and attitudes people maintain? For a long time, social movement literature neglected the discussion of grievances; the existence of grievances in a society had been taken for granted. It was assumed that grievances abound and that their existence is not a sufficient reason for protest movements to develop. More recently, the formation of grievances again gained attention of social movement scholars (Neidhardt and Rucht 1993; Klandermans 1997). Klandermans (2004) distinguishes between the demand side of participation, which refers to the potential for protest in a society, and the supply side of participation, which refers to the opportunities offered by the protest organizers. Attempts to understand the thoughts and emotions that fuel people's willingness to take part in political action concern the demand side of protest. Demand for protest begins with dissatisfaction, be it the experience of inequality, feelings of relative deprivation or of injustice, moral indignation regarding some state of affairs, or suddenly imposed grievances (Klandermans 1997). Protest organizations are—more or less—successful in responding to demand for protest, and we may assume that organizations that supply what potential participants demand obtain more support than those that fail to do so. Mobilization is the process that links demand and supply; studies about participation tend to concentrate on this and to neglect the development of demand and supply factors. To take either for granted is unjustifiable.

In this chapter, I focus on the demand side of the protest against the war in Iraq. I am interested in the opinions, attitudes, values, and ideologies that characterize the participants; I maintain that motivations to engage in protest are more complex than the proximate goals of a protest event suggests and that this is to be found more so in the case of large-scale events (Oegema and Klandermans 1994). I assume that attitudes in support of protest goals are embedded in broader oppositional sentiments, which have their own histories, as antiwar sentiments have (Neidhardt and Rucht 1993). While they frame the issue they are mobilizing for, social movement organizations try to connect the issues to such broader sentiments. The more successful these attempts to amplify the collective action frame are, the larger the demand for protest in a society will be (Snow et al. 1986).

In Chapter 4 of this book, I described how politics of peace and war have evolved since the early 1980s in the eight countries included in our study (see also Ruzza 2004). Typically, antiwar sentiments and support for antiwar and peace protests are more frequently observed among people at the (far) left side of the political spectrum (Klandermans 1991). In chapter 5, it was shown that, indeed, there was a clear mobilization surplus at the left side of the spectrum. Depending on the government in office, antiwar and peace protests can turn into antigovernment coalitions quite easily (Oegema and Klandermans 1994). Chances for such coalitions appear to be highest if the government in office is right-wing. The game becomes more complicated if a right-wing government takes on an antiwar position or if a left-wing government takes on an anti-peace position (Kriesi et al. 1995), but we maintain that the hypothesized mechanism holds in that political context as well. Even in the case of a left-wing government with an antiwar position, I contend that antiwar protest can become large, provided that a more general antigovernment sentiment exists.

Hence, the hypothesis I will test more specifically in this chapter maintains that in addition to support for the proximate goal of the demonstration—against the war in Iraq—broader sentiments of opposition account for successful mobilization. In other words, for the demonstration to grow big, more general oppositional sentiments must exist in a country. The more these exist, the larger the demonstration will become. As discussed in chapter 1, standardized for population size, the size of the demonstrations in the eight countries differed substantially. I will here test our assumption that these different levels of mobilization can be explained by differences in broader oppositional sentiment.

I will begin exhibiting these findings with a discussion of the attitudes directly related to the war: the degree of opposition to the war and the opinion about each national government's policy regarding the war. To explore the broader oppositional sentiments that these attitudes are embedded in, I will first discuss the degree of opposition against neoliberal globalization. The core section of this chapter, however, concerns people's attitudes about their national government: the ways they perceive the functioning of democracy within their own country, their feelings of political efficacy, as well as their trust in their country's social and political institutions. I will assess the extent to which the attitudes about the war are embedded in a broader oppositional sentiment, and then I will close the chapter with a discussion of the roots of oppositional sentiment by relating it to political identity and demographic background.

Opposition to War

It will come as no surprise that the participants in the demonstrations were opposed to the war in Iraq. We presented our respondents with eight opinions about the war in Iraq that were frequently expressed in those days and asked them whether they agreed or disagreed. The means for the eight countries are given in Table 6.1. The first section of the table, together with a measure (Eta^2), indicates the degree of differentiation between the eight countries.

The one opinion shared by almost all participants is that the United States wants to invade Iraq to secure its oil supply. Note that a large share of the population in the eight countries also agreed on precisely the same statement, as was shown in chapter 3. But that is where agreement ends. Two frequently heard justifications of military intervention, namely, the potential threat of Saddam Hussein and his regime to the world and the suffering of the Iraqi people, are both rejected and accepted by substantial numbers of participants in the demonstrations. However, such assessments—even to those who agreed with these statements—did not justify a war, not even with the authorization of the United Nations. In the eyes of the majority of the demonstrators, "war is always wrong." Note, however, that participants from the two countries that were in fact preparing for war—the United States and the United Kingdom—in that respect are less determined. If the United Nations were to authorize intervention, they would be less opposed to the war, and they were much less of the opinion that war is always wrong. Did Bush and Blair persuade their people? Two other arguments against the war were much less appealing to the participants: that it is racist and a crusade against Islam. Predominantly, the participants are opposed to war as a means to solve the conflict with Iraq.

We computed a scale consisting of all eight items. The resulting scale indicates "opposition to the war in Iraq." A score of five indicates that someone is opposed to war as a political means, views the war against Iraq as a war between civilizations, and does not believe that the allegations against the Iraqi regime are sufficient to begin a war against the country. A score of one indicates the opposite. Assessed with this scale, the opposition was strongest among the demonstrators in Italy and Spain and weakest among those in the Netherlands, as shown in Table 6.1.b. The differences, though, are not spectacular. On the whole, the opposition to war is strong among participants in all countries, and that, of course, is what one would expect.

Dissatisfaction with the Government's Efforts to Prevent War

How satisfied or dissatisfied were these people with how their government dealt with the imminent war? This, of course, depends on the government's stance and on how active it was—in the participants' view—in pursuing this stance. Chapter 3 discussed the positions taken by the governments of the eight countries included in our study. Against that background, we may expect significant differences between Belgium, Germany, and Switzerland on the one hand, and the United States, the United Kingdom, Spain, Italy, and the Netherlands on the other. This is exactly what we found (see Table 6.1.b). Country alone can explain no less than 68 percent of the variance in dissatisfaction with government policy. The means per country are what one would expect: very high levels of dissatisfaction were found in the nations where governments were preparing for war or took a supportive stand; low levels of dissatisfaction in those where governments—more or less explicitly—declared their opposition to war.

In all countries, dissatisfaction was positively correlated to the "opposition to war" scale. In this respect Spain is somewhat of an outlier. Its relatively low correlation is due to a lack of variance: 90 percent of the Spanish participants are completely dissatisfied with the government's policy. By and large, even in the countries whose governments opposed the war, demonstrators who were more opposed to the war wanted their governments to take firmer stands.

Widening the Blame

Negative opinions about the war in Iraq were the obvious motivators of participation. Yet, as indicated, we believe that the situation is more complicated.

Table 6.1. Attitudes toward the war in Iraq, government policy, and participation in protests

	US	UK	SP	IT	NL	SW	BE	GE	Eta²[a]
a. Attitudes toward the war in Iraq: Means[b]									
"A war is justified to bring down a dictatorial regime."[c]	1.8	2.0	1.7	1.6	2.0	1.6	1.8	1.7	.03
"A war against Iraq is justified when authorized by the UN Security Council."[c]	2.3	2.3	2.0	1.6	2.3	1.8	2.0	2.0	.06
"War is always wrong."	3.2	3.2	4.5	4.5	3.9	4.3	4.2	4.1	.16
"This is a racist war."	3.3	3.1	2.8	2.9	2.7	3.0	2.8	2.9	.02
"The USA is conducting a crusade against Islam."	2.9	3.1	3.3	3.1	3.3	3.2	3.1	3.1	.01
"Saddam Hussein and the Iraqi regime are a threat to world peace."[c]	2.9	2.8	2.5	2.6	3.2	2.7	2.6	3.0	.04
"The Iraqi regime must be brought down to end the suffering of the Iraqi people."[c]	2.7	3.5	3.6	3.1	4.0	3.6	3.2	3.3	.10
"The USA wants to invade Iraq to secure national oil supply."	4.2	4.2	4.7	4.5	4.1	4.3	4.4	4.3	.04
b. Opposition to war and dissatisfaction with government's policy									
Opposition to war in Iraq[d]	3.5	3.4	3.7	3.8	3.3	3.6	3.6	3.6	.07
Dissatisfaction with government's efforts to prevent war[e]	4.8	4.5	4.9	4.8	4.5	3.0	2.0	2.4	0.68
Pearson correlation between "opposition" and "dissatisfaction"	.22	.41	.05	.26	.16	.08	.18	.08	

Table 6.1. (continued)

	US	UK	SF	IT	NL	SW	BE	GE	Eta²[a]
c. Participation as expression of global justice sentiment									
Participation as expression of global justice sentiment[b]	2.9	2.8	3.2	3.9	3.1	3.1	3.5	3.0	.08
Pearson correlation with "opposition to war"	.34	.32	.22	.25	.18	.26	.29	.29	
Pearson correlation with "dissatisfaction with government policy"	.05	.18	.00	.20	.06	.04	.19	.13	
N	705	1129	452	1016	542	637	510	781	

Notes: [a]All Eta² are significant at p<.000.

[b]On a scale from 1 ("completely disagree") to 5 ("completely agree").

[c]Coding reversed for scale construction.

[d]On a scale from 1 ("completely not opposed") to 5 ("completely opposed").

[e]On a scale from 1 ("completely satisfied") to 5 ("completely dissatisfied").

We hypothesized that demonstrations of the size that we witnessed on February 15 do not have a single cause, which suggests that the driving force behind demonstrations of that size is more complex than the proximate goal suggests. I will test the hypothesis that greater dissatisfaction in general with the government and how politics work generates protests to the extent that we witnessed on February 15.

Opposition to Neoliberal Globalization

A first test of that hypothesis regards the possible embeddedness of the opposition to the war in Iraq in the opposition against neoliberal globalization. After all, as described in chapter 1, the European Social Forum—the global justice platform in Europe—played a significant role in the organization of the demonstrations throughout Europe (see also chapter 10, which describes the organizational backbone of February 15). In other words, aversion to neoliberal globalization may have been on the agenda of many a participant as well. In view of this possibility, we asked our respondents whether the antiwar protest was a way for them to express their negative feelings about neoliberal globalization. For quite a few participants, it obviously was, especially those from Belgium and Italy (Table 6.1.c). In each country, moreover, feelings against neoliberal globalization were significantly correlated with the "opposition to war" scale. Opposition to war in Iraq was clearly embedded in sentiment against neoliberal globalization, but there is more. Indeed, this sentiment was much less associated with dissatisfaction with one's government's policy toward the war; this observation underscores that this opposition to neoliberalism is not directed at national governments in particular. That, of course, limits the potential of these sentiments as a viable explanation for the success of the national demonstrations. Obviously, global justice sentiment was not participants' only frame of reference.

A Voice against One's Government

This brings us to the central tenet of this chapter—that the success of the demonstrations against war in Iraq must be explained by oppositional sentiment broader than opposition to the war or the national government's policy toward that war. To test that hypothesis, I assessed whether participants in the demonstrations felt at home in the political landscape of their country in various ways: How did they feel about the working of democracy? Did they experience some feeling of political efficacy? And did they trust the social and political institutions of their society (Table 6.2)?

As for the working of democracy, we asked our respondents the extent to which they were satisfied with the functioning of democracy in their country.

Table 6.2. Oppositional sentiment (means)

	US	UK	SP	IT	NL	SW	BE	GE	Eta^{2a}
Satisfaction with functioning democracy[b]	1.8	2.1	2.3	1.5	2.5	2.7	2.6	2.3	.25
Political efficacy[c]	2.7	2.6	2.6	2.2	3.2	3.1	3.0	2.8	.22
Trust in institutions[d]	2.3	–	–	2.2	2.9	2.6	2.5	–	.18
N[e]	705	1129	452	1016	542	637	510	781	

Notes: [a]All Eta^2 are significant at p<.000.

[b]On a scale from 1 ("not at all satisfied") to 4 ("very satisfied").

[c]On a scale from 1 ("hardly effective") to 5 ("highly effective").

[d]On a scale from 1 ("very little trust") to 5 ("trust completely").

[e]Approximate numbers, since numbers differed slightly for the three variables.

Their assessments differed substantially depending on which country they were from (25 percent of the variance in satisfaction can be explained by country alone). Italian and U.S. demonstrators were the least satisfied with the working of democracy in their home countries. In all other countries, means were on the positive side of our four-point scale. In Switzerland, Belgium, and the Netherlands, people evaluated the political system more positively than in the five other countries.

Political efficacy was measured with a scale based on eight statements about politics and politicians (Cronbach's alpha .80). Two examples are "I don't see the use of voting; parties do whatever they want anyway" (reversed coding) and "People like myself do have an influence on what the political authorities do." "One" on the scale represents a low level of political efficacy, and "five" represents a high level. The scores on the scale reveal this pattern: relatively high levels of political efficacy were found in the Netherlands, Belgium, and Switzerland, and relatively low levels were found in Italy. Respondents from the United States, United Kingdom, Spain, and Germany occupy intermittent positions.

In five countries—the United States, Italy, the Netherlands, Switzerland, and Germany—we included a set of questions in the questionnaire about trust in social and political institutions. We constructed a scale (Cronbach's alpha .86) that measured trust in many social and political institutions. Examples are judiciary, police, employers, press, parties, banks, government, parliament, and political parties. On the whole, as the figures in Table 6.2 show, the level of trust is the highest in the Netherlands and the lowest in Italy, which may confirm the stereotype, but the story is certainly more complicated than that. In the United States, anything that has to do with national government and national politics is not trusted at all; this goes for the administration, the parties, national government, and, most of all, the president. In Italy, though, people distrust the private sector, banks, employers, and the government, but not the president. The four institutions that reveal the largest differences among the countries are the president (Eta^2 .38), the national government (Eta^2 .32), the administration (Eta^2 .18), and the national parliament (Eta^2 .16). To reiterate: the participants from the United States do not trust their president at all, while those from Italy and Germany trust theirs highly. The two kingdoms, Belgium and the Netherlands, generate intermediate levels of trust in their head of state. With regard to the other three (government, administration, and congress or parliament) the demonstrators from the United States and Italy always reveal the lowest levels of trust, while the three other countries are at more or less identical levels.

However, the evaluation of the working of social and political institutions, although interesting, is not what occupies us here. Our main concern is whether these evaluations amplified the drive to participate in the demonstration against the war in Iraq.

Broader Opposition

We maintained that demonstrations of the size we witnessed on February 15 against the war in Iraq are embedded in broader opposition to the national government. One way of testing this hypothesis is to assess whether opposition to the war was embedded in more general discontent about the way social and political institutions work. Therefore, I conducted principal component analyses that included the two opinions about the war (opposition to the war, and dissatisfaction with the government's policy vis-à-vis the war), and the opinion about democracy, political efficacy, and trust in the core social and political institutions in Western societies. As trust was only measured in some countries, I conducted separate analyses with and without trust (Table 6.3).

The results are very consistent. Opposition to the war and the policy of the national government is embedded in broader sentiments of resistance in all eight countries. The loadings on the principal component are invariably high, and the proportion of variance explained ranges between 40 and 50 percent. Spain deviates from this pattern; dissatisfaction with its government's policy loads on a separate factor. This, however, is predominantly due to a lack of variance. Indeed, more than 90 percent of Spanish demonstrators were dissatisfied with their government's policy, irrespective of their own political sentiments. The meaning of this is straightforward. The five attitudes belong to a single underlying dimension: the more the participants are opposed to the war and the more dissatisfied they are with their national government's policy, the less happy they are with the functioning of democracy in their country, the less politically effective they feel, and the less trust they have in the social and political institutions of their country.

Note that our findings do not imply any causal relationship and, in fact, this is not what we were after either. Our point is that the protests are clearly embedded in broader opposition to national governments. Such embeddedness does not so much have a monocausal signification but rather is of a recurrent manner. That is to say, opposition to the war and dissatisfaction with the government's policy reinforce an existent oppositional sentiment toward the national government and its institutions. In its turn, those sentiments work together to produce an ever-larger demonstration.

Table 6.3. Embeddedness of opposition: Principal component analysis (loadings)

	US	UK	SP	IT	NL	SW	BE	GE	All
Analysis without trust									
"Opposition to war" scale	.75	.70	.52	.64	.57	.49	.49	.51	.50
"Dissatisfaction with government policy"	.45	.70	.12	.61	.46	.51	.69	.58	.62
"Functioning of democracy"	-.75	-.73	-.79	-.70	-.76	-.78	-.82	-.80	-.83
"Political efficacy"	-.69	-.74	-.79	-.54	-.75	-.73	-.78	-.81	-.79
Percentage of variance explained	44.8	51.4	38.3	39.2	41.8	40.8	49.8	47.6	48.8
N	705	1129	452	1016	542	637	510	781	
Analysis with trust									
"Opposition to war" scale	.69	—	—	.53	.47	—	.43	.48	.52
"Dissatisfaction with government policy"	.36	—	—	.47	.40	—	.61	.54	.53
"Functioning of democracy"	-.73	—	—	-.67	-.74	—	-.82	-.79	-.83
"Political efficacy"	-.72	—	—	-.64	-.78	—	-.80	-.80	-.81
"Trust in institutions"	-.80	—	—	-.75	-.84	—	-.83	-.82	-.81
Percentage of variance explained	45.5	—	—	38.2	44.6	—	51.0	49.1	50.9
N	705			1016	542		510	781	

Levels of Mobilization

If, indeed, opposition to war and dissatisfaction with the government's effort to prevent war are embedded in a broader such sentiment, one would assume that this oppositional sentiment accounts for the diverging mobilization levels in the eight countries. Thus the questions arise: Does such a link between oppositional sentiment and mobilization levels indeed exist? Are participants in the demonstration more negative about politics in general than non-participants are? The answers to these questions, of course, are crucial to the test of my assumption that massive protest reflects a broader oppositional sentiment than the immediate issue of the demonstration does. To answer the latter question, we exploited the fact that the question regarding the functioning of democracy was included in several waves of the Eurobarometer.[1] Although this poses the drawback that we have no information on the United States and Switzerland, we assume that a comparison of the remaining six European countries, nonetheless, will be relevant and revealing—and indeed it is. In Table 6.4, I compare the findings of two Eurobarometers and our own survey. The question regarding the functioning of democracy was not included in the surveys of 2003, yet it was asked in November 2001 and again in April 2004. Hence, we have two standards of comparison, one roughly a year prior and another a year later.

The figures in the table show the proportions of the respondents who indicate that they are "not very satisfied" or "not at all satisfied" with the functioning of democracy in their country. First, participants in the demonstrations in all six countries appear less satisfied than the average citizen, certainly if one takes 2001 as the standard of comparison. Second, the six countries included in the comparison clearly fall into two broad categories: the Netherlands, Belgium, and Germany, on the one hand, where the differences

Table 6.4. Dissatisfaction with the functioning of democracy: Percentage not satisfied

	UK	SP	IT	NL	BE	GE
Eurobarometer November 2001	27	30	60	26	31	36
Eurobarometer April 2004	34	29	60	33	35	48
Iraq demonstration survey	70	62	93	40	37	58
Survey-Eurobaromenter 2001 discrepancy	43	32	33	14	6	22
Survey-Eurobarometer 2004 discrepancy	36	33	33	7	2	10
Mobilization level at Iraq demonstration	1.6	2.5	2.6	.04	.07	.06

Note: This table represents the percentage of respondents who were "not very satisfied" or "not at all satisfied."

Source: Eurobarometer (2001; 2004).

are relatively small, and the United Kingdom, Spain, and Italy, on the other, where the differences are great. The bottom row shows the mobilization level of the six countries; the dichotomy in terms of satisfaction with the functioning of democracy is strikingly reproduced in terms of the corresponding mobilization level. In those countries where the discrepancy between participants and citizens is the greatest, the mobilization level is the highest. That, of course, makes sense. If the demonstrators were only as dissatisfied as those who did not demonstrate, such discontent could not explain their participation. That the biggest demonstrations were in countries where, compared to non-participants, participants were more dissatisfied with the ways their democracy supports our argument that the demonstrations were about more than opposition to war alone.

But the question, naturally, is whether this is a real or a spurious correlation. One could argue that the opposition to war was very strong in Italy and Spain and that the mobilization levels in those two countries therefore were high, but opposition was strong in Belgium as well, though turnout was lower, while negative attitudes toward war among the populace in the United Kingdom was of the same level as that in the Netherlands and Germany, where turnout was significantly lower. One could also argue that the level of dissatisfaction with the national government's efforts to prevent war was very high in the United Kingdom, Spain, and Italy, but it was high in the Netherlands too. Finally, one could argue that the discrepancy in Belgium was so low because the Belgian government was against the war, but the German government was against the war as well, and the Dutch government was not. These and other considerations are addressed in Table 6.5, which presents multiple regression analyses, with the mobilization level of a country as the dependent variable and the attitudes about the war and national politics as the independent variables.

The number of cases in this analysis is very small, hence one must be cautious regarding the interpretations and conclusions. Yet, the pattern is consistent and allows for a clear conclusion. The differences in mobilization levels among the six countries in the analysis can be nearly completely accounted for by the combined influence of opposition to war and dissatisfaction about the functioning of democracy. Note, however, that the discrepancy between the level of dissatisfaction among the general population and that among our respondents, rather than the absolute level of dissatisfaction, makes the difference. The presence of many people who are more dissatisfied than the average citizen about how democracy works in their country is linked to demonstration size. Note also that being more dissatisfied with the functioning of democracy rather than satisfied with the government's

Table 6.5. Level of mobilization and attitudes about the war and national politics

| | Multiple regression: Standardized betas | | | | |
	Model 1	Model 2	Model 3	Model 4	Pearson's r
Opposition to war	.56	.64**	.54*	.50	.75*
Dissatisfaction with government's policy	.43	.27	.25	.51	.67
Dissatisfaction with functioning of democracy	.26	–	–	–	.88**
Discrepancy with Eurobarometer November 2001	–	.44**	–	–	.77*
Discrepancy with Eurobarometer April 2004	–	–	.48**	–	.88**
Political efficacy	–	–	–	-.29	-.84**
N	6	6	6	6	–
Adjusted R^2	.85	.98*	.99**	.88*	–

*p < .10; **p < .05

efforts to prevent war accounts for the different mobilization levels. Indeed, the lowering of the beta coefficient compared to the Pearson correlation suggests that dissatisfaction with one's government's efforts feeds into more general dissatisfaction about the functioning of democracy. In its turn, that broader dissatisfaction made the mobilization increase.

Political Identity

The embeddedness of the resistance to the war in Iraq in oppositional sentiment is further evidenced by the political identity of the average demonstrator. The vast majority of the participants in the demonstrations are of a leftist political orientation. On a self-placement scale from 0, "left," to 10, "right," scores range from 1.8 in Italy to 2.8 in Belgium and the United Kingdom. Indeed, more than 90 percent of the participants occupy the left end (0–4) of the scale. This orientation is confirmed by the participants' self-reported voting behavior—both in the past and in the future. The political landscape clearly differs in the eight countries, but very few of our respondents voted or intended to vote for parties at the right end or even in the center of the political spectrum. Basically, the Social Democrats, the Greens, and the Far Left populated the demonstrations, although the exact mix of the three groups varied, depending on the national political configuration. The partisan affiliation of the demonstrators will be much further elaborated in chapter 8 of this volume.

In the context of this chapter, neither political identity nor voting be-havior per se interests me. My objective is to show that the participants in the demonstration were opposed to more than the imminent war in Iraq. In that respect, it is obviously relevant that the political identity of the major-ity is oppositional; the demonstrators voted for parties in the opposition, and if they did not, they planned to vote for them in the future (see chapter 8). Thus, even though we lack information on nonparticipants, it is safe to conclude that compared to the remainder of the population in their coun-try, the participants in the demonstrations were from a specific range of the political spectrum.

Embedded Opposition

In a final step to demonstrate the embeddedness of the opposition to the war in Iraq in more general oppositional sentiments, we conducted regression analyses and multivariate analyses of variance reported in Table 6.6.[2] In these analyses, we attempted to assess the extent to which opposition to the war in Iraq and to the government's policy regarding it were influenced by people's political identity and political attitudes. We assessed the influence of these political attitudes alone and controlling for country and voting in the past, with all the countries included, and with only those countries in-cluded in which the questions about trust were asked.

Table 6.6 summarizes the results of several regression analyses (Models 1 and 3) and multivariate analyses of variance (Models 2 and 4). In Models 1 and 3, the opposition to war and dissatisfaction with one's government's policy are regressed in a stepwise manner on left-right placement, the assess-ment of democracy and political efficacy, and a rejection of neoliberal glob-alization as motivation to take part in the demonstration. Models 2 and 4 report results from multivariate analyses of variance with country and past vote as factors and, in three separate steps, left-right placement, the assessment of democracy and political efficacy, in addition to anti-neoliberal globaliza-tion sentiment as covariates. The table presents the cumulative R-squares for the subsequent steps.[3] As we are predominantly interested in the question of whether opposition to war and one's government's policy vis-à-vis the war were embedded in a more general oppositional sentiment, we restrict our presentation of results to these summary figures.

Models 1 and 3 show that even among the leftist-oriented people who participated in the demonstration, left-right placement continues to have an impact. Put simply: the more left the demonstrators, the more opposed to the war they are, and the more dissatisfied with their government's policy. But left-right placement does not exhaust the differences in opinion regarding

Table 6.6. Embedded opposition: Regression analyses and multivariate analyses of variance (R-squares)

	Opposition to war				Dissatisfaction with government policy			
	Model 1[a]	Model 2[b]	Model 3[c]	Model 4[b]	Model 1[a]	Model 2[b]	Model 3[a]	Model 4[b]
Country	–	.07	–	.08	–	.72	–	.75
Vote / country x vote[c]	–	.12	–	.12	–	.77	–	.80
Left–right placement[d]	.07	.16	.07	.16	.03	.78	.05	.82
Functioning of democracy / political efficacy	.14	.21	–	–	.14	.79	–	–
Against neoliberal globalization	.17	.23	–	–	.15	.79	–	–
Functioning of democracy / political efficacy / trust	–	–	.18	.23	–	–	.16	.83
Against neoliberal globalization	–	–	.21	.25	–	–	.16	.83
N[e]	3932	2808	2010[f]	1899[f]	4125	2808	2080[f]	1899

Notes: R-squares if variables and the variables noted in the top of each the column are included. Models 1 and 2 include all countries, Models 3 and 4 include the countries that answered the questions about trust (the United States, Italy, the Netherlands, Belgium, and Germany).

[a]Stepwise regression analysis.

[b]Multivariate analysis of variance.

[c]Based on past vote.

[d]On a scale from 0 ("left") to 10 ("right").

[e]Number of cases in the last step when all variables are included.

[f]Model based on sample that completed the trust questionnaire.

national politics relevant in this context. Significant proportions of variance explained are added when differences in opinion about democracy, political efficacy, and trust in sociopolitical institutions are entered into the equation for both opposition to war and dissatisfaction with the government's policy. The less satisfied the demonstrators were with the functioning of democracy in their country, the less politically effective they felt, and the less they trusted the sociopolitical institutions in their country, the more they were opposed to the war in Iraq and the more dissatisfied they were about their government's policy regarding the war. Opposition to neoliberal globalization added significantly in the case of opposition to war but did not have an impact in the case of dissatisfaction with the government's policy vis-à-vis the war. I observed this when discussing the zero-order correlations (Table 6.4). I explained this finding, which is now reconfirmed in multivariate analyses, by arguing that neoliberal globalization implies global dynamics that a national government controls only to a very limited extent.

Models 2 and 4 show that the relationships between political identity and attitudes and opposition to war hold, irrespective of the respondents' nations and of voting patterns. Left-right placement and political attitudes continue to add significantly to the variance explained, beyond country and past vote. Even in the case of dissatisfaction with government policy, political attitudes add beyond the large proportions of variance explained by voting patterns and country variation. The proportion of variance added is, of necessity, modest, as 75 and 80 percent of the variance is explained by country and voting alone, but both are statistically significant improvements of the models. Opposition to neoliberal globalization, however, does not add further. This was to be expected on the basis of previous analyses.

I also found significant interactions of country and voting patterns. This indicates that the impact of voting patterns differed by country. For a further exploration of these interactions, I will focus on the parties to the left: the Far Left, the Greens, and the Social Democrats. As support for the remaining parties is too limited in all or most countries to generate a reliable comparison, I collapsed those parties into one category, namely "others," which comprises the parties further to the right on the political spectrum. To explore the individual interactions, I computed the means for opposition to war and dissatisfaction with government's policy vis-à-vis the war for these three parties and the remaining parties in the eight countries.

In most countries, opposition to war is strongest among supporters of the Far Left, followed by the Greens, and then the Social Democrats. Opposition to war is weakest among supporters of the parties farther to the right. However, the differences among the party supporters vary across countries.

Although they follow the general pattern, the differences in Italy and the Netherlands are not significant. The impact of voting patterns on the opposition to war is the strongest in Germany and Switzerland. In Switzerland, this is because the opposition is significantly lower among supporters from the parties farther to the right than among those of parties to the left; this holds for Germany as well. But in addition, German supporters of the Far Left are significantly more opposed to the war than those of the Greens and the Social Democrats. We found a pattern similar to that in Germany in Spain, though slightly less prominent. In the United States, supporters of Ralph Nader (27 percent) were more opposed to the war than supporters of Al Gore. In the United Kingdom, supporters of any but the leftist parties did not differ from supporters of the social democrats.

As far as dissatisfaction with government's policy is concerned, the picture is more complicated. First, there are the demonstrators from the United States, the United Kingdom, and Italy who are equally annoyed, regardless of which party they choose. Second, there are the demonstrators from the Netherlands and Spain who are annoyed as well, but at different levels, depending on party preference; that is to say, the more left, the more annoyed. Finally, there are demonstrators from Belgium, Germany, and Switzerland who are much more satisfied with their government's policy. In Belgium, however, supporters of the Far Left are far more dissatisfied with their government's policy than are those of the other parties. Also in Germany, supporters of the two parties in office (Greens and Social Democrats) are the predominantly satisfied ones. Members of the remaining parties (including the Far Left) are significantly less satisfied.

The Demographics of Opposition

My analyses thus far support the argument that opposition to the war in Iraq and dissatisfaction with one's government's policy in that regard are part of a broader sentiment of opposition—against neoliberal globalization and/or how politics are working in the participants' country, or both. Such opinions are embedded in a broader political identity, as reflected in left-right placement and voting behavior. The last step in this chapter concerns the demographic correlates of these political attitudes. How are they related to such factors as gender, age, education, and religion? To assess these relationships, I conducted multivariate analyses with the opposition to the war and one's government's policy regarding the war as the dependent variables; country and religion as fixed factors; and age, gender, and level of education as covariates of country and religion.

Although the effects are never very strong, the analyses suggest that the two attitudes—opposition to war and dissatisfaction with government—are distributed differentially among the categories of gender, age, education, and religion. Women are more opposed to the war in Iraq than men are. More educated people are less opposed to the war than less educated people. Age did not influence the degree of opposition to war. These findings hold for all eight countries. In most countries, participants from Protestant or Roman Catholic backgrounds are less opposed to the war than those who adhere to no religion or adherents of other religions, but in Spain and Switzerland we found the opposite pattern in some instances. Dissatisfaction with the government's policy vis-à-vis the war increased if demonstrators were older, but gender and level of education were unrelated to such feelings of dissatisfaction. In Spain, participants belonging to Protestant or Catholic churches are more dissatisfied with their government's war policy.

Conclusion

It's not surprising that we found strong opposition to the war in Iraq among participants in the demonstrations in all eight countries, although we observed differences in degree of opposition among the countries. Rejection of war as a means to solving an international conflict brought the people to the streets even though many of the demonstrators believed that the Iraqi regime deserved no sympathy.

Dissatisfaction with the government's policy vis-à-vis the war was, to a large extent, dependent on the actual policy of the government of someone's country: very high levels of dissatisfaction in the countries that were preparing for war or that took a supportive stance and satisfaction in the countries whose governments rejected war. The more opposed demonstrators were to the war, the more dissatisfied they were with their government's policy, even in those countries where governments declared their opposition to the war. For obvious reasons, the correlation between opposition and dissatisfaction was the strongest in the two countries that were planning for war: the United States and the United Kingdom.

The frames of reference of the demonstrators, however, were much broader than opposition to the war and dissatisfaction with the government's policy; these were clearly embedded in broader oppositional sentiments. On the one hand, for many people, the demonstration was also a way of expressing their opposition to neoliberal globalization. On the other hand, the demonstration signaled more general opposition to national governments expressed by citizens opposed to the powers in office. The different levels of mobilization in the eight countries can largely be explained by their opposition to the war and by their dissatisfaction with how democracy functioned in their country. The embeddedness of the opposition to the war in broader oppositional sentiments is further underscored by the political identity of the participants, who invariably came from the leftist side of the political spectrum and disproportionately voted for opposition parties. The governments' policies vis-à-vis the war reinforced existing oppositional sentiments and made people take to the streets in unprecedented numbers.

Notes

1. The Eurobarometer also includes questions about trust in the national government and parliament. Unfortunately, the 1999 survey was the last one that included these questions. We did not feel that a comparison of our data with these data would be valuable. However, our own data show that the level of satisfaction with the functioning of democracy is strongly correlated with these two indicators of trust and also feelings of political efficacy (Pearson $r = .60, .55,$ and $.53$ for trust in government, trust in parliament, and political efficacy, respectively). Hence, we believe that our findings regarding the functioning of democracy are a reliable indicator of people's attitude toward national politics.

2. As country and vote were nominal variables, it was more appropriate to treat them as fixed factors in a multivariate analysis of variance.

3. We chose to report R-squares rather than full models, which would have meant including many more figures without necessarily providing more information. After all, we were interested in the R-squares as indicators of variance explained, and the R-square changes as indicators of the increase of explained variance when a group of variables was entered in the equation.

Works Cited

Klandermans, Bert. 1991. "The Peace Movement and Social Movement Theory." In *Peace Movement in International Perspective. International Social Movement Research* 3, ed. Bert Klandermans, 1–42. Greenwich, Conn.: JAI Press.

———. 1997. *The Social Psychology of Protest.* Oxford: Blackwell.

———. 2004. "The Demand and Supply of Participation: Social Psychological Correlates of Participation in a Social Movement." In *Blackwell Companion to Social Movements,* ed. David A. Snow, Sarah A. Soule, and Hanspeter Kriesi, 360–79. Oxford: Blackwell.

Kriesi, Hanspeter, Ruud Koopmans, Jan Willem Duyvendak, and Marco G. Giugni. 1995. *New Social Movements in Western Europe: A Comparative Analysis.* Minneapolis: University of Minnesota Press.

Neidhardt, Friedhelm, and Dieter Rucht. 1993. "Auf dem Weg in die Bewegungsgesellschaft? Ueber die Stabilisierbarkeit sozialer Bewegungen." *Soziale Welt* 44: 305–26.

Oegema, Dirk, and Bert Klandermans. 1994. "Why Social Movement Sympathiz-
     ers Don't Participate: Erosion and Nonconversion of Support." *American Soci-
     ological Review* 59: 703–22.
Ruzza, Carlo. 2004. "Peace Movements." In *Democracy and Protest: Popular Protest and
     New Social Movements,* ed. Gary Taylor and Malcolm Todd, 290–306. London:
     Merlin.
Snow, David A., E. Burke Rochford Jr., Steve K. Worden, and Robert D. Benford.
     1986. "Frame Alignment Processes, Micro-Mobilization, and Movement Par-
     ticipation." *American Sociological Review* 51: 464–81.

7

Paths to the February 15 Protest:
Social or Political Determinants?

Donatella della Porta

This chapter analyzes the degrees and forms of participation among February 15 demonstrators. The questions of participants' previous experiences in anti-war demonstrations is particularly relevant, because of the very characteristics of the peace movements—small nuclei of committed pacifists—and the capacity to at times mobilize very large and heterogeneous networks rooted in various movements; and the involvement of citizens with mainly ethical or religious stances who are not (or not yet) politicized (see chapter 4). The issues of diversity in participants' backgrounds as well as the presence of large numbers of first-timers were particularly relevant for the 2003 demonstrations against the war in Iraq, which did not confirm the paths of cross-national strengths and weaknesses in mobilization capacity that had emerged in previous waves of political mobilization: for instance, the protest remained weak in the Netherlands (where the protest against the deployment of cruise missiles had been very strong in the early 1980s) but was impressively widespread in Spain, where no previous large mobilization had existed (although the anti-militarist movement was very active). In several countries, the mobilizations against Iraq attracted not only already mobilized activists but also new generations of protestors as well as many "first timers." Called for by the Assembly of European Social Movements, held at the end of the first European Social Forum, the Global Day of Action was strongly supported by a broad and at that time particularly visible global justice movement (della Porta 2007). An analysis of the social and political backgrounds of demonstrators could help us understand the extraordinary mobilization capacity of that protest (see chapter 2) and also its differential success in mobilizing "on the street."

In this chapter, I will focus on two dependent variables: frequency and action repertoires of previous protest participation. Beyond the description of the February 15 marchers, I also want to examine the various degrees and forms of participation previously engaged in by those citizens who took to the street on the Global Day of Action. In social movement studies, repertoires of protest have usually been explained by political opportunities, either structural or contingent. Cross-nationally, the institutional closure or openness toward challengers as well as toward the coalitions in government are expected to have an impact on the degree and forms of mobilization. In general, the presence of allies in government supports the use of "insiders' strategies" (lobbying or codecision) rather than mass protest—unless those allies look for public expressions of support, in particular through contentious collective actions that address an international organization or foreign government. Since the peace demonstrations mobilized different social and political groups in the countries under study (see chapters 5 and 6 in this volume), the cross-national analysis has to be supplemented by an analysis of individual paths of participation. Especially in research on political participation, sociodemographic background and political attitudes are the most often discussed sets of variables. In this analysis, I will single out the individual characteristics of more or less frequent demonstrators, as well as moderate and more radical ones, in terms of their sociodemographic backgrounds and their political attitudes, all of which converge in forming their political identities.[1] In what follows, I will observe country characteristics and discuss the extent to which they can be explained by national political opportunities.

In this chapter, I shall discuss these hypotheses and also take a step forward, beyond causal explanation of individual choices and toward the analysis of the dynamics of militantism, that is, the presence of long-term paths. After introducing the explanatory model, I will devote a second section to a cross-national comparison of degrees and forms of commitment. I shall then discuss the hypotheses about the socioeconomic centrality of activists, looking mainly at profession, age, gender, and education. In the fourth section, I shall address the hypotheses about the construction of a militant career, looking at the previous experiences of activists, in terms of both participation in organizations and activities promoted by different movements. In the concluding section, I will reflect on the impact of environmental variables, filtered via activists' experiences, on the specific paths of militancy of different generations. Throughout, I will consider political opportunity structure (measured by the country in which the demonstration was held) as an intervening variable.

What Do We Want to Explain: Degrees and Forms of Participation

Political participation has been defined as all citizens' behavior oriented to influence the political process (Axford, Huggins, and Turner 1997, 109). There are, however, many different degrees of political participation and various means for influencing the political process, from minimal forms, such as voluntary exposure to political messages (reading newspapers, listening to news), to activation in specific activities—from "ballots to bullets." Research on political participation initially explicitly excluded protest, focusing on conventional forms of participation, such as being exposed to political messages, voting, carrying political buttons, contacting public officers, contributing money for a party or candidate, assisting in a public speech, engaging in a political campaign, or occupying electoral public office (Milbrath 1965, 18). Since the 1970s, however, surveys have included nonconventional forms of political participation, such as letters to newspapers, boycotts, self-reduction of tax and rent, occupations of public buildings, traffic blocks, petitions, sit-ins, wildcat strikes, marches, damage to property, and violence against persons (Dalton 1996).

Protest forms can be more or less radical in nature, ranging from conventional petitioning to more conflictual activities, including violent forms of action. Russell Dalton has suggested several thresholds on the continuum, from the least to the most radical forms: "The first threshold indicates the transition from conventional to unconventional politics. Signing petitions and participating in lawful demonstrations are unorthodox political activities but still within the bounds of accepted democratic norms. The second threshold represents the shift to direct action techniques, such as boycotts. A third level of political activities involves illegal, but nonviolent, acts. Unofficial strikes or a peaceful occupation of a building typify this step. Finally, a fourth threshold includes violent activities such as personal injury or physical damage (Dalton 1996). Recent surveys of participants in large protest events—such as the 2001 protest against the G8 in Genoa (Andretta et al. 2002; 2003), the 2002 European Social Forum in Florence (della Porta et al. 2006), and the 2003 European Social Forum in Paris (Agrikoliansky and Sommier 2004)—indicate that the activists had a rich and various repertoire that combines many forms of action.

None of these studies has gone in depth into the analysis of the contextual, sociodemographic or attitudinal determinants of activists' choices of protest repertoire nor systematically compared activists of different countries. This is indeed what I want to do in what follows, by looking at the degree and repertoires of previous experiences with political participation of those who mobilized on February 15. I will measure *frequency of participation* by the question "Can you estimate how often in the past five years you took part in a local, national or international demonstration or public protest?" coded into three categories: "first time," "two to ten times" and "more than ten times." I measure *protest repertoires* by an extensive set of questions referring to forms of action used in the past, which (on the basis of previous research in the field as well as factor analysis, see below) I have recoded: First, *semi-conventional forms* include contacting a politician, an organization or association, or a civil servant; wearing a pin or hanging a flyer, poster, or sticker of a political campaign; making a donation; raising funds; contacting the media or appearing in the media; and abstaining from an election for reasons of protest. Second, *demonstrative forms* include signing a people's initiative, a referendum, or a petition; setting up or gathering signatures for a petition; and taking part in a strike. Third, *political consumerism* includes activities such as taking part in a product boycott or buying a product for political, ethical, or ecological reasons. Fourth, *disruptive action* is operationalized as occupying a public building, school, or university or squatting in houses or abandoned areas. Finally, *violent action* is defined as the engagement in forms of action that imply violence against property or persons.

Research on social movements suggests that national political opportunities influence national repertoires of action. As I shall argue in the next section, however, the relevance of political opportunities for the explanation of the country-specific dominant repertoire is not confirmed when one looks at the activist backgrounds of those who participate in specific protest events. Moving from aggregate to individual data, there are two classical explanations for individual political participation. The first focuses on the individual availability of resources, such as, in particular, money (and, consequently, time) as well as education (and, consequently, the sense of having the "right to speak up"), taking some sociodemographic characteristics as indicators. These hypotheses have been put forward in the pioneering research on political participation, especially stressing participation as a middle-class activity, but also confirmed later on, particularly regarding level of education. However, these studies referred in particular to conventional forms of participation. Research on unconventional forms has already indicated some different patterns. Regarding the labor movement, theories of political participation have stressed the role of class consciousness more than class position. Analyses of new social movements, although mentioning the high presence of segments of the middle classes, have also emphasized the role of beliefs more than belonging to a specific social group. Research on social movements has emphasized the importance of political socialization—both primary socialization, as in the family, and secondary socialization, as in peer groups—in facilitating political activism.

Repertoires of Action and Political Opportunities

Looking at the political opportunities for protest, comparative studies have considered the degree of centralization of the state apparatus, government control over market participation, and the dependence of the judiciary on other arms of government (Kitschelt 1986, 61–64); regime structure (Rucht 1994, 303–12); and territorial decentralization, the functional division of powers, and direct democracy (Kriesi 1995). Institutional variables influence the strategies adopted by national social movement families: social movements tend to use the channels of access made available to them by "weak" states, reducing their availability for more disruptive protest; and, in reverse, closed political institutions trigger an escalation of political conflicts (della Porta and Rucht 1995). In this volume, Beyeler and Rucht present some indicators of power sharing and potential alliance for progressive movements as important political dimensions. Additionally, Mario Diani links the mobilization capacity of the peace marches to the position of their respective national governments on the Iraq War, with open opportunities in Germany and Belgium (and in some ways also Switzerland), and, in contrast, very closed opportunities in the United States, the United Kingdom, Italy, and Spain (and, although less so, in the Netherlands). But how do political opportunities relate to frequency and repertoire of previous participation among the mobilized activists? Do traditionally closed systems tend to produce more radical demonstrators? And do open opportunities facilitate the participation of "first timers," as well as unconventional participation in general? Or, is it when a danger appears as more menacing (for instance, with an adversary in government) that even previously nonmobilized people take to the street? Our data confirm the difficulty, mentioned in chapter 2, of easily translating general political opportunities in terms of characteristics of mobilized protestors at specific marches.

As for *frequency of participation,* answers to the question "How often did you participate in protest activities in the last five years?" indicate that Italians are much more highly mobilized (average 10.56), followed by Belgians (6.64), Spaniards (5.74), Swiss (6.66), and Germans (5.17) with moderate values, and Americans (4.79), Brits and Scots (3.55), and Dutch (3.22) on the less mobilized side.[2] Relevant country differences are also visible as far as "first timers" are concerned: against an average of about a third (30 percent), the Netherlands presents a very high percentage of first timers (54 percent), followed by the United Kingdom (49 percent), while first timers are rare in

Italy (9 percent, with an even slightly lower 8 percent for the postal sample). The frequency of previous participation seems to reflect the strength of recent mobilizations in the global justice movements in various countries (see della Porta 2007) more than the position of each country in terms of distribution of power (as reported in Table 2.1, this volume). Hypotheses suggesting higher levels of mobilization when the right is in government are also not clearly confirmed—for example, look at the positions of the Belgians and the Germans, whose center-left governments had taken strong stances against the war. Frequency of participation is explained neither by the influence of left-wing parties in terms of access to power (Table 2.2) nor by indicators of the strength of labor organizations (Table 2.3), while (with the exception of Belgium) frequency tends to increase with the percentage of citizens that locate themselves on the left of the political spectrum (Table 2.4), with scores high in Spain and Italy and low in the United States and the United Kingdom.

To investigate the *specific repertoires of participation* belonging to the protest repertoires of activists from different countries, we have recoded the question regarding the use of various forms of action, singling out conventional, semi-conventional, political consumerism, disruptive, and violent forms and comparing actual values with expected counts by country. A factor analysis we ran confirmed that our theoretically based aggregation in sub-types reflected the statistical structure hidden behind our set of data.[3]

According to our data (see Table 7.1), most activists from various countries have a very high degree of experience with *semi-conventional* forms of participation, with almost all U.S. activists, at the highest level, having experiences in semi-conventional actions (98 percent) and Spaniards with the lowest (although certainly not low in absolute terms), at 80 percent. The Belgians and Dutch are slightly lower than average, with all other countries very near the average of 88 percent. I can therefore state that, with some exceptions, almost all of those who took part in the February 15 marches have experiences in semi-conventional forms of action as well. If the two outliers seem to provide some leverage for the hypothesis that "weak" states (such as the United States) facilitate more conventional forms of participation (and "strong" states such as Spain do the opposite), the analysis of the patterns of our countries does not confirm such a clear picture.

More differences emerge if we look at the *demonstrative* forms of participation that have been used more than the average by the Italians and Swiss (91 percent), followed by the Americans (89 percent) and then Spaniards, Belgians, and British, while the Germans and the Dutch have values well below the average. Also in this case, traditional political opportunity structure hypotheses are of little help (suffice it to say that the top position is

Table 7.1. Repertoires of participation by countries: Positive responses ("yes" in percent)

	Semi-conventional	Direct forms	Political consumerism	Disruptive action	Violent
United States	98	89	80	4	1
United Kingdom	90	85	79	4	1
Spain	80	87	62	7	1
Italy	90	91	84	28	4
Netherlands	83	69	66	5	1
Switzerland	91	92	91	7	2
Belgium	83	87	82	6	1
Germany	86	68	70	6	2
Total	88	84	78	10	2
N	4,552	4,315	3,998	495	96

occupied by activists from the "most different" Italy and Switzerland). The same is true if one looks at a set of demonstrative forms that I have kept separate because of their increasing relevance for contemporary movements: *political consumerism,* especially boycott and ethically driven consumption. In this case as well, there are significant differences that cannot be understood in terms of political opportunities as defined by distribution of power: boycott is used more by the Swiss but also by participants in the February 15 marches in Italy, Belgium, the United Kingdom, and the United States—significantly less, again, in the Netherlands and Germany (della Porta 2003).

If we look at *disruptive action* (illegal but not violent, in Dalton's definition), the Italian case emerges as exceptionally different from the others (with almost 28 percent of the marchers responding that they have used disruptive protest), while differences are much lower among the other countries (ranging from 4 percent in the United Kingdom and United States to 7 percent in Switzerland).[4] Very low are the values related to the use of *violent actions:* 1.9 percent of the total number of participants, with a higher (but still not high) 4 percent in Italy.

We can account for the difficulty in using political opportunities to explain the previous protest experiences of the marchers if we consider that the peace marches involved a quite different social and political base in the various cases. In particular, political opportunities could be expected to have an effect ceteris paribus, that is, in explaining differing strategic propensities of similar social and political groups. Here, the countries differ a great deal in terms of the capacity of the February 15 demonstration to mobilize activists from various social movements. Looking at previous experiences in specific types of demonstrations (Table 7.2), we can observe the relevant participation of Italians in almost all types of demonstrations; of Belgians especially in new global, antiracist, and third-world events; and of Germans in pacifist and antiracist, but also environmentalist protest. The Spaniards have especially frequent experiences in demonstrations on social issues; citizens of the United Kingdom on antiracism; and Americans on women's and peace issues; while there is relatively less mobilization on the various issues among the Swiss and Dutch. Comparing these data with those from the World Values Survey, we note that the differential presence of activists with experiences regarding various issues does not seem to be explained by the mere strength of memberships in related movements in the national population (Table 2.5).

Social Centrality and Participation

Moving from the macro to the micro, these are the first questions to investigate: What are the characteristics, within each country, of the activists with different degrees of participation? What explains the choices among the different repertoires of activism? Are the same explanations valid across countries? A first set of variables necessary to consider refers to individual socioeconomic resources. The early research on political participation, based on surveys, reveals very low levels of participation (for a review, see Lagroye 1993, 312).[5] Moreover, the number of citizens involved diminished dramatically for the more demanding forms of participation. The normative problems involved in this selectivity were increased by the nonrepresentativeness of those who participated: in fact, higher levels of participation were singled out, ceteris paribus, for those who were socially central, that is, the better educated, middle-class, male, medium-age cohort, married people, city residents, ethnic majorities, and citizens involved in voluntary associations (Milbrath and Goel 1977). Similarly, in their research on participation in the United States, Verba and Nie (1972) observed that the higher the social status of an individual, the higher the probability that she or he will participate; Verba, Nie, and Kim (1978) have confirmed this observation in a seven-nation comparison that concluded that social inequalities are reflected in unequal political influence. Usually, higher social status implies more material resources (and free time) to invest in political participation, a higher probability of being successful (via personal relationships with powerful individuals), and especially a higher sense of personal achievement. Psychological disadvantages overlap with social disadvantages, reducing the perception of one's own "right to speak up" (Bourdieu 1979, 180). If participation responds to demands for equality, it does tend to reproduce inequalities, since "any individual participates, at least potentially, with the differential (or unequal) influence (if we do not want to use the word 'privilege,' which would have an

Table 7.2. Respondents with experiences in previous demonstrations by country (percent)

	Peace	Antiracism	Human Rights	Third world	Social	Ecology	Global justice	Women's rights	Regionalist
United States	67	24	28	9	28	22	17	21	3
United Kingdom	46	26	17	10	27	15	12	8	6
Spain	43	15	15	16	58	15	15	14	2
Italy	71	39	37	20	71	23	55	15	6
Netherlands	46	21	16	8	18	16	9	6	1
Switzerland	48	32	26	14	38	22	25	16	4
Belgium	55	44	24	21	38	20	35	10	2
Germany	66	44	21	6	39	23	15	9	2
Total	56	31	24	13	42	20	24	13	4

ancien régime flavor) that characterizes his or her position in the system of private interests" (Pizzorno 1966, 90).

Research on social movements has also looked at the social characteristics of activists from at least two points of view. First, it has often been observed that the new social movements recruit in a specific social base, made up mainly of some components of the middle class. Second, to account for the overrepresentation of young and student activists, I used the conception of biographical availability to point to the circumstances that increase free time and reduce family responsibility, reducing constraints on participation in movement actions (see McAdam 1988). Because of adolescent enthusiasm and the lack of social inhibitions, young people are also expected to be more radical in their forms of action.

To what extent does an adapted version of social centrality explain the degree and forms of participation in a highly active population such as the one we have surveyed, which is, however, quite heterogeneous at least (and not only) for gender and age? To answer this question, I have crossed our dependent variables with gender, age, professional situation, education, and religion.[6] Our data tell us that, in our highly mobilized population, sociobiographical data have little explanatory value in accounting for the frequency and repertoire of participation (see Table 7.3). Gender, class, and religion are unable to tell us how much and in which forms demonstrators have mobilized in the past. As for frequency of participation, the only significant correlation we found is that the lower the age, the higher the frequency of previous participation (rho = .04). Notably, however, not only the strength of correlation but also its direction changes in different countries: participation increases with age in Belgium but decreases in Germany and the Netherlands, and age is irrelevant in the remaining countries. Education has some effect only in

Table 7.3. Correlations between sociodemographic characteristics and forms of action (Cramér's v)

	Semi-conventional	Demonstrative	Political consumerism	Disruptive	Violent
Sex	.01	.05	.07	.04	.06
Age	.06	.09	.15	.26	.10
Profession	.09	.06	.11	.25	.07
Working sector	.13	.11	.18	.16	.08
Education	.08	.06	.04	.12	.07
Religion	.05	.05	.04	.04	.04
N	4,552	4,315	3,998	495	96

Note: All values are significant at least at the .05 level.

Belgium and Switzerland. Sociodemographic background has no explanatory power as far as first timers are concerned: they have the same gender, age, professional, and educational characteristics as other demonstrators.

Sociodemographic characteristics (with the exception of gender, which seems to play absolutely no role) are slightly more useful for explaining the preference for some forms of action—not so much conventional (used by almost all marchers) or violent forms (used by almost none), but political consumerism and disruptive forms. As expected, the last are more popular among the young and students (especially among Italians and Americans, less among Spaniards). Age and profession also have some explanatory power as far as political consumerism is concerned.

Political Attitudes, Networks, and Participation

While sociobiographical data tell little about protestors' frequency of participation and choice of repertoire, more relevant results emerge if one looks at some specific attitudes, as well as membership in associations and protest groups (a sort of social capital for protest) and previous experiences with movement activism on causes congruent with the targets and demands of the February 15 demonstrations.

Those who marched against the war in Iraq had frequent and intense previous experiences with various forms of political participation—living testimony for the "participatory revolution" that social scientists had already identified in the 1970s and has been reassessed since the 1990s (Meyer and Tarrow 1998; Norris 2002). After the path-breaking research of the 1950s and 1960s, more recent research started to note increasing degrees and reduced selectivity of participation. Particularly in Western Europe, at least until 1990, political participation increased and the percentage of passive citizens declined (from 85 percent in 1959 to 44 percent in 1990) (Topf 1995, 68). Additionally, while conventional participation remained stable, unconventional forms have drastically increased, with decreasing inequality as far as gender, age, and education are concerned. When labor mobilization seemed to decline, research on the global justice movement pointed at a remobilization of the class cleavage, with increased participation from the labor movement (della Porta 2003).

Especially with the growth of political participation and the increase of research on its less conventional forms, the debate about the degree and sources of selectivity reemerged. Alessandro Pizzorno (1966) has already noted that characteristics of political participation are rooted in the systems of solidarity at the basis of the very definition of interest: interests can in fact be identified only with reference to a specific value system; values push individuals to identify with wider groups in society, providing a sense of belonging and willingness to mobilize. From this perspective, participation is an action in solidarity with others that aims to protect or transform the dominant values and interest systems; it therefore requires the construction of solidarity communities within which individuals perceive themselves and are recognized as equals. Political participation aims at this identity construction: before mobilizing as a worker, I have to identify myself as a worker and feel that I belong to a working class. Identification as awareness of being part of a collective *us* facilitates political participation that, stated Pizzorno, "increases (it is more intense, clearer, more precise) the higher is class consciousness" (1966, 109). In this sense, it is not the social centrality mentioned by Milbrath (1965) but the centrality with respect to a class (or group)—as linked to identification with that class (or group)—that defines an individual's propensity to political participation. This explains why some groups composed of individuals who are endowed with low status are able, under some conditions, to mobilize more effectively than other groups. Participation is therefore explained by not only individual but also collective resources.

While the construction of a collective identity is a precondition for action, it is also a consequence of it. In fact, participation itself changes individual identity, increasing the sense of belonging to some groups and weakening other potential identifications. In collective action, identity is produced and reproduced (della Porta and Diani 2006, chapter 3). Revolutionaries' barricades, workers' strikes, and students' occupations are actions oriented to influence public authorities and also have an internal function of strengthening class consciousness—or, in more modern words, collective identification. Participation, then, in a sort of virtuous circle, strengthens the sense of belonging, which promotes more participation. During action, participants identify not only themselves (the "we" they identify with) but also the targeted adversaries ("them"). It is indeed in action that the process of cognitive liberation develops (McAdam 1988, della Porta and Diani 2006). And it is in the course of actions that the struggle for the recognition of emerging identities evolves—a recognition that is part and parcel of identity building (Pizzorno 1991; della Porta, Greco, and Szacolczai 2000). Specific experiences of intense protest participation determine subsequent choices, and militant identities develop during long-lasting activist "careers" (McAdam 1988; della Porta 1995). *Persistent activism* has been explained as an effect of attitudinal availability (deriving from socialization) and situational availability (flexible careers, part-time jobs, no children), but also of the reflexive effects of movement participation in terms of strengthening an alternative value system (Downton and Wehr 1997).

Our data can be useful in testing the extent to which the degree of participation increases within the processes of development of specific political values and in various types of movement organizations and activities. In this direction, they can help us to determine the mobilization potential of the peace demonstrations and identify how beliefs, networks, and previous activism influence patterns of participation. That peace demonstrations have a quite heterogeneous social and political base could be related to the location of the peace marches in various national social movement sectors—particularly left-libertarian families and labor movements—with related effects on the construction of collective identities. In particular, in some countries the February 15 marches can be located within periods of intense protest, mainly focused around global issues. In Italy and Spain, and also in Switzerland and Belgium, the organization of transnational counter-summits contributed to the identity construction of the global justice movement, which then provided a basis for bloc recruitment in the peace movement. The February 15 protest therefore inherited from the global justice movement mobilizations their nationally specific characteristics (della Porta 2007): for example, the larger presence of the labor movement in Italy and Spain, and of left-libertarians in Switzerland and Belgium. In the United States and the Netherlands, in contrast, the marches seem to have remained more within the tradition of national movements.

Looking at the various components of the development of (broadly defined) collective identities as movement activists, we have therefore crossed our dependent variables with two sets of variables indicating political attitudes (political interest in politics; location on the left-right continuum; judgment about parties, police, and the global justice movement; trust in various actors); membership in various organizations; participation in protest events by different types of movement (not the frequencies of participation in demonstration, which is our dependent variable).

In general, our analysis confirms the role of some values and beliefs in explaining prior mobilization. First, in all countries, the most committed hard core of demonstrators is formed by staunch leftists. If we look at the rho value (which indicates the strength of correlation), in particular, high level of participation is related to political position: The farther left the respondent, the higher the previous participation in demonstrations (rho = .31). In particular, the mobilizations on global issues have constituted the main reservoir of committed activists. In fact—and, again, consistently for all countries—a relevant explanation for a high level of participation is the demonstrators' attitude toward the global justice movement: the higher the sympathy for the movement, the higher previous participation in demonstrations (rho = .28).

In the same direction, the more the respondent agrees with the statement "For me, this antiwar protest is another way to express my feelings against neo-liberal globalization," the higher the amount of his or her previous participation in demonstrations (rho = .22). The connection between trust in social movements and participation in demonstrations is also confirmed by the answers to a battery of questions addressing trust in civil society: the higher the trust in civil society, the higher the previous participation in demonstrations (rho = .16).

Previous participation is also strongly correlated with attitudes toward police. In fact: the less necessary police attendance is considered, the higher the previous participation in demonstrations (rho = .28); and the lower the trust in the police, the higher the previous participation in demonstrations (rho = .29). Demonstrators with high levels of participation had negative judgments of police in all countries, confirming that the more frequent the interaction with police, the less the confidence in them. It is also confirmed that demonstrators are not antipolitical people; to the contrary, the more committed they are to demonstrating, the more they express interest in politics. In fact, less strong, but still relevant (and relevant for all countries), is the correlation of frequency of participation with interest in politics (the higher the interest in politics, the higher the previous participation in demonstrations; rho = .20). Confirming a tense relationship with institutional politics, the more participation increases, the more trust in political institutions (rho = .15) and other institutions (rho = .16) is lowered.[7] This is particularly true in Italy and the United States, but also in the Netherlands, Belgium, and Spain.

Additionally, the more protest-experienced the marchers, the less they expressed antipolitical feelings. There is no systematic correlation between agreement with a statement such as "Political parties are only interested in my vote, not in my ideas and opinions" and previous participation in demonstrations (rho = .02). Items addressing a sense of personal or collective efficacy ("When people like myself voice opinions to politicians, these are taken into account"; or "Political parties are only interested in my votes") are unable to explain the differences in frequency of previous participation in most countries (and sometimes the existing correlations have different directions in different countries)—probably because they tend to mix criticism of "old politics" and sense of efficacy of politics "from below."

The data indicates that participation feeds on itself but also that participation in some types of demonstrations (such as the peace movement, but also demonstrations on social rights and global justice) explains February 15 marchers' degree of participation especially strongly. To compare the importance of the type of previous demonstrations, it is sufficient to look at the absolute z-values in the test statistics of separate Mann-Whitney U tests. Previous participation in peace demonstrations had the strongest effect on the number of previous demonstrations (that is, peace demonstrators are frequent demonstrators), whereas previous participation in regionalist demonstrations has the least effect (that is, regionalists are not very frequent demonstrators). Particularly interesting is the relevant role of participation in the global justice and social or labor demonstrations. There are, however, telling differences among countries: previous participation in demonstrations for global justice is a very good predictor of high levels of participation in Italy and Belgium (although in both countries antiracist demonstrations are even more correlated with participation at the February 15 demonstrations), as well as in the United Kingdom; but also in Switzerland, Spain, and the United States (where, however, the best predictor is participation in social or labor demonstrations); and much less in the Netherlands (where antiracist, human rights, and environmental demonstrations come first). Table 7.4 gives the order of importance of the single types of demonstrations in each country as explanation of frequency of participation in the February 15 protests. Similarly, together with membership in peace movement organizations, membership in global justice organizations is also relevant in explaining the degree of previous mobilization.

In summary, the most committed demonstrators are leftist, with sympathies for the new global movement and low confidence in the police, and with high interest in politics but mistrust of institutions. But can the same variables also explain the choice of specific repertoires? As mentioned, while almost all demonstrators used conventional forms of action and almost none used violence, there are interesting differences in the use of disruptive forms of action and of the specific repertoire of political consumerism (data not shown but available on request). Those having experience with the most disruptive forms of action are, in general, more likely to be leftists and to have participated in demonstrations with various goals (particularly global justice, but also third world and labor; the only exception are the women's and regionalist movements). Moreover, in parallel with what has already been said for degree of political participation, the use of disruptive forms of action is also related to (negative) judgments about police attendance at demonstrations and distrust in political institutions; this does not, however, reduce confidence in the capacity of "people like myself" to have an impact on politics. Participation in student organizations has a high explanatory value. A similar explanatory model emerges for the use of political consumerist repertoires, which are also positively correlated with interest in politics and membership in church, environmental, charitable, human rights, and peace organizations, as well as participation in new global organizations.

Table 7.4. Participation in specific types of demonstrations by country (rank order of z-values in statistical test of separate Mann-Whitney U tests)

	US	UK	SP	IT	NL	SW	BE	GE	Total
Peace	1	1	2	3	1	1	5	1	1
Social	2	5	1	4	6	2	3	4	2
Global justice	3	3	3	2	5	4	2	3	3
Anti-racism	5	4	5	1	2	3	1	2	4
Human rights	4	2	8	5	3	5	6	5	5
Third world	6	7	4	6	7	7	4	9	6
Environment	7	6	7	8	4	6	7	6	7
Women's rights	8	8	6	7	8	8	8	7	8
Regional issues	9	9	9	9	9	9	9	8	9

Note: The table gives the rank order of z-values for separate Mann-Whitney U tests for every type of demonstration (independent variable: participation in type of demonstration, yes or no; dependent variable: frequency of demonstration activity). Z-values are standardized values of a normal distribution. Every single data point is standardized by subtracting its arithmetic mean and dividing the result by the standard deviation. A $z = 0$ indicates that the original value is equal to the mean of the distribution. All z-values below -1.645 make up the lowest 5 percent of the distribution, whereas all those above $+1.645$ mark the highest percentage of the distribution. The Mann-Whitney U test, of course, does not rely on a normal distribution but uses its parameters.

Also in this case, however, differences emerge among countries, which could be interpreted by looking at the differences in the social movement sectors. For instance, in countries with (relatively) weak global justice movements, political consumerism seems to have remained a typical repertoire of religious groups and voluntary associations active particularly on third-world issues. In contrast, in countries such as Italy or Belgium, a very similar model accounts for the use of both disruptive (but not violent) repertoires and boycotts, or conscientious consumption. Also very dissimilar cross-nationally is the impact of membership in environmental or labor organizations, which in some cases increases and in others decreases (or has no effect on) the tendency to use disruptive forms of action: for instance, in Italy, membership in environmental organizations does not affect the propensity to use disruptive forms of action, as it does in Germany; in Belgium, Switzerland, the Netherlands, Spain, and the United Kingdom, membership in labor movements has no effect on the use of disruptive repertoires, as it does in Italy or the United States.

If one compares the explanatory capacity of the two models as a whole, "political attitudes" (defined in terms of political attitudes and experiences of mobilization, leaving out participation in specific types of demonstrations in order to avoid the risk of endogeneity) appears much more effective than "social centrality" in explaining both frequency of participation at demonstrations and repertoire of political participation (see Table 7.5). After standardizing the number of variables included in the two models (which were originally six for the first model and twenty-nine for the second) by running a factor analysis for reducing the twenty-nine original variables in six latent factors, to deal with mixed-scale-level models, ordered logit models and classical logit models were calculated.[8] Since the numbers of respondents were highly unbalanced among the countries, every single analysis was conducted by "blocking" for the countries (i.e., giving equal weight to each country). In conclusion, in all analyses, the model based upon activists' attitudes and networks was superior to the social centrality model, which has significance only for the explanation of disruptive behavior; even in this case, however, it performs worse than the second model. This is, above all, the case for the dependent variable "frequency of demonstrations."

Conclusion

Our analysis of the degrees and forms of participation indicates that most of those who demonstrated on February 15 had used a large repertoire of political participation. While most participants had experiences with conventional forms of participation, they often combined these with less conventional forms

Table 7.5. Comparison of the two models via ordered logit models (pseudo R squares)

	Social centrality	Political attitudes
Frequency of demonstrations	.00	.19
Semi-conventional forms	.06	.14
Demonstrative	.08	.16
Political consumerism	.06	.08
Disruptive	.15	.16
Violent action	.09	.11

Note: The adjusted R squares indicate how well the model explains. The cell entries can be read as shares. All values are significant at least at the .01 level.

and sometimes with disruptive forms of action—but almost never with violent repertoires. They are neither troublemakers nor inexperienced protestors. To the contrary, the national characteristics of the February 15 marches (and marchers) seemed to be influenced less by political opportunities (distribution of institutional power and coalition in government) than by the (step and degree of) development of other convergent movements, in particular those on global issues.

The differences in the social and political base of the peace marches called for an examination of the degrees and forms of participation in terms of participants' social backgrounds and political attitudes. My analysis indicated that the social centrality of the individuals is not particularly telling in terms of frequency of participation (with the exception of age, which is inversely correlated with degree of participation) and only partially related to the forms of action (again, with youths and students more likely to use disruptive forms of protest and religious behaviors sometimes related to "political consumerism").

The attitudinal model provided stronger explanations. High degrees of participation emerged as significantly and strongly correlated with being leftist and identifying with the global justice movement as well as related mobilization (on social and labor issues, third-world solidarity or antiracism). Strong identification with and deep embeddedness in movement networks are the best predictors of degree of participation. Marchers are not antipolitical: they have an interest in politics and believe in their capacity to affect public decisions. However, they are very critical of institutional politics. Similar constellations of variables—although with significant cross-national differences— also explain the use of more innovative (political consumerism) and/or risky (disruptive) forms of action.

The dynamics of collective activism cannot be understood simply in terms of individual choices. If persistent activists keep their militancy during periods of latency of protest, thereby nurturing movements' identities (Melucci

1989), individual paths are strongly influenced by macro trends in the evolution of social movements. Experiences with social protest produce generations of activists, but the form of their commitment is influenced by the shifting involvements of public versus private concerns, or, more directly, by cycles of protest (Tarrow 1989).

Notes

1. A methodological note is in order. In this analysis, I have used different correlation indexes, according to the level of scale of the variables. In particular, I have used the "Spearman Rank Order Correlation" (or simpler: "Spearman's rho") for two ordinal variables. Usually, little variance in one of the two decreases the values of correlation indexes; as in my analysis, the variables very often only take on about three values, and the rho values tend to be quite low. However, the tests of significance that have been developed for Spearman's rho work well, no matter how much (or little) variance can be observed in the variables, and no matter how many cases are involved. For nominal data (cross tables) I used "Cramér's v," a standardization of the more commonly known "phi coefficient," to get values between −1 and 1 and to make results comparable to each other. Respecting the ordinal character of most of the variables, I have also used Mann-Whitney U tests (for dichotomous independent variables) and Kruskal-Wallis tests (for independent variables with more than two values). The classically known correlation, going back to Bravais and Pearson (also known as "product moment correlation"), is of little use, since it should only be applied if both variables have interval scale level, or, in other words, if both variables are truly quantitative. This was hardly ever the case in our survey. I have also abstained from other methods (such as analysis of variance or t-tests), as they assume a meaningful calculation of means, which is not possible for ordinal values.

2. Values are estimates, based on assumptions of equal distribution within the categories. Similar results come from the mean rank (Kruskal-Wallis test), which indicates a quite varied picture, with Italy showing a very strong level of participation (in first place, with a mean rank of 3928), followed by Belgium, Spain, Germany, and Switzerland (with quite similar values, between 3219 and 3023), and then the United States (with 2859) and then, by quite a distance, the United Kingdom (2283) and the Netherlands (with 2137).

3. In fact, we have extracted four factors that largely confirmed our categorization: Factor 1 largely corresponds to semi-conventional forms (including contacting a politician or a civil servant; contacting/appearing on the media, contacting an organization); in Factor 2 the main forms of political consumerism (buy a product, boycott a product) converge; Factor 3 designs direct forms of action (with strikes and sit-ins); Factor 4 the disruptive squatting and occupation of building.

4. To explain the Italian exceptionalism, I have considered the strategy of sampling:

on the streets, in most countries; in part on the special trains leading to the march; and in part at the march itself, in the Italian case. A comparison of the two Italian subsamples (one with the questionnaires collected on the trains, one with those collected at the demonstration in Rome) indicates, however, no significant difference in any of the variables I have used in this chapter—with the only exception of participation in environmental organizations.

5. In the United States, according to Lester Milbrath (1965), as many as 60 percent of the citizens had until the early 1960s just a minimal level of participation, and 30 percent were totally uninterested in politics. Similar results on the United States are presented in Verba and Nie (1972), and on the United States, the United Kingdom, Germany, Italy, and Mexico at the beginning of the 1960s in Almond and Verba (1963, 474).

6. Age groups have been recoded: 0–17, 18–24, 25–34, 35–44, 45–54, 55–64, and 65+. Religion is coded thus: one group without faith, including declared freethinkers; one Christian group; and one religious, but non-Christian, group. In the social centrality approach, belonging to the dominant religion should increase propensity to political participation.

7. In particular we recoded trust in political institutions (king, queen, or president; public administration; local government; national government; national parliament; European Union; United Nations); the police; other institutions (educational system or legal system, political parties, church, press, banks); and civil society (trade unions, social movements, or citizens' groups).

8. In the model of centrality, one variable was nominal dichotomous, four were multinomial, and the sixth was interval. In the second model, eighteen nominal dichotomous variables and eleven ordinal variables were brought together. This usually makes a multivariate estimation rather difficult, not least since the dependent variables were not on an interval scale (which would have improved the situation), but on an ordinal scale (frequency of demonstration activities) or a nominal dichotomous level (forms of participation, yes or no). Bivariate correlations between each independent variable and each dependent one gave values very similar to those in the aggregated model (data not shown, but available on request).

Works Cited

Agrikoliansky, Eric, and Isabelle Sommier, eds. 2005. *Radiographie du mouvement altermondialiste*. Paris: La dispute.

Almond, Gabriel, and Sidney Verba. 1963. *The Civic Culture: Political Attitudes and Democracy in Five Nations*. Princeton, N.J.: Princeton University Press.

Andretta, Massimiliano, Donatella della Porta, Lorenzo Mosca, and Herbert Reiter. 2002. *Global, Noglobal, New Global: La protesta contro il G8 a Genova*. Rome: Laterza.

————. 2003. *Global—New Global: Identität und Strategien der Antiglobalisierungs-bewegung.* Frankfurt a.M.: Campus Verlag.

Axford, Barrie, Richard Huggins, and John Turner. 1997. *Politics: An Introduction.* London: Routledge.

Bourdieu, Pierre. 1979. *La distinction.* Paris: Minuit.

Dalton, Russell. 1996. *Citizen Politics in Western Democracy: Public Opinion and Political Parties in Advanced Western Societies.* Chatham, N.J.: Chatham House.

della Porta, Donatella. 1995. *Social Movements, Political Violence, and the State: A Comparative Analysis of Italy and Germany.* New York: Cambridge University Press.

————. 2003. *I New Global.* Bologna: Il Mulino.

————, ed. 2007. *The Global Justice Movement: Cross-National and Transnational Perspectives.* New York: Paradigm.

della Porta, Donatella, Massimiliano Andretta, Lorenzo Mosca, and Herbert Reiter. 2006. *Globalization from Below: Transnational Activists and Protest Networks.* Minneapolis: University of Minnesota Press.

della Porta, Donatella, and Mario Diani. 2006. *Social Movements: An Introduction.* Oxford: Blackwell.

della Porta, Donatella, Monica Greco, and Arpad Szacolczai, eds. 2000. *Identità, riconoscimento e scambio: Saggi in onore di Alessandro Pizzorno.* Rome: Laterza.

della Porta, Donatella, and Dieter Rucht. 1995. "Left-Libertarian Movements in Context: Comparing Italy and West Germany, 1965–1990." In *The Politics of Social Protest: Comparative Perspectives on States and Social Movements,* ed. J. Craig Jenkins and Bert Klandermans, 229–72. Minneapolis: University of Minnesota Press.

Downton, James, Jr., and Paul Wehr. 1997. *The Persistent Activist: How Peace Commitment Develops and Survives.* Boulder, Colo.: Westview.

Kitschelt, Herbert. 1986. "Political Opportunity Structures and Political Protest: Anti-Nuclear Movements in Four Democracies." *British Journal of Political Science* 16: 57–85.

Kriesi, Hanspeter. 1995. "The Political Opportunity Structure of New Social Movements: Its Impact on Their Mobilization." In *The Politics of Social Protest: Comparative Perspectives on States and Social Movements,* ed. J. Craig Jenkins and Bert Klandermans, 167–98. Minneapolis: University of Minnesota Press.

Lagroye, Jacques. 1993. *Sociologie politique.* Paris: Presse de la Fondation Nationale de Sciences Politiques.

McAdam, Doug. 1988. *Freedom Summer.* New York: Oxford University Press.

Melucci, Alberto. 1989. *Nomads of the Present: Social Movements and Individual Needs in Contemporary Society.* London: Century Hutchinson.

Meyer, David S., and Sidney Tarrow. 1998. "A Movement Society: Contentious Politics for the New Century." In *The Social Movement Society: Contentious Politics for a New Century,* ed. David S. Meyer and Sidney Tarrow, 1–28. Lanham, Md.: Rowman & Littlefield.

Milbrath, Lester W. 1965. *Political Participation: How and Why Do People Get Involved in Politics?* Chicago: Rand McNally.

Milbrath, Lester W., and Madan Lal Goel. 1977. *Political Participation: How and Why Do People Get Involved in Politics?* 2nd ed. Chicago: Rand McNally.

Norris, Pippa. 2002. *Democratic Phoenix: Reinventing Political Activism.* New York: Cambridge University Press.

Pizzorno, Alessandro. 1966 [1993]. "Introduzione allo studio della partecipazione politica." Repr., in Allesandro Pizzorno, *Le radici della politica assoluta,* 85–128. Milan: Feltrinelli.

———. 1991. "On the Individualistic Theory of Social Order." In *Social Theory for a Changing Society,* ed. Pierre Bourdieu and James S. Coleman, 209–31. Boulder, Colo.: Westview.

Rucht, Dieter. 1994. *Modernisierung und neue soziale Bewegungen.* Frankfurt a.M.: Campus Verlag.

Tarrow, Sidney. 1989. *Democracy and Disorder: Protest and Politics in Italy. 1965–1975.* New York: Clarendon.

Topf, Richard. 1995. "Beyond Electoral Participation." In *Citizens and the State,* ed. Hans-Dieter Klingemann and Dieter Fuchs, 52–91. New York: Oxford University Press.

Verba, Sidney, and Norman H. Nie. 1972. *Participation in America: Political Democracy and Social Equality.* New York: Harper and Row.

Verba, Sidney, Norman H. Nie, and Jae-On Kim. 1978. *Participation and Political Equality: A Seven-Nation Comparison.* New York: Cambridge University Press.

8

Boon or Burden?
Antiwar Protest and Political Parties

Wolfgang Rüdig

The enormous size of the demonstrations on February 15, 2003, gives rise to the question of whether this marks a turning point in the relationship between protest and parties. Political protest has sometimes been seen as a challenge to representative democracy and the dominant role of political parties in aggregating political demands. Others regard protest behavior as just one of a range of forms of political behavior that also includes voting and working within political parties. The question thus arises of whether the unprecedented mobilization over the Iraq War has provided political parties with a new challenge or a new opportunity: did the demonstrations signify more alienation from party politics, or did they provide a fertile recruiting ground for parties in search of new supporters?

Peace protests have traditionally been associated with parties of the Left. Past debates have, in particular, seen conflicts between the main parties of the Left, such as Labor, Social Democratic, or Socialist parties, and smaller parties competing for left-of-center voters; this includes Communist and former Communist parties as well as various parties of the New Left that emerged out of the student and ecological protest movements of the 1960s and 1970s. In a few cases, peace issues were of key importance for the formation and development of small parties, such as in the Netherlands and Germany. Liberal parties also supported key demands of the peace movement, such as, in Britain and the Netherlands, opposition to the deployment of medium-range nuclear missiles in the early 1980s. Overall, the political spectrum of parties that potentially seize on "peace" issues is thus quite wide, including liberals, greens, social democrats, socialists, and communists (Rochon 1988, 156–78).

The events surrounding the campaign against the Iraq War could be seen as just the latest installment of a long-running saga of party competition on peace issues. However, the political constellation in some cases has changed rather radically. Of particular interest must be the reversal of the situation between Britain and some continental European countries. While the British Labour Party spearheaded the antinuclear campaign of the early 1980s, Social Democratic governments in Germany and elsewhere supported the stationing of nuclear missiles. In 2003, Socialist and Social Democratic parties in continental Europe were critical of the Iraq War, while the Labour Party supported the U.S.-led war movement.

In terms of party competition, the main issue is thus the extent to which small, leftist parties have been able to attract supporters who otherwise would associate themselves with the main party of the Left. But apart from choosing between one party and another, the question arises as to what extent political parties feature at all in the political world of the peace demonstrator. In this chapter, I will address two choices: that between party and nonparty political activity, and that between support for one party or another.

The first specific questions to be addressed concern the role of political parties before and during the demonstration. What was their role for the mobilization of demonstrators? How important were parties—as compared to nonparty organizations—in the process of people turning up for the demonstrations?

The second question concerns the impact of the antiwar movement in general and the February 15 demonstrations in particular on party politics. What choices about their association with political parties did demonstrators express in terms of future electoral participation, voting preference, and possible future party membership? And to what extent are these choices reflected in the actual development of party preferences and membership following the 2003 antiwar protest?

These questions raise a number of theoretical issues that will be explored in the next section. After this, I briefly discuss the data I will use to examine these questions and then present the results in two main empirical parts: The first will look at the background of demonstrators and their previous political affiliations. The second one will analyze any changes of party political orientation the antiwar movement has precipitated and look at the impact of these processes on the electoral fortunes of antiwar parties as well as their possible success or failure in attracting demonstrators as new members and activists.

Theoretical Reflections

Political parties are said to be in crisis: Party membership is declining in most Western European countries. Moreover, the attachment of voters to the major political parties has declined sharply. What people think about political issues is less and less dependent on the views held by "their" parties. Parties are thus losing their grip on the political process. But how correct is this assessment? Are we really seeing a general decline in party affiliation or, rather, a reshaping, a realignment of political action, including party politics?

The evidence on the current state and future of political parties is rather contradictory. On the one hand, there is a lot of evidence that suggests a process of political alienation is in progress, with decreasing electoral turnout (Franklin 2004), decreasing party membership (Scarrow 2000; Mair and van Biezen 2001), and reduced trust in governments and parties (Dalton 2004). On the other hand, there is also evidence that this decline is by no means even. Some elections attract high turnouts; some parties have managed to increase members. The thesis of a linear road to apathy regarding party politics might thus be premature (Norris 2002).

Two different aspects of the alienation literature must be distinguished. The first concerns alternative forms of political participation that bypass or challenge the dominance of parties. The theme of "antiparty" sentiment belongs here (e.g., Seyd 1995; Poguntke 1996) as well as the issue of party linkage (Lawson and Merkl 1988; Poguntke 2002). Do parties lose their ability to link the concerns of citizens with the decision-making process? Is there a fundamental rejection of political parties that challenges not just individual parties but the whole system of decision-making based on elections contested by political parties? Faced with greater competition from interest groups and social movements for the attention of activists, parties may lose out in such a "market of activism" (Richardson 1995).

The second dimension has to do with party competition. Much of the literature on alienation from parties is essentially concerned with the major parties, which face challenges from within the party system in the form of small and/or new parties. Disillusionment with the large parties should promote the rise of new and small ones, either to challenge the large ones to reform and respond to popular demands or to replace them altogether. In this context, protest movements are not primarily challengers to the dominance of parties per se but they act as a conduit for the spawning of new political parties and/or the promotion of small parties to provide the basis of a new party system and/or a new relationship between parties and civic society. The protest movements of the 1960s and 1970s, and the rise of new parties like the Greens in the 1980s and 1990s were the early foci of this literature (see Dalton and Kuechler 1990; Müller-Rommel and Pridham 1991)

Considering the publication dates of some of the literature referred to so far, it is clear that this debate is not particularly new. Successes of small parties in more recent elections have revived interest in their study in some countries, for example, in Germany (Jun, Kreikenbom, and Neu 2006), but the trend of reduced turnout and declining party membership started some time ago. New movements and parties have emerged at fairly regular intervals since the 1960s and 1970s. Despite facing all these challenges, the established parties have not crumbled—small parties on the whole have remained small; many new parties have risen, fallen, and disappeared.

One explanation may lie in the way the large parties have responded. In fact, the major parties have been fighting back, reorganizing and restructuring to stabilize their operations in the face of new challenges. Katz and Mair's (1995) theory of the "cartel party" is perhaps the best known analysis of this fighting back. The flipside of this is how stable an electorate the challenging parties can rely on. At least for the "new politics" parties that have arisen since the 1970s, Inglehart (1990) predicts problems in securing a stable electorate on the basis of the notion of "cognitive mobilization" (see also Dalton 1984). The highly educated "new politics" voter sees no need to form firm ties with one party but prefers to decide election by election, issue by issue, policy by policy, which party to vote for. The result appears to be a system of party competition where the large parties do not have the security of old and need to fight harder to defend their position, and the smaller parties have more to gain but remain on fairly shaky ground, with little inherent stability.

Inglehart's basic analysis has changed little over the years. The spectacular upsurge of antiwar protest accompanied by a loss of support for mass parties and increasing challenges from new and small parties in the early twenty-first century seems to follow the same basic principles first used to diagnose the student protest of the 1960s and the rise of new social movements in the 1970s and 1980s (Inglehart 1977; 1990; 1997). How well do protest movements against the Iraq War fit into this scheme?

The failure of previous movements to challenge the predominance of parties in political life should make one cautious about readily embracing an "antiparty" argument. Looking at the issue in question here, party systems could be expected to be well positioned to absorb this new wave of activism. While most previous movements—such as the student movement, the antinuclear movement, and also the feminist movement—faced a phalanx of hostile parties when they first emerged in the 1970s in most countries, the antiwar position in 2003 found a ready home in several parties in all countries covered. In Western Europe, "peace" and "war" have historically been linked to the Left, and have divided the Left on numerous occasions. Throughout the twentieth century, different parts of the Left located themselves on the continuum between radical pacifism and support for war in a series of different contexts, with the antiwar position usually associated with the left-wing part of the spectrum and the pro-war position linked to the right of the Socialist/Social Democratic spectrum. The peace movements of the 1950s were strongly based in the traditional left; the New Left that arose with the student movement and took on a strong antiwar message in opposition to Vietnam added a second dimension. As a result of these developments, the antiwar issue could be expected to be picked up by at least two party families: One is the Old Left, which covers both the left-wing part of any Socialist or Social Democratic party and any parties farther to the left, in particular parties that stand in the tradition of Communist party organizations. The second party group open to antiwar campaigning are the New Left parties, arising from the student movement and new social movements of the 1960s and 1970s.

As the party system is thus better placed in the 2000s to absorb peace mobilization than it was in earlier protest cycles, the focus of attention then shifts to the question of which parties will benefit from this phenomenon. The key battleground is, of course, between the main party of the Left and the "challenger" parties of the Old and New Left. What factors are likely to play a role here?

I broadly distinguish between external, factors outside the control of Old or New Left challenger parties, such as electoral systems and the policy positions of the main parties, and internal factors, consisting of attributes of the parties themselves.

To start with external factors, the position of the main party of the Left clearly could be expected to be of major importance. We should expect that Old or New Left challenger parties would be particularly successful in the United Kingdom, where the Labour Party has not only moved sharply to the right in recent years over economic and social issues but also provided strong political and military support for the U.S.-led war in Iraq. In contrast, the main center-left parties in the other countries invariably opposed the war, either in government (Belgium, Germany) or in opposition (Spain, Italy, the Netherlands, and the United States). Small challenger parties should find it more difficult to mobilize effectively on the antiwar issue if the main left-wing party is also committed to the same agenda.

While Green and Far Left parties could thus be expected to benefit, we have to ask the extent to which antiwar mobilization has transcended the realm of left-wing politics. Unlike opposition to stationing nuclear missiles in the early 1980s, which was supported only by a minority (Flynn and Rattinger 1985), the Iraq War was unpopular among large sections of the population throughout Western Europe. While those radically opposed to any kind of military action might have been a minority, the perceived lack of United Nations sanction for the war potentially broadened the range of recruits to the antiwar movement across the entire left-right spectrum. This is shown empirically in chapter 3, where Joris Verhulst and Stefaan Walgrave establish that even among right-wing voters war opposition was widespread. Therefore, if the antiwar movement involves a broader political spectrum, members of other parties might enter the picture as potential players. In Britain, it was the Liberal Democrats as well as Welsh and Scottish Nationalist parties who expressed opposition to the war and took part in the demonstrations. Protesters and voters thus had the choice between no fewer than four left-of-center antiwar parties in Scotland. Among the other countries, only in Spain could we expect a stronger role for regional parties, but as separate demonstrations in regional centers were not covered, their influence is unlikely to show in the Madrid data.

Does it matter whether the main party of the Left, taking an antiwar position, is in government or in opposition at the time of the demonstration? This is quite a tricky issue: as far as antiwar voters are concerned, a rational choice would be to support the antiwar party most likely to be able to recapture government and change government policy. This should benefit the major party of the Left, and thus we might expect less support for Old or New Left challenger parties where the main party of the Left is in opposition to the government. However, calculations are made more complex if we consider the process of government formation: small parties that are likely coalition partners of the major party of the Left are less likely to experience a loss of support to the major party. The Italian Greens fall into this category while the Spanish United Left as well as the Dutch Socialist Party and Green Left Party were not seen as likely future coalition partners.

In both cases where the main parties of the Left were in government opposing the war, Green parties were also part of the governing coalition (Belgium, Germany). One might argue that a vote for the smaller antiwar parties might send a strong signal to the main party of the Left to maintain its antiwar position. At the same time, without a government to oppose, the stakes of the antiwar issue for left-wing politics could be expected to be much lower. Indeed, demonstrations were largest in countries where the government supported the war (Britain, Spain, the Netherlands, Italy) as was shown in chapter 1 of this volume.

Calculations that might be sensible for voters, however, do not necessarily apply to demonstrators. For a low-saliency protest issue with no strong domestic polarization, in particular, one might expect that only those very committed to the issue would make the effort to come out for a demonstration. This would lead one to expect that demonstrators in countries whose government opposed the war are more likely to represent the "usual suspects" of committed peace activists, that is, those partisan or at least sympathetic to the parties of the Old or New Left. On the other hand, in high-saliency protest demonstrators, one would expect a far larger cross-section of the population to be mobilized. In Britain, Spain, Italy, and the Netherlands, we could thus expect the political-party profile of demonstrators to be less likely to be dominated by small parties of the Old or New Left.

Turning to matters of the parties themselves, differences in the positioning of parties on the war issue seem to be a poor predictor of attracting support. Antiwar parties were generally opposed to the Iraq War under any circumstances, with or without a UN Security Council resolution. For antiwar protesters, there was little to choose here in most cases, the only exception is the British Liberal Democrats, who were rather reluctant to take part in the demonstration and were less vociferous in their condemnation, focusing very much on the UN Security Council issue in their arguments.

With little or no policy differences between and Old Left and Green parties on the war issue, what could account for their relative fortunes? One possible factor is the strength of each party group. Green parties have been relatively weak in Southern Europe (Italy and Spain), leaving the Far Left in a better position to benefit. Greens have played a very important role as challengers to the main party of the Left in Belgium, Germany, and Switzerland, with antiwar positions being significant, and thus we could expect the Greens to be high-profile beneficiaries of antiwar mobilization in these countries. Finally, neither Greens nor Far Left parties have been particularly strong forces in either British or U.S. party politics. However, the strong rightward movement of the British Labour Party, combined with constitutional and electoral reform offering new opportunities for small parties in European and regional elections, has triggered increased support for Green parties as well as a revival of the Far Left, in particular with the Scottish Socialist Party.

Beyond taking a specific position on the war, other political choices could affect the attractiveness of these parties to antiwar protesters. While some small parties seem happy to be perpetual challengers, others have sought to pass through the party lifecycle and move from outsider status to be considered potential coalition partners in government (see Rihoux and Rüdig 2006). The German Green Party is perhaps the most obvious example; it grew in prominence at the height of the antinuclear movement of the early 1980s and made nonviolence part of its political identity. By the late 1990s, however, it had gone through a transition process that saw it change from an opposition party rejecting any form of German military intervention abroad to a government party that backed the first combat mission of the German military since World War II in the 1999 Kosovo conflict (Rüdig 2002). Having, in the view of some, thus disowned its roots in the peace movement, it will be interesting to see to what extent the party can command the support of antiwar activists on the Iraq War issue, which sees Greens back in the antiwar camp.

What, then, can we expect? First, members associated with the Green and Far Left parties can be expected at demonstrations, as these parties generally try to play prominent roles in the organization and mobilization of antiwar protest in all countries concerned. Data on the presence of party members will give us some clues as to their relative importance. Their national membership numbers are normally quite low, so we cannot expect huge figures. As they are traditional mass parties, it will be interesting to see how well antiwar Social Democratic or Socialist parties can mobilize members to attend demonstrations.

Looking to future political action, how successful will these small parties be in attracting voters and members from the pool of potential new activists that present themselves in these demonstrations? Much of the media hype has been about how people who never protested before were moved to turn out on this occasion. The results presented in chapter 7 show that the number of protest novices was not quite as high as some media reports suggested, and quite a few people who had demonstrated years before were mobilized again. But despite this, small parties clearly must have seen the demonstrations as a major recruiting ground: how successful were they?

This is a crucial question in the context of the debate over the future of party politics. If people are motivated to come out and demonstrate in the hundreds of thousands, are they happy to leave it at that, or is this a stepping stone for a reinvigoration of party politics with a generation of activists politicized in the antiwar campaign going beyond one-off single-issue politics to become immersed in politics involving both unconventional and conventional forms of action? In the absence of panel data on the political preferences of peace protesters over time, there are two ways one might examine their party political impact. First, to what extent are the changes in party preferences expressed by peace demonstrators typical of the electorate as a whole? Did antiwar protesters form a vanguard that led the way in terms of electoral realignment? Second, to what extent were parties able to attract new members from the ranks of the peace movement? The decision to join a political party is likely to have a greater medium- to long-term effect than just changing voting preferences. Based on membership data from 2002 and 2003, I will assess the role antiwar protesters played in this regard.

Data

The main focus of this chapter is voters and party members. Excluded from this analysis are thus demonstrators who were too young to vote in the last general election. Also excluded are those ineligible to vote because they are not citizens of the countries in which they are demonstrating. As the electoral choices are different in England and Scotland, in this chapter, unlike in most other chapters in this volume, they are considered separate countries for the purposes of electoral analysis. About 10 percent of demonstrators in Glasgow came from England, and these were reallocated to "England."

In addition to the survey data on the demonstrators taking part in the protest marches on February 15, 2003, I use a range of other data sources (e.g., European Social Survey, World Values Surveys, general election data, party membership data). One particularly important aspect is the comparison of the demonstrators with the general population, and I use survey evidence from a variety of polling organizations to identify how typical demonstrators were of a general trend in public opinion and voting choice. Party membership data have been gathered mainly from party reports and accounts.

The Role of Parties in Mobilizing Demonstrators

A first indication of the involvement of political parties is the number of party members that took part in the demonstration. We asked demonstrators about their present and past involvement with political parties, offering four options: active member, passive member, previous member and, lastly, not a party member at present or in the past. In order to compare demonstrators with the general public, we also compiled the results of a general public opinion survey carried out shortly before the demonstration, the 2002 European Social Survey, which asked about current party membership as well as the result of an attempt to compile national membership data on the basis of membership information gathered from the parties themselves. The results are displayed in Table 8.1.

Demonstrators are substantially more heavily involved with "conventional" party politics than the general public. In Western Europe, between 11 and 27 percent of demonstrators were members of a political party at the time of the demonstration.[1] The European Social Survey data as well as the data compiled by Mair and van Biezen (2001) suggests that party membership is

Table 8.1. Party membership among the February 15 demonstrators and the population (percent)

Party Member		US	EN	SC	SP	IT	NL	SW	BE	GE
Demonstrators	Active	23	8	5	6	10	13	15	13	7
	Passive	32	5	10	7	10	13	5	7	4
	Former	3	17	15	9	10	6	5	6	12
Population	European Social Survey 2002	19	3	2	3	4	5	9	7	4
	Mair and Van Biezen 1997–2000	–	1.92[ab]	1.92[ab]	3.42[c]	4.05[a]	2.51[c]	6.38[d]	6.55[e]	2.93[e]

Notes: The European Social Survey population percentages for the United States and Sweden are taken from the World Values Survey (1999, 1991).

[a] 1998.

[b] Great Britain.

[c] 2000.

[d] 1997.

[e] 1999.

Sources: European Social Survey 2002; World Values Survey (Inglehart et al. 2004, 1068). Party membership figures based on party records (Mair and Van Biezen 2001).

an activity involving a rather small minority of the public at large. There are some interesting individual results. Taking into account past party membership reveals that about one third of demonstrators have been a member of a party at one time or another. There is relatively little cross-national variation. The only striking difference is that past party membership is rather more pronounced in the United Kingdom than elsewhere. This might be an indication of a particularly severe decline in party membership in Britain, but also of a high degree of mobilization on the Iraq issue there.

While we have no data on the parties that demonstrators were members of, we did ask specifically about links demonstrators had to groups involved in the organization of the demonstration. Most demonstrators were not members of any of these groups, but a substantial minority was—and political parties were one of the most frequently cited groups (see Table 8.2).

Upon analyzing the importance of different types of groups, some interesting patterns emerge. In the Netherlands, 17 percent of the respondents were members of political parties that (co)organized the demonstration. In no other country are political parties the most important type of organizing group demonstrators were involved in. Parties play a more marginal role in other countries: they are practically not mentioned at all in England and the United States. In Belgium, Switzerland, Germany, Spain, and especially Italy, trade unions play the most dominant role, with parties less important but still mentioned more frequently than in the English-speaking countries. Chapter 10 in this volume elaborates the organizational membership of the demonstrators in more detail.

Parties may, of course, have not only mobilized members and those with a strong sense of party identification, but also elements of the general public with clear preferences or attachments to specific antiwar parties. While we did not ask a question about party identification or the degree of attachment to particular parties, we can use information collected about past voting behavior to gauge the relative mobilizing power of antiwar parties. A look at previous voting behavior also should tell something about the degree of alienation from the political process (see Table 8.3).

If we exclude those who were too young and those who simply refuse to reveal anything about their previous electoral behavior, it is clear that comparatively few demonstrators abstain from the electoral process on principle: in total, only about 4 percent of demonstrators said they did not vote because there was no political party available they wanted to vote for, and just 1 percent indicated they did not vote out of a fundamental objection to representative democracy. There is some limited cross-national variation: Twelve percent of Swiss, 9 percent of Spanish, and 8 percent of English demonstrators cite a

Table 8.2. Voting behavior of demonstrators versus population: Abstention, blank votes, turnout (percentage)

Party Member	US	EN	SC	SP	IT	NL	SW	BE	GE
Demonstrators who did not take part in an election for protest reasons	6	9	5	10	10	3	6	1	3
Demonstrators who voted in last general election	91	77	86	76	83	95	77	86	90
Population turnout in last general election	51	59	58	69	81	80	43	91	79
N (IPPS)	572	261	220	441	921	506	534	456	726

Sources: International Peace Protest Survey (IPPS) 2003; Belgian general elections, 1999: http://polling2003.belgium.be; Dutch general elections, January 22, 2003: http://statline.cbs.nl; Swiss general elections, 1999: http://www.parlament.ch; German general elections, 2002: http://www.bundeswahlleiter.de; Spanish general elections, 2000: http://www.congreso.es; Italian general elections, 2001: Di Virgilio 2001; Parker and Natale 2002; U.S. presidential elections, 2000: http://www.fes.gov; British general elections, 2001: Morgan 2001.

Table 8.3. Recalled vote in last parliamentary elections compared with actual election results

Party family	US Feb. 15	US +/- pop	EN Feb. 15	EN +/- pop	SC Feb. 15	SC +/- pop	SP Feb. 15	SP +/- pop	IT Feb. 15	IT +/- pop	NL Feb. 15	NL +/- pop	SW Feb. 15	SW +/- pop	BE Feb. 15	BE +/- pop	GE Feb. 15	GE +/- pop
Far Left	–	–	5	+5	13	+10	27	+31	43	+38	33	+27	–	–	7	+6	23	+19
Green	33	+30	7	+6	4	+4	2	+1	2	0	40	+35	16	+11	54	+40	35	+26
Social Democrat	65	+16	59	+18	48	+5	57	+22	49	+32	19	–8	79	+56	24	–5	39	0
Liberal	–	–	29	+11	14	–2	–	–	5	–10	5	–13	2	–18	4	–20	2	–5
Conservative	1	–47	–	–32	–	–16	13	–44	1	–28	2	–27	13	–7	6	–14	1	–38
Regional	–	–	–	–	20	0	–	–10	–	–5	–	–	–	–	3	–7	–	–
N (IPPS)	562		193		182		327		388		437		400		385		647	

Note: For each country, the first column indicates the percentage of February 15, 2003, demonstrators who stated they voted for a party indicated at the last national elections (nonvoters excluded); the second column indicates the percentage difference between the recalled vote of demonstrators and the recorded vote of all voters at the last election.

The comparison of percentages between a general population sample and a sample of demonstrators obviously must take into account the differences in confidence intervals; general population surveys with a thousand or more randomly selected respondents normally have a confidence interval of about plus/minus 3 percent (with 95 percent probability); for the much smaller sample sizes for demonstrators, the confidence intervals will be somewhat higher; taking the smallest sample (Scotland) as an example, the figure of 48 percent Labour voters would, with 95 percent probability, be accurate within a confidence interval of plus/minus 7.25 percent (assuming a total population of eighty thousand demonstrators). Only major percentage differences would thus pass statistical significance tests.

Sources: International Peace Protest Survey (IPPS) 2003; Belgian general elections, 1999: http://polling2003.belgium.be; Dutch general elections, January 22, 2003: http://statline.cbs.nl; Swiss general elections, 1999: http://www.parlament.ch; German general elections, 2002: http://www.bundeswahlleiter.de; Spanish general elections, 2000: http://www.congreso.es; Italian general elections, 2001: Di Virgilio 2001; Parker and Natale 2002; U.S. presidential elections, 2000: http://www.fec.gov; British general elections, 2001: Morgan 2001.

lack of a suitable political party. A lacking belief in representative democracy is indicated by 3 percent of Spanish and English demonstrators. Five percent of Spanish and 4 percent of English demonstrators also said they had spoiled their vote. There is a similar pattern in the responses to the statement about not taking part in an election for reasons of protest.

Very few demonstrators have not taken part in an election for reasons of protest in Belgium, Netherlands, and Germany; Swiss voters with 6 percent are already somewhat more inclined to "protest" by abstaining, on roughly the same level as voters in the United Kingdom and the United States. Spain and Italy top the bill with 10 percent electoral protesters. When one compares past turnout differences between demonstrators and the general public, it is generally much higher among demonstrators, suggesting that these are people more politically active than the average population, even considering that recalled turnout in any survey is always somewhat higher than the actual turnout. But, apart from Belgium and Italy, the differential turnout is substantial: there is thus no evidence that demonstrators are alienated from the electoral process: to the contrary, they are more involved in traditional, conventional political participation than the general public (see also chapter 7 about previous activism).

Overall, there is little evidence here to suggest that antiwar demonstrators display what Poguntke (1996) calls generalized antipartyism. Is "specific antipartyism" as expressed in the rejection of major parties more common? To gain a picture of the main pattern in party preference among demonstrators in different countries, let us look at the vote in the last election (as recalled by our respondents) and compare it with the actual election results (Table 8.3).

These data first of all show that the demonstrators were not a representative cross-section of the population. Voters of center-right parties are heavily underrepresented. Very few demonstrators indicated having voted for parties to the right of the main Socialist or Social Democratic parties. Spain did have a significant number of votes (more than 10 percent) for the conservative party, the People's Party (PP); and in Belgium, 6 percent recalled having voted for a Christian Democratic party.[2]

Demonstrators were associated mostly with the main parties of the Left, such as the Socialist or Social Democratic party, the Greens, and parties of the Far Left. The only major exception is the Liberal Democrats in England and Scotland, and the Nationalists in Scotland. Both Liberal Democrats and the Scottish National Party can be considered to stand to the left of the ruling Labour Party, which sets them apart rather sharply from some Far-Right wing regional parties in Belgium and Italy, for example, as well as most Liberal parties in continental Europe, which generally have moved to the right (see Benoit and Laver 2006).

There are a number of important differences in the respective importance of the main parties of the Left, the Greens, and the Far Left. Social Democratic voters are most dominant in Switzerland, followed by England, Spain, Italy, and Scotland. Green Party supporters are most strongly represented in Belgium, the Netherlands, and Germany. Far Left parties are most dominant in Italy, the Netherlands, Spain, and Germany.

In summary, demonstrators are thus clearly not individuals alienated from party politics; to the contrary, they display very high levels of conventional participation. Also, as shown in data on political interest (not reported here in detail), demonstrators generally pay close attention to politics, again far more than by the general public by a substantial margin in all countries (except the Netherlands).

The Impact of February 15 on Party Politics

What happened after demonstrators had gone home? Did the experience have any impact on their post-demonstration behavior? Ideally, I would discuss here the results of a follow-up of demonstrators months or years after the event, trying to trace their behavior and possible link to the demonstration. In the absence of this type of individual-level data, I will try to do two things: first, interpret the results of questions we asked the demonstrators about their likely future political behavior, and second, turn to aggregate data on party membership and voting behavior to gauge the possible impact of the demonstrations.[3]

First, did the demonstration lead demonstrators to be more alienated from conventional party and electoral politics, or is the opposite the case: did taking part in the demonstration strengthen the involvement in conventional political participation? The data does not suggest that demonstrators have been turned off the electoral process: just 2 percent overall indicated they would abstain or issue an invalid vote. More of a constraint on my analysis are those who said they did not know whom to vote for in the future: they amount to 7 percent of demonstrators eligible to vote, with a particularly high incidence of voters uncertain about their future party choice in Spain (18 percent), England (16 percent), Scotland (15 percent), and Belgium (13 percent).

Second, what were the voting intentions of demonstrators at a future general election? Compared with their past voting record, there are some changes but also some continuities. The main continuity perhaps is that also on this score, demonstrators are not representative of the population as a whole. Comparing the voting intentions of demonstrators with those of the general population, I find huge discrepancies in most cases (see Table 8.4). Even more than in the case of past voting, voters of Center-Right parties are almost completely absent. In some countries, this contrasts quite starkly with the then-current trend of voting in favor of Conservative parties, for example, in Germany. Even in Britain, Labour's vote held up very strongly: there is no sign that the Iraq War adversely affected its vote. Clearly, in the population at large, the Iraq War was not necessarily the dominant issue.

Among demonstrators, the general picture is one in which the main party of the Left loses support and smaller antiwar parties—such as the Greens, the Far Left, and, in England and Scotland, the Liberal Democrats—pick up additional support. However, the scale of the loss differs quite markedly; it is highest in England and Scotland. But, importantly, Social Democratic parties are also losing much support in other countries, namely in Switzerland and in Germany. Losses are much smaller in Italy and the Netherlands, while the balance is positive for the Belgian and Spanish Socialists. This might suggest that the position of the Social Democrats on the war is not necessarily a determining factor: not supporting the war has not protected the German and Swiss Social Democrats from losing support to smaller parties among demonstrators.

What, then, determines whether a demonstrator turned his or her back on the main party of the Left and embraced smaller parties like the Greens and the Far Left? I can try to predict demonstrators' intended votes with reference to a variety of attributes: one might expect that young, cognitively mobilized voters might be more willing to turn to smaller parties; demonstrators with some previous engagement in social movement activities might be expected to be more easily persuaded to vote Green or Far Left. Perhaps most interesting would be a look at the influence of ideology and the strength of feeling about the justification for the war in Iraq.

I conducted a series of multinomial logistic regressions to answer these questions, with both the overall data and individual national datasets, comparing voters of Green, Far Left (and, in Britain, the Liberal Democrats) with those expressing a voting preference for the main party of the Left (Socialist/Social Democratic/Labor parties). To reduce the complexity of the model, I removed variables that did not make any impact in any country or in the overall analysis of all countries. In terms of party choice, some countries did not have well-established Green or Far Left parties, and the number of demonstrators expressing a preference for these parties was too small for a reliable analysis; in these cases, I only considered the main small party alternatives.[4] The results of a simplified model with just six independent variables are presented in Table 8.5. What did I find?

Table 8.4. Voting intentions for next parliamentary elections: Comparison between demonstrators and entire populations

	ENG		SCO		SP		IT		NL		SW		BE		GE	
Party family	Feb. 15	+/- pop	Feb. 15	+/- pop	Feb. 15	+/- pop	Feb. 15	+/- pop	Feb. 15	+/- pop	Feb. 15	+/- pop	Feb. 15	+/- pop	Feb. 15	+/- pop
Far Left	11	+11	23	+19	25	+10	44	+38	38	+32	8	+8	9	+9	21	+17
Green	24	+23	9	+9	3	+3	8	+5	44	+39	32	+27	46	+33	54	+45
Social Democrat	16	-28	11	-31	69	+29	44	+25	11	-16	54	+30	31	+3	20	-10
Liberal	46	+24	35	+20	-	-	1	-12	6	-12	2	-19	5	-18	1	-5
Conservative	-	-25	1	-11	2	-38	-	-44	1	-28	2	-13	6	-13	1	-47
Regional	1	-2	21	-4	-	-5	-	-4	-	-	1	-1	2	-8	-	-
N (IPPS)	207		68		331		637		477		521		395		604	

Note: For each country, the first column indicates the percentage of February 15, 2003, demonstrators who stated their intention to vote for a party belonging to the party group indicated whether there was a national election immediately (nonvoters excluded); the second column indicates the percentage difference between the voting intentions of demonstrators of the population as a whole as shown in general surveys of voting intention carried out by polling institutes; poll results chosen were based on fieldwork undertaken as closely as possible to the of the date of the demonstration. For the interpretation of the results, please note that confidence intervals for demonstrator data may be as high as plus or minus 7 percent, as it is for Scotland (see Table 8.3 note).

Sources: International Peace Protest Survey (IPPS) 2003; Belgium: La Libre Belgique, "Sondage trimestriel," March 2003, http://www.lalibre.be. Netherlands: the general election took place only three weeks before the demonstration, so the actual election result is entered here. Switzerland: Longchamp and Golder 2003. Germany: Forschungsgruppe Wahlen, survey conducted February 17–20, 2003, http://www.wahlrecht.de/umfragen/politbar.htm. Spain: Gallup Poll, conducted February 3–24, 2003, http://www.gallup.es/encu/opp/feb03/intro.asp [accessed March 11, 2004]; Greens not listed separately. Italy: average of three national polls conducted during February 2003 (ISPO, SWG, Abacus). http://brunik/altervista.org/riepilogo.html [accessed April 11, 2004]. England: MORI polling for entire United Kingdom, February 2003, http://www.mori.com; Far Left (Socialist Alliance) not listed. Scotland: System3 poll, voting preference in UK Parliament, March 7, 2003, http://www.alba.org.uk; Greens not listed separately.

Table 8.5. Determinants of Green and Far Left voting vs. Social Democrat/Labor voting (multinomial logistic regression)

	UK			IT	NL		SW	BE	GE		Totals	
	Greens	Far Left	Liberals	Far Left	Greens	Far Left	Greens	Greens	Greens	Far Left	Greens	Far Left
Demographics												
Age (Ref.: 55+):												
Age 18–34	5.674**	4.619*	4.607**	2.404	1.661	1.213	1.829	1.522	2.562**	.860	2.608***	1.726**
Age 35–54	3.569*	2.598	2.676*	2.406	2.034	1.654	1.202	1.656	2.040*	1.334	1.938***	1.423*
Political Action												
Participation in demonstrations:												
Social/labor	.329	2.278	.683	1.047	.527	.836	.704	1.658	.723	.928	.762*	1.198
environmental	2.047	.684	.450	1.566	7.981*	6.779	2.420**	3.791***	1.732	.842	2.674***	1.621**
Ideology												
Sympathy with global justice movement	.676	1.079	1.008	2.175	2.179*	2.533*	1.564	2.525*	2.177**	1.323	2.103***	2.010***
Self-positioning as Far Left	2.514	1.687	.430	3.971***	3.391**	4.784***	1.079	.653	1.395	4.903***	1.195	2.844***
"War not justified with UN approval" (strongly agree)	7.638	20.977**	9.380*	1.614	.786	1.929	1.268	1.115	.687	.023*	1.125	2.381***
Country dummies	—	—	—	—	—	—	—	—	—	—	(not shown)	(not shown)
Pseudo R² (Nagelkerke)		.253		.208	.205		.183	.271	.166		.441	
N (valid)		329		572	440		455	391	586		3264	

* p<.05; ** p<.01; *** p<.001

Note: Cell entries are odds ratios. The baseline choice is a voting preference for the main left-wing party.

Inglehart's notion of the cognitively mobilized voter could not be substantially confirmed, as education and interest in politics failed to account for party choice. Of course, demonstrators constitute a subgroup of the population distinguished by very high levels of education and political interest, and thus, within a group so homogeneous in these terms, these variables may not have the expected effects. Age, however, was quite an important predictor in most countries. A preference for small antiwar parties was consistently associated with younger voters, with the single exception of the Party of Democratic Socialism in Germany. Relative youth was a particularly pronounced factor in Italy and Great Britain, with demonstrators aged eighteen to thirty four particularly ready to vote for small parties. Overall, this is consistent with the long-established idea that party identification is particularly weak among younger voters, and thus such voters are more likely to be attracted by protest and challenger parties.

Previous protest frequency and other indicators of political activity failed to make any difference regarding variables associated with previous political activity. The only variable that appeared fairly consistently associated with party choice was having participated in specific demonstrations that had Left or Green socialization: in all countries but Belgium, having taken part in a demonstration on issues of social justice, such as a trade union march, made it less likely for a demonstrator to express a preference vote for a Green party. By contrast, having participated in such an activity did not generally provide a great boost for voting for a Far Left party: it made it slightly more likely in most cases, but nowhere is the effect statistically significant. By contrast, having participated in an environmental demonstration provided a good predictor of Green party choice in all countries.

Turning to ideology, sympathy with the global justice movement fairly consistently was a factor for both Green and Far Left voting; positioning on the left-right scale was particularly important for Far Left parties. Opposition to the idea that the war might be justified if sanctioned by the UN Security Council was more important for Far Left than Green parties.

In the overall analysis—using weighted data, giving each country the same number of cases, and using country dummies to ensure that country-specific relationships do not skew the overall model—the picture emerges that Green voters tend to be younger than supporters of the main party of the Left, less likely to have attended demonstrations on social issues but far more likely to have attended environmental ones, and have more sympathy with the global justice movement. For Far Left party voters, youth is less significant than for Greens, as is previous involvement in protest, while sympathy for the global justice movement has a similar effect. What sets Far Left voters apart in particular is a stronger ideological left commitment and a stronger opposition to UN-approved military action in Iraq.

But what about the country-by-country picture? Are there differences in terms of whether the main party of the Left is in government or in opposition? When one compares the models on a country-by-country basis, the U.K. case stands out as fundamentally different from the rest. Here, two variables clearly dominate the model, namely age and opposition to a war justified by the United Nations. Strangely, perhaps, the model is more or less the same for all three antiwar parties. There are differences in terms of previous protest behavior and left-right positioning, which go broadly into the expected directions.

If I compare the countries with governments supporting the war (the Netherlands, Spain, and Italy) with those who do not (Belgium, Switzerland, Germany), I do not find any major differences. Certainly ideology as measured by left-right position and sympathy with the global justice movement play far more important roles than they do in the United Kingdom, while the issue of UN sanctioning of the war is fairly marginal. With the exception of Italy, age also plays a rather minor role in the other countries.

One possible interpretation of this finding is simply that, except in the case of Britain, the results are a manifestation of how voters of Green and Far Left parties are fairly settled and stable in their orientation. Demonstrators who express a future voting preference for these parties are similar to the voters who would generally be expected to vote for these parties in any case, and, thus, the Iraq issue makes relatively little difference in this context. In Britain, by contrast, the justification of the Iraq War has a dominance that in particular affects younger voters who have no settled party preference. In that sense, the British picture is one of greater change and instability.

One problem with the analysis presented so far is that it does not try to measure changes in voter preferences. We also conducted a detailed analysis of what determined whether previous voters of the main party of the Left either stayed loyal to their party or changed to one of the smaller parties. A series of multinomial logistic regressions were conducted (coefficients not shown) with the variables used in Table 8.5. The main problem encountered with this analysis is the small number of cases; very few coefficients reach the basic level of statistical significance ($p<.05$). Thus, the results could at best be seen as indicators of trends. Essentially, the analyses of changes in voter preferences do not lead to any different results. In terms of the direction and size of coefficients, all of the conclusions reached on basis of the previous analysis are confirmed. In other words, new voters of Green and Far Left parties display essentially the same attributes as all voters of these parties.

This result thus confirms a general trend in our analysis that deemphasizes the potential change associated with the events of February 15: it is the "usual suspects" who attend these demonstrations and make the expected voting choices. Looking beyond the data gathered on demonstrators, however, is there any evidence of changes in the electoral fortunes of antiwar parties as a result of the protest events?

The answer, in short, is "no": an analysis of the poll rating of antiwar parties (detailed results not shown) demonstrates that while some parties experienced brief increases in their ratings after the February 15 demonstrations, this was only a blip—in no case was the political standing of any of the antiwar parties transformed by the Iraq issue.

The actual election results following the Iraq War generally confirm this trend. In some countries, the Iraq issue was completely marginal to elections; in others, elections were heavily influenced by the debate on Iraq. The only national elections in which the Iraq conflict played a major role were those in Spain and the United Kingdom. The Spanish parliamentary elections of 2004 were strongly influenced by the terrorist attack immediately preceding election day, which brought the Spanish Socialist policy on Iraq back to the fore (Ordeix i Rigo 2005); in the British general election of 2005, the Iraq War also was a major issue. In Britain, there was a realignment of the Far Left, with the Socialist Alliance dissolved to be replaced by a new Respect Party mainly associated with the former Labour member of Parliament and prominent antiwar campaigner George Galloway. While Galloway won a seat in the House of Commons, Labour's losses to antiwar parties and candidates were not major enough to deny the party a renewal of its governmental mandate (Kavanagh and Butler 2005). Small antiwar parties might have expected to do particularly well in the European elections of 2004 (Lodge 2005), as second-order elections normally provide a good basis for protest voting, but even on this occasion, the results were not entirely positive for the antiwar camp. Some antiwar parties did quite well, but others had disappointing, and in some cases, catastrophic results (i.e., the Greens in Belgium). Overall, it is difficult to escape the conclusion that the antiwar issue was, at best, of marginal importance in terms of influencing the electoral fortunes of antiwar parties.

Finally, did the demonstration lead to an increase in the party membership of antiwar parties? To assess the possible impact of the antiwar campaign on the recruitment of party members by antiwar parties, I compiled the national party membership figures of all major antiwar parties at the end of 2002 and 2003, that is, the months during which the main antiwar mobilization took place. While this is admittedly a rather crude measure, it allows a first look at what could be expected to be a major membership increase of these parties following the 2003 demonstrations. The results are compiled in Table 8.6.

Yes, there is a major change in membership for quite a few parties. In Scotland, parties of the Far Left (SSP and Socialist Alliance) and the Greens appear to have benefited strongly; the Liberal Democrats and the Scottish National Party, in contrast, were not among the winners of 2003. Other countries in which antiwar parties appear to have had increased memberships are England, Spain, Italy, and the Netherlands. In Germany, Belgium, and Switzerland, however, membership developments were mostly negative.

Overall, the figures support the interpretation that in countries where the antiwar issue attained a high salience, namely those where the government supported the Iraq War, antiwar parties benefited from a significant mobilization process. Virtually all Old and New Left antiwar parties in these countries managed to increase their membership, in some cases substantially, between the end of 2002 and of 2003. In contrast, for countries with a low salience of the issue, the mobilization potential in terms of attracting new members was obviously low. Here, membership levels seem virtually unaffected by the antiwar issue.

While there is thus some evidence suggesting that the antiwar demonstrations of 2003 have not been completely without impact on party politics, further research is needed to assess how important the Iraq issue really was for the new members who joined during 2003. Another open question is how stable an addition to party membership the antiwar mobilization cycle produced has been. Even if the impression of a mobilization effect in countries whose government supported the Iraq War can be confirmed, it is important to note that while antiwar parties benefited by quite substantial margins in relative terms, the actual numbers involved are quite small. In Britain, the high percentage changes involve just a few hundred additional members, as opposed to the hundreds of thousands who demonstrated. In Italy and the Netherlands, some antiwar parties had net increases of a few thousand, and in Spain, the United Left could add at best a few thousand members over a longer time period. Only the Spanish Socialists could mobilize new members in the tens of thousands. However, most of these appear to have joined after their election victory in 2004 and thus could hardly be claimed as antiwar movement related.

If one compares the net membership increases with the number of demonstrators, then the mismatch is particular strong in Britain, Italy, and Spain. In the Netherlands, however, a comparatively tiny mobilization is associated with a quite sizeable net increase in antiwar party membership of several thousand. The Netherlands also stands out here, thus reconfirming the status of

Table 8.6. Party Membership: December 2002 to December 2003

Country	Party	Membership— end of 2002	Membership— end of 2003	Difference (percent)[a]
Scotland	Scottish Labour Party	21,046	22,153	+5.2
	Scottish National Party	16,122	13,382	−17.0
	Scottish Liberal Democrats	4,352	4,171	−4.2
	Scottish Socialist Party	2,300	2,800	+21.7
	Scottish Green Party	531	759	+42.9
England and Wales	Labour Party	227,248	192,789	−15.2
	Liberal Democrat	67,284	69,134	+2.7
	Green Party	5,268	5,858	+11.2
	Socialist Alliance	2,000	2,400	+20.0
Germany	Social Democrats (SPD)	693,894	650,798	−6.2
	Party of Democratic Socialism (PDS)	70,805	65,753	−7.1
	Alliance '90/Greens	43,881	44,052	+0.5
Spain	Socialists(PSOE)	484,321	546,746 (2004)	(+12.9)
	United Left (IU)	65,000 (2000)	69,000 (2004)	(+6.2)
Italy	Democrats of the Left (DS)	534,358	549,372	+2.8
	Federation of Greens	16,000	20,000	+25.0
	Party of Italian Communists (PdCI)	23,747	30,932	+30.3
	Communist Refoundation (PRC)	89,124	85,770	−3.8
The Netherlands	Labour Party (PvdA)	57,374 (2001)	60,062	(+4.7)
	Green Left	18,469	20,503	+11.0
	Socialist Party (SP)	36,406	43,389	+19.2
Belgium	Flemish Socialists (SP.a)	63,898 (2001)	61,637	(−3.5)
	Walloon Socialists (PS)	82,470	83,105 (2004)	(+0.8)
	AGALEV	5,348	5,955	+11.4
	ECOLO	4,463	3,751	−16.0
Switzerland	Social Democrats (SPS)	35,150	34,509	−1.8
	Greens	5,000 (1998)	4,757 (2005)	(−4.9)

Note: [a]The numbers are in parentheses if the data available do not match exactly the annual figures immediately pre- and postdating the demonstration.

Sources: Great Britain: Annual Accounts submitted to Electoral Commission, http://www .electoralcommission.org.uk; except for Scottish Labour Party in 2002: Annual Report 2003 figures supplied by Scottish Labour Party, September 5, 2005; 2003: *Scotsman*, February 24, 2005 (figures for England and Wales for Labour and Liberal Democrats were calculated by subtracting the Scottish membership from the national membership); *Germany:* Niedermayer 2005; *Spain*: Méndez, Morales, and Ramiro 2004; *Italy*: Archivio dati sulle elezione e la partecipazione politica (ADELE), Istituto Carlo Cattaneo, http://www.istcattaneo.org; *Netherlands:* Documentatiecentrum Nederlandse Politieke Partijen, http://www.rug/nl/dnpp; *Belgium*: Agalev/Groen: Personal communication, Jo Buelens, February 2006; ECOLO. Van Haute 2005; Socialist Parties: Personal communication, Stefaan Walgrave, December 2006; *Switzerland:* SPS, personal communication Rosmarie Bürki, SPS, October 2, 2006; Greens 1998: Ladner and Brändle 2001; 2005: Swiss Green Party: only figures available for 2005 and 2006; personal communication, Simon Grossenbacher, Sekretariat Les Verts-Grüne, Bern, September 5, 2006.

a country that was already marked by the importance parties played in the organization of the demonstration (see chapter 10). Exploring the reasons for this may raise some interesting research questions. The country has not stood out so far in terms of the size of party membership: comparisons here place it just slightly above average (see Table 8.1). In one other area, namely environmental NGO membership, the Dutch are a clear outlier and display levels of membership that far outstrip any rival (Dalton 2005). If Dutch political activists are thus generally "joiners," then this might provide a nation-specific cultural basis where small political parties are better placed in using new issues to mobilize new members.

Conclusion

The antiwar demonstrators of February 2003 displayed political allegiances and preferences that indicated increased support for Green and Far Left parties. Demonstrators were not turned away completely from the electoral process and party politics; rather, they were prepared to vote and express preferences. Beyond this, however, there was very little evidence of a major increase in party political activity generated by the protest events.

Despite the extraordinary size of the February 15 demonstrations, it is quite obvious that they were not pivotal in terms of changing the political fortunes of many political parties. In some countries, the issue was simply too marginal to affect party development in a more sustained way; in others, there was an "Iraq effect," which had taken hold in late summer or autumn of 2002; some cases can be identified in which antiwar parties received a boost in February and March, but in most instances, this was just a temporary result. No major political earthquake effect on parties can be detected.

Also, in terms of general political behavior patterns, such as participation in elections and joining political parties, the evidence suggests that the antiwar movement was not an earth-shattering event that changed the face of politics. Some parties did experience a new influx of members that may, at least in part, have been associated with the events of February 15, 2003, but the evidence available suggests only fairly minor changes. The antiwar movement apparently did not constitute an experience that politicized substantial percentages of the population not previous involved in politics.

Were the February 15 events of thus a boon or a burden for the parties? There is no evidence to suggest that alienation from electoral politics played a major role in the protests; demonstrators in all countries had been active voters and were also eager to take part in future elections. There is more evidence that the demonstration was associated with a move away from the major parties to smaller Green and Far Left parties. But even here, the benefits experienced by these parties in terms of additional voters and members were on quite a small scale. They were a boon, but a whimper rather than a big bang.

What I thus find is a discrepancy between the unprecedented degree of protest mobilization on the one hand, and the feebleness of the impact of such mobilization on elections and party politics on the other. Why did the events of 2003 not have a more profound effect? One interpretation is that demonstrators predominantly were engaged in some form of identity or gesture politics and did not regard electoral or party political activity to be particularly relevant in this context. If, indeed, even such a major issue cannot revive interest in political parties among at most a small minority of those mobilized to demonstrate, then this episode might provide further evidence for theories of a post-party politics. However, there are some indications that an instrumental element was present in some cases, namely in these countries where there was realistic prospect of a change of government leading to a change of policy on Iraq. In Spain, the Socialists were the main vehicle of change and they received overwhelming support from demonstrators, while the United Left, an outsider party that was not part of the governmental project, benefited only weakly. In Italy, though, the Far Left was part of the broad left-wing alliance, and a vote for parties belonging to the alliance indicated support for an alternative government, not just a protest vote for an outsider party. The membership figures, significantly, suggest that the Party of Italian Communists (PdCI) rather than the Communist Refoundation (RC) benefited most. This would be compatible with an instrumentalist explanation of party choice, as the PdCI had remained faithful members of the left-wing bloc while the RC had a more ambivalent attitude to government.[5] The gesture politics interpretation thus predominantly applies to countries where either the government already was opposed to the Iraq War or, as in Britain, both major parties supported the war effort with no practical prospect of a change of government that would be linked with a change of policy.

A note of caution might be appropriate, however: I have analyzed data gathered on one specific political event that, to those who witnessed the unbelievable number of people who moved through the streets of cities around the world that day, seemed to be special. Being so close to the event might raise expectations in one's mind of an appropriate impact on party politics that might exceed what could reasonably be expected. Some past protest events that were seen as significant, such as the May 1968 protests, did not immediately produce major political realignments, new parties, or the like but nevertheless had a profound political effect. The current assessment of the February 15 protests not having a major impact on party politics may thus be premature.

Notes

1. The very high figure of 55 percent for the United States most likely indicates that "party membership" is understood in very different terms in the U.S. context. Political parties in the United States are structured very differently from those in Europe, and the concept of party "membership" in a European sense does not exist in the United States, at least as far as the main parties are concerned. Some state Green parties have established "membership" that is comparable to that in European Green parties, but practices vary widely among states. The respondents most likely understood the question to relate to being a registered supporter of a particular party.

2. We obviously have to consider that voting recall is likely to be affected by rationalizations of previous behavior as well as social desirability factors: it thus could be expected that these figures not only overestimate the number of people who voted but also the number of demonstrators who voted for antiwar parties.

3. The U.S. surveys did not include a question on intended future voting choice, and as no data are thus available, the United States is not included in the subsequent analyses.

4. The dependent variable used for this analysis was future voting preference, with the categories "Green," "Far Left," "other," and "Socialist/Social Democrat/Labor Parties," with the last as reference category. For the United Kingdom, the data of England and Scotland were combined, and a separate category for the Liberal Democrats was used. The coefficients for the "other" parties are not displayed because the small number of cases renders them largely meaningless. The small number of cases also imposed limitations on the number and complexity of independent variables. The independent variables used were (a) Age, with three categories: 18–34, 35–54, and 55 or older, with the last used as reference category; (b) Previous attendance of demonstration: Social/Labour, recoded with the nonparticipants as reference category; (c) Previous attendance of demonstration: Environmental, coded as b; (d) Sympathy for antiglobalization movement, recoded to make those without sympathy the reference category; (e) Far Left: those who scored 0, 1, or 2 on the 0–10 left-right scale are categorized as Far Left, with everybody else as reference category; (f) Justification of Iraq War: those who "completely disagree" that war against Iraq would be justified if sanctioned by the UN Security Council are pitted against everybody else (i.e., those who only moderately disagree with this statement, are undecided, or agree with this position).

5. I am grateful to Daniele Albertazzi (University of Birmingham) for this point.

Works Cited

Benoit, Kenneth, and Michael Laver. 2006. *Party Policy in Modern Democracies*. London: Routledge.

Dalton, Russell J. 1984. "Cognitive Mobilisation and Partisan Dealignment in Advanced Industrial Democracy." *Journal of Politics* 46: 264–84.

———. 2004. *Democratic Challenges, Democratic Choices: The Erosion of Political Support in Industrial Democracies.* Oxford: Oxford University Press.

———. 2005. "The Greening of the Globe? Cross-National Levels of Environmental Group Membership." *Environmental Politics* 14: 441–59.

Dalton, Russell J., and Manfred Kuechler, eds. 1990. *Challenging the Political Order: New Social and Political Movements in Western Democracies.* Cambridge: Polity.

Di Virgilio, Aldo. 2001. "Le elezioni politiche del 13 maggio 2001." *Quaderni dell'Osservatario Elettorale* 46: 155–82.

Flynn, Gregory, and Hans Rattinger, eds. 1985. *The Public and Atlantic Defense.* Totowa, N.J.: Rowman & Allanheld.

Franklin, Mark N. 2004. *Voter Turnout and the Dynamics of Electoral Competition in Established Democracies since 1945.* Cambridge: Cambridge University Press.

Inglehart, Ronald. 1977. *The Silent Revolution: Changing Values and Political Styles among Western Publics.* Princeton, N.J.: Princeton University Press.

———. 1990. *Culture Shift in Advanced Industrial Society.* Princeton, N.J.: Princeton University Press.

———. 1997. *Modernization and Postmodernization: Cultural, Economic, and Political Change in Forty-three Societies.* Princeton, N.J.: Princeton University Press.

Inglehart, Ronald, Miguel Basáñez, Jaime Díez-Medrano, Loek Halman, and Ruud Luijkx, eds. 2004. *Human Beliefs and Values: A Cross-Cultural Sourcebook Based on the 1999–2002 Values Surveys.* Mexico City: Siglo XXI Editores.

Jun, Uwe, Henry Kreikenbom, and Viola Neu, eds. 2006. *Kleine Parteien im Aufwind: Zur Veränderung der deutschen Parteienlandschaft.* Frankfurt a.M.: Campus.

Katz, Richard S., and Peter Mair. 1995. "Changing Models of Party Organization and Part Democracy: The emergence of the Cartel Party." *Party Politics* 1: 5–28.

Kavanagh, Dennis, and David Butler. 2005. *The British General Election of 2005.* London: Palgrave Macmillan.

Ladner, Andreas, and Michael Brändle. 2001. *Die Schweizer Parteien im Wandel: Von Mitgliederparteien zu professionalisierten Wählerparteien?* Zurich: Seismo.

Lawson, Kay, and Peter H. Merkl, eds. 1988. *When Parties Fail: Emerging Alternative Organizations.* Princeton, N.J.: Princeton University Press.

Lodge, Juliet, ed. 2005. *The 2004 Elections to the European Parliament.* London: Palgrave Macmillan.

Longchamp, Claude, and Lukas Golder. 2003. *SVP-Aufstieg erstmals gebremst: Medienbericht zum 3. SRG SSR Wahlbarometer '03.* Bern: GfS-Forschungsinstitut, Politik, und Staat. http://www.polittrends.ch/wahlen/wahlbarometer.

Mair, Peter, and Ingrid van Biezen. 2001. "Party Membership in Twenty European Democracies, 1980–2000." *Party Politics* 7: 5–21.

Méndez, Mónica, Laura Morales, and Luis Ramiro. 2004. "Los afiliados y su papel en los partidos políticos españoles." *Zona Abierta* 108/09: 153–207

Morgan, Bryn. 2001. *General Election Results, 7 June 2001.* (Research Paper 01/54). London: House of Commons.

Müller-Rommel, Ferdinand, and Geoffrey Pridham, eds. 1991. *Small Parties in Western Europe: Comparative and National Perspectives.* London: Sage.

Niedermayer, Oskar. 2005. "Parteimitgliedschaften im Jahre 2004." *Zeitschrift für Parlamentsfragen* 36: 382–89

Norris, Pippa. 2002. *Democratic Phoenix: Reinventing Political Activism.* Cambridge: Cambridge University Press.

Ordeix i Rigo, Enric. 2005. "Aznar's Political Failure or Punishment for Supporting the Iraq War? Hypotheses about the Causes of the 2004 Spanish Election Results. *American Behavioral Scientist* 49: 610–15.

Parker, Simon, and Paolo Natale. 2002. "Parliamentary Elections in Italy, May 2001." *Electoral Studies* 21: 649–80.

Poguntke, Thomas. 1996. "Anti-Party Sentiment—Conceptual Thoughts and Empirical Evidence: Explorations into a Minefield." *European Journal of Political Research* 29: 319–44.

———. 2002. "Party Organisational Linkage: Parties without Firm Social Roots?" In *Political Parties in the New Europe: Political and Analytical Challenges,* ed. Kurt Richard Luther and Ferdinand Müller-Rommel, 43–62. Oxford: Oxford University Press.

Richardson, Jeremy. 1995. "The Market for Political Activism: Interest Groups as Challenge to Political Parties." *West European Politics* 18: 116–39.

Rihoux, Benoît, and Wolfgang Rüdig. 2006. "Analysing Greens in Power: Setting the Agenda." *European Journal of Political Research* 45: S1–S33.

Rochon, Thomas R. 1988. *Mobilizing for Peace: The Antinuclear Movements in Western Europe.* Princeton, N.J.: Princeton University Press.

Rüdig, Wolfgang. 2002. "Germany." In *Green Parties in National Government,* ed. Ferdinand Müller-Rommel and Thomas Poguntke, 78–111. London: Frank Cass.

Scarrow, Susan. 2000. "Parties without Members? Party Organization in a Changing Electoral Environment." In *Parties without Partisans: Political Change in Advanced Industrial Democracies,* ed. Russell J. Dalton, and Martin P. Wattenberg, 79–101. Oxford: Oxford University Press.

Seyd, Patrick. 1995. "Anti-Party Politics in Britain: An Assessment." *Jahrbuch für Politik/Yearbook of Politics* 5: 21–41.

Van Haute, Emilie. 2005. "After Governmental Participation: Still the Age of Cohesion between Green Members and Activists? The Case of Ecolo, Belgian French-speaking Green Party." Paper presented at 3rd ECPR General Conference, Budapest, September.

9

Open and Closed Mobilization Patterns: The Role of Channels and Ties

Stefaan Walgrave and Bert Klandermans

Mobilization can usefully be discussed in terms of the demand and supply metaphor. "Demand" refers to the will of (a segment of) the population to protest and show its discontent, while "supply" refers to the offer of a certain collective action event staged by organizations and social movements. Mobilization brings demand and supply together. To be sure, this economic metaphor does not apply entirely to collective action events—both "parties" are not exchanging different types of goods, they essentially want the same (collective action), and there can be demand without supply, in the case of spontaneous collective actions. Yet, it is a very useful way of speaking about collective action in general and mobilization in particular. Mobilization, then, is one side of the demand, supply, and mobilization triangle that accounts for the ebb and flow of social movements (Klandermans 2004). Mobilization is the process that gets the movement going and links a certain demand for protest among the population in a country to a supply or offer from the protest market in that country. Demand and supply would remain potentials, if processes of mobilization were not to bring the two together. This makes it understandable why so much of the literature on social movements is devoted to mobilization processes. Yet, it would be a mistake to neglect demand or supply factors. Mobilization is only possible on the basis of some demand and supply being developed over the course of time; if neither of them existed in a society, mobilization would be inconceivable and in vain. In this chapter, after a theoretical introduction developing two mobilization typologies, we will focus on the assessment of mobilization patterns in the eight nations studied. Next, we will assess the extent to which mobilization patterns make a difference and affect the features of the demonstrators. Finally, we will attempt to account for these differences in mobilization patterns by associating them to diverging patterns of supply and demand in the eight countries under study.

Open and Closed Channels, Strong and Weak Ties

According to Klandermans, social movements face two separate mobilization challenges: consensus mobilization, that is, persuading people of the good cause, and action mobilization, that is, actually bringing people to the streets (Klandermans 1984; Klandermans 1997). Our focus here will be on action mobilization and what can be learned about it from the demonstrations of February 15.

Action mobilization is a funneling process with different stages in which generalized preparedness to act in support of a cause must be transformed into specific preparedness to participate in a particular protest event, and finally into actual participation (Oegema and Klandermans 1994). This activation process has three aspects: getting in touch with people to get the message about the event across (informing them about what, where, and when), motivating people to participate (making sure that the pros of participation outweigh the cons), and helping motivated participants overcome barriers to participation (Klandermans and Oegema 1987; Oegema and Klandermans 1994). A whole range of social movement organizations, political parties, associations, and NGOs staged the protests of February 15. In chapter 1, we described the organizers in each country, and chapter 10 shows how the actual protesters were organizationally embedded. Obviously, the organizational makeup of the antiwar coalition affected the process of mobilization, if only because organizations differ in how they mobilize. Our aim here is not to compare mobilization strategies employed by the various organizations in the countries of our study; rather, in this chapter, we are interested in the opposite end of the mobilization chain—the people targeted. As we only interviewed people who actually showed up for the demonstration, we cannot contrast successful and unsuccessful mobilization attempts but can only sketch action mobilization attempts that succeeded, as it was participants who reported back. In this context, our focus is on information dissemination. Certainly, being targeted with information is not a sufficient precondition for participation, but for obvious reasons it is a necessary condition. For example, research by Klandermans and Oegema (1987) showed that in the specific case they investigated, simply *none* of those who a movement organization failed to target participated in the event. Our respondents were necessarily reached by information about the demonstration. Our core question in this chapter is of how they were reached: which people were successfully targeted for mobilization through what kind of information channels?

Since the first formulation of resource mobilization theory (McCarthy and Zald 1976), social movement literature has acknowledged the organized character of mobilization. Numerous studies have since documented the crucial significance of social networks for understanding mobilization and differential recruitment (see Diani 2002; Diani and McAdam 2003; Gould 1993; Kitts 2000; Tindall 2004). However, most of the available research focuses not on the specific information channels but rather on the general sociostructural embeddedness of mobilization. Resource mobilization theory, for example, emphasizes the necessity of formal organizations for mobilization (McCarthy and Zald 1976). People have to be more or less integrated in social movement organizations to enable large and successful mobilization processes. Via learning processes that develop participatory skills, via the generation of social networks reducing information costs and expanding weak ties, and via intentional mobilization does membership in formal associations foster protest participation (Morales 2008; Tindall 2004). Movement organizations are mobilization machines specialized in helping people eliminate the barriers that lie between willingness to participate and actual participation. Some scholars, in contrast, claimed that informal networks could do the mobilization job as well and that, rather, informal preexisting networks are the sociostructural requirement for collective action. McAdams's concept of a micromobilization context proved especially influential in this respect (McAdam 1988; McAdam, McCarthy, and Zald, 1996).

Although the role of formal and informal networks is widely documented, it is perfectly conceivable that the actual targeting and information dissemination are not embedded in a social network. Research in Belgium, for example, showed that the media, not formal organizations or informal networks, brought the demonstration message across and thus played a central role in making the White March the biggest demonstration ever held in Belgium. At least in targeting the population, but probably even in motivating potential participants and lowering the barriers for participation, the mass media played a major role (Walgrave and Manssens 2000). Thus, mobilization, certainly the information dissemination aspect of it, can happen outside of organizational networks or, better, reach beyond them. Based on this general idea, we propose two different dimensions of mobilization: strong versus weak ties and open versus closed mobilization channels.

Granovetter first launched the idea of the strength of ties in a seminal article (1973) elaborating on the importance of strong and weak ties for social movement mobilization (see also Putnam [2000], who speaks about "bridging" and "bonding" social capital). The strength of weak ties, so writes Granovet-ter, is that they connect cliques (that is, groups with strong ties). Therefore, it is the weak ties that are crucial in spreading information among cliques. Without weak ties, information would not travel beyond group boundaries. Strong ties, though, while not very effective in disseminating information, are more effective than weak ties when it comes to activation (McAdam 1986; see also Marwell and Oliver 1993).

The open-closed distinction is based on various typologies we encoun-tered in the social movement literature. Klandermans and Oegema (1987), for instance, discern four routes to target individuals for mobilization: mass media, direct mail, and organization and friendship ties. They distinguish between formal and informal mobilization attempts, the first being deliber-ate mobilization efforts of the movement (via flyers, posters, stands, adver-tisements, and so on), and the second being personal links with someone who planned to participate in the upcoming demonstration. They conclude that although more people are reached by formal channels, the informal links are especially crucial for stimulating actual participation, since they yield much more participation motivation than formal information channels (see also Gould 1991; 1993). Snow and colleagues distinguish face-to-face dissemi-nation from mediated dissemination (Snow, Zurcher, and Ekland-Olson 1980). Face-to-face dissemination requires the physical presence of a source of information, and mediated dissemination implies the use of media—like newspapers, television, mail, the Internet, and telephones. Furthermore, Snow and colleagues distinguish private channels for mobilization and recruit-ment from public channels. Snow, Zurcher, and Ekland-Olson's taxonomy of recruitment channels suggests that some channels can reach the public at large, while others only reach certain segments of the population.

Elaborating on these ideas, we distinguish also their openness versus closedness. The characteristic that defines the openness or closedness of a communication channel is the target: open mobilization channels have no restriction regarding whom they target, while closed mobilization channels only target people with certain characteristics, for instance, members of an organization. The broader the target groups, the less specific personal char-acteristics, the more open the mobilization channel. An organization that primarily targets its own members is an example of closed mobilization. Labor union demonstrations are typical examples of recruitment via closed chan-nels. As a rule, such demonstrations are crowded with union members, and hardly any nonmembers show up at these protests. Closed channels are typ-ically employed in so-called en-bloc recruitment (McAdam 1986), where members of a group or organization are recruited as a whole. The mass media, on the other hand, are probably the best example of an open mobilization channel. Although there are some notable biases in media use—coinciding largely with organization membership—mass media can be considered a ubiquitous mobilizer because a vast majority of the population is confronted with mass media outlets.

Theoretically, the two dimensions—kinds of ties and openness or closedness of channels—are independent from one another, as they refer to different facets of the mobilization process. This is not to say that they are not correlated in practice. Obviously, membership in an organization (strong tie) makes it more likely for one to be targeted by mobilization attempts from that organization (closed channel). Thus, we expect both dimensions to be associated to some extent. To complicate matters further, the same channel might function differently in different countries and under different circumstances. For example, we considered newspapers as open mobilization channels, but they can be explicitly partisan, owned and controlled by a social organization or political party. Hence, the readership of such newspaper probably tends to be selective, offering certain social and political features. The decision to read this specific newspaper most likely is based on ideological beliefs. As a consequence, mobilization via this newspaper is less open than would be the case via more neutral ones. In a similar vein, friendship networks or links with colleagues can be more open depending on the issue. For work-related and bread-and-butter issues, colleagues act as closed channels referring to specific interests. Yet for universal issues, such as the protest against the war in Iraq, colleagues are more likely to act as an open mobilization channel. Here is another example of the contingent nature of mobilization channels: some people are informed about a demonstration by flyers, ads, or posters. Are these open or closed mobilization channels? The answer depends on the strategy of the organizers. If they decide to distribute flyers in train stations or on the streets, this technique is fairly open. If, in contrast, they focus their distribution on political meetings, obviously only some specific groups are targeted. The same applies to posters: are they suspended on the streets or, rather, in specific places like universities, schools, and clubs?

During a mobilization campaign, a movement organization minimally tends to target its own members. This pattern of mobilization via closed channels and through strong ties Marwell and Oliver (1993) identifies as the pattern most likely to be adopted by organizers. Yet, unless an organizer is satisfied to stay within the boundaries of the organization's constituency, weak ties and open channels must be employed. After all, not every citizen has strong ties, or any ties at all, to the organizations staging the events. If the movement is engaged in a battle for universal values—such as the antiwar demonstrations of February 15—chances are that the message gets across to a broader segment of the population. In this process, the mass media play a crucial part. Although their normal role is not a mobilizing one and the media seldom take sides in a controversy or urge people to participate in any protest, they do convey the message that there will be a protest event, certainly when it is anticipated to be a large-scale one, such as a mass demonstration in the country's capital. Therefore, we expect open channels to have played a substantial role in the making of February 15. In chapter 3, indeed, it was documented that there was massive attention to the war in all covered countries, and chapter 12 will show that in many countries the protests against war also got a lot of attention in the media.

Patterns of Mobilization

What kind of links did people have to the organizations staging the demonstration? We asked our respondents whether they were members of one of those organizations or whether they knew people who were members. If the answer to either question was affirmative, we asked them how they maintained contact with these organizations—indirectly, through such media as the Internet or newsletters, or directly, by attending meetings. We used the answers to these three questions to construct an indicator of the strength of the ties that an individual has with relevant movement organizations. We distinguished five levels of strength: no ties, and weak, moderate, strong, and very strong ones.[1] Table 9.1 shows the findings with regard to the five different levels of connectedness for the eight countries.

Half of the participants had no ties with organizations that staged the demonstrations in their country. The remaining half had ties ranging from weak to very strong. Overall, we observed considerable variation in the strength of ties among countries. For example, in the United States and the United Kingdom—the two countries that went to war—close to two thirds of the demonstrators had no ties to the protest-staging organizations. In the Netherlands and Germany, also relatively few participants were tied to the mobilizing organizations. In Belgium and Switzerland, the degree of embeddedness was almost identical and, in contrast, shifted toward stronger ties. Spanish demonstrators predominantly had weak or moderate ties. In Italy, no fewer than 70 percent of the participants had some ties to antiwar organizations, while more than one third even had strong or very strong ties. These very strong ties reported deserve a special commentary. We first suspected this might be an artifact of the sampling procedure employed in Italy, where respondents to the survey were approached during the train ride to Rome from the north part of the country. (This is explained in full detail in the

Table 9.1. Ties to organizations staging the demonstration (percent)

	US	UK	SP	IT	NL	SW	BE	GE	Total
No ties	61.9	62.2	44.9	26.9	58.5	49.6	49.5	58.4	50.8
Weak ties	7.6	14.1	33.0	20.9	13.3	11.9	13.1	16.0	16.4
Moderate ties	11.2	6.9	15.3	14.9	7.1	11.7	12.1	9.0	11.3
Strong ties	5.7	5.3	5.6	10.5	6.6	9.6	8.6	5.1	7.2
Very strong ties	11.5	11.5	1.1	26.8	14.5	17.2	16.7	11.5	14.2
N	666	116	448	1002	582	629	503	769	5661

Note: Chi-square 1086.47; df 28; p<.001.

methodological appendix at the end of this volume.) As a consequence, one might expect these participants to be mobilized more in advance and to take part in a more organized way than those from the other countries who were surveyed at the demonstration venue. This is what our data show.[2] Yet, tests specially aimed at discovering method biases for the Italian survey showed no systematic differences between postal and face-to-face surveys in Italy (see appendix A).

To compare the degree of openness of the mobilization in the various countries, we asked our respondents how they came to know about the demonstration. We recoded their answers into four categories ranging from more open to more closed: via television, radio, and newspapers; family, friends, school, and work; Web sites, ads/flyers, mailing lists, and posters; and organizations. Table 9.2 presents our findings regarding these channels.

Close to one tenth of the participants learned about the demonstration via some organization, while the remaining nine tenths were equally distributed over the three other types of channels. The utilized mix of channels varied per country. In the United States, interpersonal networks and ads, flyers, et cetera had equal importance and were more important than the other channels. The same holds for Belgium, though less prominently. In the United Kingdom, the vast majority of the participants were reached by ads et cetera, and in Spain the mass media served that purpose. In Italy and Germany, either mass media or interpersonal networks informed equal proportions of the participants. Italy also had highest proportion of the participants informed via organizational networks. In the Netherlands, mass media and ads and so forth were approximately equally prominent. Switzerland was the only country where interpersonal networks were the most important. In terms of openness versus closedness of mobilization channels, our data suggest that Spain experienced the most open campaign, followed by Germany and the Netherlands, whereas the campaigns in the United States, the United Kingdom, and Belgium seem to have been the most closed.

Having presented our focal variables grasping the two dimensions of mobilization, we explore the relationship between the two. We argue that both dimensions, although probably statistically associated, are theoretically independent of one another. We expected to find every possible pattern among the five levels of ties and the four levels of openness; this turned out to be the case. The moderate correlation (Pearson's r = .27) suggests that, although correlated, the two factors are not identical.

However, the dominant pattern is of people without ties to movement organizations who have learned about the demonstration via open communication channels (be they mass media or interpersonal networks). Substantial

Table 9.2. Most important information channels to mobilize demonstrators (percent)

	US	UK	SP	IT	NL	SW	BE	GE	Total
Radio/television/newspapers	18.3	10.4	55.8	33.9	34.6	26.4	26.2	33.8	30.0
Family/friends/school/work	36.8	16.1	24.3	30.6	26.9	37.8	30.2	32.7	29.4
Ads/flyers/posters/et cetera	37.0	69.1	15.0	19.2	30.3	27.0	30.6	24.8	31.6
Organizations	7.9	4.5	4.9	16.3	8.0	8.8	12.9	8.7	9.0
N	666	1116	448	1002	528	629	503	769	5661

proportions of the participants without any ties to any movement organization learned about the demonstration through such relatively closed channels as ads, flyers, posters, and the Internet. Apparently, these are not closed
to the extent that they exclude those not tied to the organizations that are
the sources of information. This is understandable to a certain extent. Ads,
flyers, and posters may be closed, but chances are that people other than
those connected to the senders will come to see and read them. Participants
who have strong ties to movement organizations are more likely to have
learned about the demonstration through closed channels, the more so if they
have very strong ties; in fact, among those with very strong ties are participants who mostly used closed channels.

Is this general pattern present in all countries? Apparently not, as evidenced by the figures in Table 9.3. This table presents the country breakdowns
for participants who had no ties and were informed about the demonstration
through open channels (mass media or interpersonal channels) and for those
who had strong or very strong ties and were informed through closed channels
(ads, et cetera, and organizational channels). The breakdowns reveal interesting differences in mobilization patterns. Spain, the Netherlands, and Germany display a relatively open pattern of mobilization with an emphasis on
mass media channels, while in the United States, the United Kingdom, and
Switzerland, mobilization is relatively open as well, but the emphasis is on
interpersonal communication channels. And Italy and Belgium have the highest proportions of participants mobilized via closed patterns of mobilization.

The previous discussion confirms that mobilization patterns are context-
dependent. Obviously, the mobilization campaign in one country has been
more open than that in another. It is equally interesting to know whether
the mobilization campaign for the specific February 15 demonstrations have
been more open or closed than those of other demonstrations. Comparative
evidence for all eight countries is lacking, but we had at our disposal comparable data involving six other demonstrations staged in Belgium (Brussels)
between 1999 and 2002 (Van Aelst and Walgrave 2001; Norris, Walgrave,
and Van Aelst 2005). This Belgian evidence was gathered in an identical
manner but covers strongly diverging issues and movements: from typical
new social movement events like antiracist and global justice demonstrations,
to classic bread-and-butter actions staged by trade unions (nonprofit, social
sector, and education), to a new right demonstration against tolerant Belgian
drug abuse laws. Analysis shows that the differences among the seven Belgian
demonstrations are certainly much larger than those found on February 15
among countries. Protests staged by new social movements in Belgium are,
on average, characterized by a substantially more open mobilization process

Table 9.3. Mobilization patterns: ties and channels (percent)

	US	UK	SP	IT	NL	SW	BE	GE	TOTAL
No ties and mass media	15.0	15.7	27.2	10.1	25.3	14.1	16.5	24.6	18.8
No ties and interpersonal channels	23.5	22.6	11.8	11.1	17.2	20.9	14.9	18.5	17.2
(Very) strong ties and organizations, ads, flyers, et cetera	12.6	10.3	1.5	18.4	12.8	13.5	15.4	9.5	11.9
N	566	1115	448	1002	528	629	503	769	5661

than those staged by the other social movements. Apparently, issues matter a lot, much more than country differences. Compared to the other demonstrations in Belgium, the Belgian protest on February 15 against the war on Iraq was an evident and very strong case of open mobilization. Of course, this is not conclusive proof that the February 15 demonstrations in general, and not only in Belgium, were characterized by open mobilization. But since the Belgian antiwar demonstration, compared to the seven other February 15 demonstrations, was by no means an extremely open case—in fact, Belgium ranked among the more closed mobilizations—it is at least plausible to assume that the mobilization processes leading up to February 15 were in general relatively more open than for other demonstrations in the other seven countries under study as well.

Consequences of Mobilization Patterns

Do mobilization patterns make a difference? Do they influence the behavior of the participants? For example, do they affect when participants decide to participate, whether they go with others or alone, how far they travel, and so on? Or do mobilization patterns influence who is going to demonstrate in terms of age, gender, education, political attitudes, and opposition to war? In other words, do different patterns of mobilization produce different demonstrations? Oegema and Klandermans believe that mobilization processes make a difference: "Mobilization attempts, incentives, and barriers do not occur randomly throughout a population, but coincide with characteristics of movement organizations, campaign characteristics, specific actions, characteristics of individual communities, and social categories" (1994, 705). Most of the factors associated with different mobilization patterns are held constant in this study: it concerns the movement, campaign, and action form. This gives us the opportunity to focus entirely on the characteristics of the participants possibly associated with mobilization patterns as such. In this section, we will compare the characteristics of people mobilized through the six different patterns. We will do so by means of multivariate analyses of variance with the strength of ties, degree of openness, and country as factors. Such analyses enable us to disentangle the main effects of ties, channels, and countries and the interaction of these factors.

Going to the Demonstration

People may go to demonstrations alone, or with family, friends, or acquaintances. They may decide to participate long before the actual demonstration or at the very last moment. The decision to take part is, of course, also influenced by how far someone lives from the actual venue of the demonstration.

In all these matters it is conceivable that the process of mobilization affects people as it takes place. To investigate this matter, we asked our interviewees with whom they came to the demonstration, when they decided to participate, and how far they traveled (figures not presented in a table).

In all countries the majority of the participants came with family or friends. Colleagues and comembers of movement organizations were companions in much smaller proportions. One tenth of the participants came alone. Although the patterns in the eight countries are very similar, we observe some interesting variations among them. For example, almost twice the number of participants came alone in the Netherlands as in other countries. In Spain more than anywhere else, the demonstration resembles a family fair. In Italy and Germany, though, friends were the most common companions. Members of movement organizations relatively frequently accompanied participants in Italy, Belgium, and the United States.

In Italy, the United States, and the United Kingdom, a higher proportion of the people decided to participate in the protest at an earlier stage than in other countries. Belgian and Dutch participants made up their minds late, most frequently only in the last week or even the very last day before the demonstration. The farthest distance traveled on average was in Italy. In all other countries, we found the typical pattern of a relatively large proportion from within a few kilometers, smaller numbers from intermediary distances, and again larger numbers from longer distances.

Were such matters as participants' accompaniment, when they decided to participate, and the distance they traveled to the demonstration related to the way people were mobilized? To sort that out, we conducted multivariate analyses of variance, with the strength of ties, the openness of mobilization channels, and country as factors (figures not presented in a table).[3]

On the whole, one can conclude that accompaniment to the demonstration is influenced by mobilization patterns. However, the influence is not the same for each type of group. The analyses reveal a main effect of ties for colleagues and comembers only. Stronger ties more often make people come to the demonstration with colleagues and comembers of movement organizations. The strength of ties does not have an influence on whether people come with family or friends or on their own. The mobilization channel used has a significant impact on all five possible social arrangements. Follow-up analyses show that people who are mobilized via closed channels are more likely to come with comembers, while people mobilized through open channels are more likely to come alone or with family or friends. The impact of channels of mobilization on accompaniment to the demonstration is much larger than that of the strength of ties. The significant interaction of ties and mobilization channels implies that the two factors reinforce each other. We found significant interactions especially in the case of coming alone or with comembers: having no ties to movement organizations and being mobilized via mass media makes it much more likely for people to come alone, while having strong ties and being mobilized via organizations makes it much more likely for people to come with comembers of movement organizations. Obviously, these effects do not fully explain the country variation. First, a modest but significant country interactions suggest that some variation exists among the eight countries in how ties and mobilization channels influence companionship at the demonstration. However, the patterns are too unsystematic to interpret. Finally, a substantial proportion of the variation in accompaniment among the countries is due to factors other than mobilization patterns.

Mobilization patterns have a substantial impact on the timing of the decision to participate and the distance traveled. Ties have a main effect, which implies that people with strong ties decided earlier to participate and traveled farther than people with weak ones; the same holds for people with weak ties compared to people with none. We also found a main effect of degree of openness of mobilization channels: people who were mobilized through closed channels decided earlier. Mobilization channels did, however, not influence the distance traveled. The effect of ties and channels reinforced each other. Some variance in the dependent variables is due to the differential impact of mobilization patterns in the various countries. The significant main effects for a country again signify that factors other than mobilization patterns are responsible for the variance among the countries.[4] In sum, diverging mobilization patterns did, indeed, generate diverging patterns of participation. Open channels and weak ties or the absence of ties bring to the demonstrations more people who come on their own or with family and friends; these people decided more recently and traveled less far. Those who came with comembers, who decided longer ago and traveled far, were much more tied into an organizational field that staged the demonstration and were more often mobilized via the organizations.

Differential Recruitment

Did such diverging patterns result in differential recruitment, that is to say, were the people who showed up different depending on the mobilization patterns through which they were recruited? Our answer to this question begins with the distribution of demographics. With regard to gender, age, and education, we found main effects of the strength of ties and the openness of channels for all three variables. Male demonstrators were more often mobilized through ties and open channels than females. As for age, we found a curvilinear relationship: people without ties or with strong ties were older than those with weak ties. Similarly, we found that people mobilized through mass media channels and people who were mobilized through closed channels were older than those mobilized through interpersonal channels. Finally, we found no systematic pattern with regard to education.

Not only demographics such as age or gender were influenced by patterns of mobilization; the various mobilization patterns resulted in differential recruitment in terms of ideology and social and political participation as well. We assessed whether participants differed in terms of involvement in civil society organizations, interest in politics, protest frequency, left-right self-placement, and voting behavior. The results are fairly straightforward, for involvement in civil society organizations, interest in politics, and protest frequency: main effects of ties and channels and an interaction of ties and channels on all variables (results not presented in a table). Participants with stronger ties are more often involved in civil society organizations, are more interested in politics, have more frequently participated in protest, and are more leftist-oriented in terms of both self-placement and past vote. Mobilization channels have less impact. Only mobilization via closed channels had an impact on these social political attitudes and behavior: participants mobilized this way are more actively involved in civil society organizations and protest, more interested in politics, and more leftist-oriented. As for the interaction of ties and channels, we found the same pattern for all five variables: the effect of the openness of mobilization channels was the largest among people without ties or with weak or moderate ones. Among those with strong and very strong ties, the channels through which they were mobilized did not matter.

In a final attempt to allude to differences among participants contingent on mobilization patterns, we discuss the attitudes about the war (Table 9.4). We found main effects of ties on top of the main effects of country. Participants with ties to movement organizations and/or who were mobilized through closed channels were more opposed to the war and to their own government's policy regarding the war than participants who had no such ties or were mobilized through open channels. Overall, the pattern is clear. The organizations that were staging the demonstrations, obviously, were opposed to the war. People who were tied (directly or indirectly) to these organizations and/or were mobilized through closed channels by those organizations were more opposed to the war in Iraq and to their government. This is not to say that others were not opposed to the war, but it emphasizes

Table 9.4. Mobilization features per country and per mobilization type (averages; 4,089<N<4,671)

	US	UK	SP	IT	NL	SW	BE	GE
Timing of participation decision[a]								
No ties / open	2.64	2.76	2.57	2.64	2.19	2.39	2.18	2.35
No ties / closed	2.86	3.15	2.82	2.87	2.74	2.44	2.51	2.79
Ties / open	2.95	3.10	2.67	2.91	2.43	2.54	2.53	2.73
Ties / closed	3.16	3.56	3.11	3.20	3.17	3.03	3.09	2.99
Distance traveled to demonstration[b]								
No ties / open	2.98	3.27	–	7.06	3.23	4.66	3.75	3.15
No ties / closed	2.93	3.44	–	6.83	3.47	4.25	3.44	33.73
Ties / open	3.27	4.09	–	7.15	3.05	4.54	4.01	4.01
Ties / closed	2.85	4.05	–	7.25	4.23	4.55	3.96	4.76
Left-right placement[c]								
No ties / open	2.68	3.05	2.74	2.25	2.97	2.55	3.17	2.92
No ties / closed	2.35	2.87	2.33	2.04	2.41	2.40	3.13	2.68
Ties / open	2.17	2.22	2.39	1.58	2.33	2.06	2.66	2.49
Ties / closed	1.99	2.35	1.85	1.40	1.78	1.75	1.98	2.32
Involvement in civil society[d]								
No ties / open	2.25	1.05	0.72	0.72	1.00	1.01	0.82	0.53
No ties / closed	2.75	1.23	0.45	1.30	0.84	1.01	1.08	0.79
Ties / open	3.47	1.83	1.40	1.24	1.57	1.70	1.86	1.24
Ties / closed	4.06	1.92	1.89	1.75	2.28	2.46	2.10	1.63

Table 9.4. (continued)

	US	UK	SP	IT	NL	SW	BE	GE
Protest frequency[e]								
No ties / open	1.73	1.51	1.97	2.62	1.38	1.79	2.01	1.91
No ties / closed	1.95	1.63	2.37	2.48	1.62	2.02	2.04	2.39
Ties / open	2.55	2.15	2.74	3.18	1.80	2.58	2.68	2.50
Ties / closed	2.52	2.41	3.54	3.76	2.11	2.89	3.13	2.65
Satisfaction with government's efforts to prevent war[f]								
No ties / open	4.66	4.42	4.90	4.73	4.43	2.96	1.75	2.34
No ties / closed	4.77	4.57	4.80	4.75	4.54	2.76	1.96	2.35
Ties / open	4.85	4.73	4.94	4.83	4.40	3.05	2.00	2.47
Ties / closed	4.81	4.69	4.93	4.89	4.74	3.10	2.46	2.60
Opposition to war[g]								
No ties / open	3.37	3.24	3.62	3.72	3.26	3.54	3.57	3.49
No ties / closed	3.52	3.38	3.89	3.88	3.34	3.61	3.53	3.63
Ties / open	3.66	3.55	3.63	3.78	3.25	3.64	3.68	3.58
Ties / clo.sed	3.65	3.55	3.75	3.80	3.42	3.77	3.74	3.60

Notes: [a]1 = late; 5 = early.

[b]0=not far; 8 = far.

[c]1=left; 5 = less left.

[d]Number of organizations.

[e]Number in last five years.

[f]0 = satisf.ed; 5 = dissatisfied.

[g]1 = weak; 5 = strong.

that recruitment networks are reproduced in the composition of the body of participants.

Obviously, mobilization patterns differed in the eight countries included in our study. In some countries, the demonstrators' ties to organizations that staged the demonstration were much stronger than in others; in some countries, people were mobilized significantly more via open channels than in others. Such differences matter: they resulted in differential recruitment. The various modes of mobilization brought different people into the streets. People, depending on how they were mobilized, not only differed in terms of age, gender, and education but also in terms of political identity and social and political participation. Moreover, a person's accompaniment was contingent upon the mode of mobilization employed. As a consequence, the configurations of participants in the various demonstrations were diverse. All this naturally raises the question of why mobilization patterns differ among countries. We will devote the last section of this chapter to this question.

Causes of Mobilization Patterns

Mobilization patterns are neither an a priori given nor completely exogenous, but integrated parts of the societal configurations that enable protest events. The aim of this book is precisely to map those configurations and carefully investigate how they influenced the events of February 15 in the eight nations under study. As mobilization patterns appear to have affected the recruitment of the demonstration, the question arises as to what are the causes of the observed differences in mobilization patterns. In the introduction to this chapter, we stated that mobilization is the process that links demand for protest to supply. Protest organizations stage events that offer people who feel aggrieved the opportunity to protest. Mobilization, we argued, is necessary to bring demand and supply together. It is, so to say, the sales and marketing mechanism of the movement industry. Obviously, mobilization can only succeed if demand and supply are tuned into each other. The people we interviewed *were* brought together; after all, they took part in the demonstration. However, not all these people were mobilized in the same manner. Such differences in mobilization patterns among countries, we believe, are partly determined by the configuration of demand and supply factors in a country and by the extent to which they are in sync.

In terms of demand factors, the public opinion in a country vis-à-vis the cause is especially important. Mobilization, obviously, is a completely different matter when the majority of the people support the cause than it is when support is only marginal and goes against the mainstream. In the case of a supportive public opinion, dissemination about the actual location of a demonstration suffices to get people to take to the streets. In such a situation, demand for protest is high and people want to vent their anger somehow. Thus, any offer on the protest market will fall on fertile soil. People do not need to be motivated, nor do they need help to tackle any barriers. Under such circumstances, open patterns of mobilization can be extremely successful—as the White Marches in Belgium demonstrate. Indeed, strong ties to movement organizations and en masse mobilization of members of organizations are not needed in recruiting participants. Therefore, we expect that in countries where public opinion is prevailingly antiwar, the mobilization patterns will be more open, that is to say, more frequently employing open channels and less dependent on ties to movement organizations.

The mass media coverage of an issue is related to the public opinion within a country; this was established in chapter 3. We expect that mobilization becomes increasingly open the more the mass media sympathize with the cause of a protest campaign. This is due to the mobilizing role of the media as such. Since media are most effective in disseminating or spreading the protest message, they contribute to open mobilization processes. Moreover, media coverage and its tone are associated with public opinion: media might play a part in creating a sentiment among the population and/or reinforce public opinion. Either way, sympathetic coverage of a protest issue, we suspect, is linked to open mobilization. The same holds for the run-up to the Iraq War: the more the media show sympathy for antiwar protests, the more open the mobilization will be.

Supply factors refer to the set of organizations staging and supporting protest events and to their numbers, strength, activity level, history, and action repertoire. In general, we expect closed mobilization to be more important in countries where the social movement sector is dense. We believe that this density accounts for the significance of ties and closed channels in the mobilization process. Only a limited number of organizations are able to generate massive street mobilization by relying on their own networks. Traditionally, three types of actors belong to this category: labor unions, political parties, and new social movements (including the global justice movement). The antiwar coalitions in the various countries differed in the scope, composition, and strength of the organizations included and the extent to which these organizations have a track record of organizing mass demonstrations. We will use several measures that tap the density and strength of the social movement sector in a country and employ those in analyses that link density and strength of the movement sector to the openness of the mobilization process. More specifically, we expect that ties to movement organizations become more important and mobilization channels more closed the more the density and strength of the movement sector increase.

Table 9.5 contains simple Pearson's correlations between the two dependent variables (openness or closedness and strength of ties) and six independent variables at the country level. The two dependent variables are the average strength of ties and the average openness of mobilization channels in each country. The independent variables are a demand-side factor, namely the degree of opposition to the war in public opinion, and five supply-side factors, namely the activity level of new social movements, union membership, and the level of party membership in a country as indicators of the density of the movement sector; the demonstration culture and strike activity levels in a country serve as indicators of the level of contentiousness of the movement sector in a country.[5] Because the number of cases is very small (N = 8), coefficients have to be very high to be significant. Therefore, we use a lower threshold than usual.

We found support for our assumption that mobilization patterns are affected by supply and demand factors—quite a few coefficients are (modestly) significant—but the evidence is complex. First, not all correlations pass the set significance threshold. Moreover, there appears to be a significant variation in the correlation patterns. Sometimes the strength of ties is predominantly affected, sometimes the mobilization channels used, and sometimes both. We found, indeed, that mobilization patterns tend to be more open in countries where the opposition to war was stronger: participants there were more often mobilized via open channels. Furthermore, as expected, the denser the movement sector was in a country, the more closed were patterns of mobilization. In the case of new social movement activity, this was reflected in the mobilization channels used, whereas in the case of union and party membership it was reflected more in the significance of strong ties for the mobilization. Finally, if the movement sector in a country was more contentious, mobilization for the Iraq demonstration tended to increasingly work via open mobilization channels.

In summary, mobilization patterns appear to vary among countries. In some countries, the antiwar protest was characterized by an open pattern, in others it was more closed. As we expected, the process of mobilization is formed by the configuration of supply and demand factors in a country; at least this is what our findings suggest. The pattern of correlations is complex, however. Demand factors appear to influence which channels are used but not the significance of ties; some supply factors affect both indicators of the openness of mobilization, others only what channels are used or on the importance of ties. The involvement of citizens in new social movements

Table 9.5. The influence of supply and demand factors on mobilization patterns (Pearson's correlations)

	Demand	Supply: Density of movement sector			Supply: Contentiousness of movement sector	
	Opposition to war in public opinion	New social movement activity	Union membership	Party membership population	Demonstration culture	Strike activity
Strength of ties	.24	-.21	.48	.50*	.05	.36
Closedness of mobilization patterns	-.53*	.57*	.33	-.19	-.72**	-.43

* p<.20; ** p<.05.

Note: The degree of opposition to war in public opinion is based on the EOS Gallup poll on the war carried out in Europe just before February 15. General activity levels of new social movements in countries is derived from the European Social Survey (no cata on the United States or on Switzerland) asking for participation in an activity of a humanitarian or an environmental/peace organization during the last twelve months. Figures for general union membership are derived from the World Labour Report 1997–1998 of the International Labour Organization (http://www.ilo.org). General demonstration culture in a country is based on the World Values Survey answers on questions about participation in a lawful demonstration. Strike activity levels are based on figures from the ILO, taking the yearly average of the absolute number of demonstrations recorded in a country between 1998 and 2003 divided by the population size. Statistics about general partisan membership in a country are based on Mair and van Biezen (2001).

seems to increase the usage of open channels but the significance of ties does not, while involvement in traditional organizations such as labor unions and political parties seems to generate the opposite pattern. The level of contentiousness of the movement sector again seems to reinforce the use of open mobilization channels. Obviously, in order to understand the dynamics of supply, demand, and mobilization, more systematic research is called for, but this much is clear thus far: they interact in a complicated manner to generate protest.

Conclusion

In this chapter, we concentrated on patterns of mobilization and distinguished among more open and closed patterns of mobilization. Openness and closedness were defined in terms both of the communication channels employed and of the prominence of strong ties in the mobilization campaign. Closed patterns of mobilization depend more on strong ties and closed channels of communication; open patterns do not depend on strong ties or ties at all and employ open channels of communication, such as mass media or interpersonal networks.

We demonstrated that the openness or closedness of a mobilization campaign affects aspects of the mobilization process, such as the companionship of participants at the demonstration, the moment they decided to take part, and the distance they traveled. People who were mobilized in a closed rather than an open manner are accompanied by colleagues or comembers of organizations rather than with family or friends and decide earlier to participate and travel farther distances. Moreover, open and closed patterns mobilize different sorts of participants. This holds for such demographics as gender and age, political attitudes and behavior, and for attitude toward the war. We observed several striking differences between channels and ties in their impact on these participant characteristics and discovered some crucial interactions between the two aspects of openness. We found that, on the whole, participants who were tied to organizations that staged the demonstration were more involved in politics and leaned more to the left. Of the mobilization channels, only movement organizations had the same effect. The other channels did not tap into politically specific populations. It is interesting to see that the effects of channels only exist among participants without ties or with weak to moderate ties. Among people with strong ties to movement organizations, mobilization channels no longer made a difference. This, of course, makes sense, as the effect of channels only holds for organizational channels. Chances are, of course, that people who have strong ties to movement organizations are mobilized through those organizations. For obvious reasons, people who were tied to movement organizations that were staging a demonstration or who were mobilized directly through those organizations were more opposed to the war and dissatisfied with their government's policies.

We also demonstrated that countries differ in terms of mobilization patterns employed and that these differences are related to a variation in the configuration of demand and supply factors in a given country. Strong demand seems to reinforce open mobilization patterns, as does a contentious social movement sector, whereas a dense social movement sector seems to reinforce closed mobilization patterns. The evidence from our small sample of countries is far from conclusive, but it does suggest that different configurations of demand and supply generate different mobilization patterns. This is an important finding and certainly worth pursuing in further research, as it alludes to the dynamic relationship among three key factors in the emergence of protest events.

Notes

1. Weak ties imply that someone only knows people who are members of a movement organization. Moderate, strong, and very strong ties imply an increasingly dense combination of knowing someone, being a member oneself, and maintaining contact with movement organizations.

2. The Italian respondents were mobilized in a much more organizationally embedded manner: they traveled much farther than their colleagues in other countries, they most frequently mentioned organizations as their main source of information for the demonstration, more of them attended the demonstration in the company of other organization members or colleagues, and they made the decision to participate fairly early.

3. We ran the same analyses with and without Italy, and we ran separate analyses on the Italian sample to assess whether the diverging sampling strategy in Italy has biased the conclusion. As this was not the case, we included Italy in the analyses.

4. The large main effect of "country" is due to the Italian sample. If we omit Italy, the F-value reduces to 28.24. In this analysis, the remaining F-values barely change.

Works Cited

Diani, Mario. 2002. "Network Analysis." In *Methods of Social Movement Research*, ed. Bert Klandermans and Suzanne Staggenborg, 173–200. Minneapolis: University of Minnesota Press.

Diani, Mario, and Doug McAdam, eds. 2003. *Social Movements and Networks: Relational Approaches to Collective Action*. Oxford: Oxford University Press.

Gould, Roger V. 1991. "Multiple Networks and Mobilization in the Paris Commune, 1871." *American Sociological Review* 56: 716–29.

———. 1993. "Collective Action and Network Structure." *American Sociological Review* 58: 182–96.

Granovetter, Marc. 1973. "The Strength of Weak Ties." *American Journal of Sociology* 78: 1360–80.

Kitts, James A. 2000. "Mobilizing in Black Boxes: Social Networks and Participation in Social Movement Organizations." *Mobilization* 5: 241–57.

Klandermans, Bert. 1984. "Mobilization and Participation: Social Psychological Expansions of Resource Mobilization Theory." *American Sociological Review* 49: 583–600.

———. 1997. *The Social Psychology of Protest.* Oxford: Blackwell.

———. 2004. "The Demand and Supply of Participation: Social Psychological Correlates of Participation in a Social Movement." In *Blackwell Companion to Social Movements,* ed. David A. Snow, Sarah A. Soule, and Hanspeter Kriesi, 360–79. Oxford: Blackwell.

Klandermans, Bert, and Dirk Oegema. 1987. "Potentials, Networks, Motivations, and Barriers: Steps toward Participation in Social Movements." *American Sociological Review* 52: 519–31.

Mair, Peter, and Ingrid van Biezen. 2001. "Party Membership in Twenty European Democracies, 1998–2000." *Party Politics* 7: 5–21.

Marwell, Gerald, and Pamela Oliver. 1993. *The Critical Mass in Collective Action: A Micro-Social Theory.* Cambridge: Cambridge University Press.

McAdam, Doug. 1986. "Recruitment to High-Risk Activism: The Case of Freedom Summer." *American Journal of Sociology* 92: 64–90.

———. 1988. *Freedom Summer.* New York: Oxford University Press.

McAdam, Doug, John McCarthy, and Mayer N. Zald, eds. 1996. *Comparative Perspectives on Social Movements: Political Opportunities, Mobilizing Structures, and Cultural Framing.* Cambridge: Cambridge University Press.

McCarthy, John D., and Mayer N. Zald. 1976. "Resource Mobilization and Social Movements: A Partial Theory." *American Journal of Sociology* 82: 1212–41.

Morales, Laura. 2008. *Joining Political Organisations: Institutions, Mobilisation, and Participation in Western Democracies.* Colchester, England: European Consortium for Political Research Press.

Norris, Pippa, Stefaan Walgrave, and Peter Van Aelst. 2005. "Who Demonstrates? Anti-State Rebels or Conventional Participants? Or Everyone?" *Comparative Politics* 2: 251–75.

Putnam, Robert. 2000. *Bowling Alone: The Collapse and Revival of American Community.* New York: Simon & Schuster.

Oegema, Dirk, and Bert Klandermans. 1994. "Non-Conversion and Erosion: The Unwanted Effects of Action Mobilization." *American Sociological Review* 59: 703–22.

Snow, David A., Louis A. Zurcher, and Sheldon Ekland-Olson. 1980. "Social Networks and Social Movements: A Microstructural Approach to Differential Recruitment." *American Sociological Review* 45: 787–801.

Tindall, David B. 2004. "Social Movement Participation over Time: An Ego-Network Approach to Micro-Mobilization." *Sociological Focus* 37: 163–84.

Van Aelst, Peter, and Stefaan Walgrave. 2001. "Who Is That (Wo)man in the Street? From the Normalisation of Protest to the Normalisation of the Protester." *European Journal of Political Research* 39: 461–86.

Walgrave, Stefaan, and Jan Manssens. 2000. "The Making of the White March: The Mass Media as a Mobilization Alternative to Movement Organizations." *Mobilization* 5: 217–40.

10

Promoting the Protest:
The Organizational Embeddedness of the Demonstrators

Mario Diani

Although they have been frequently associated with peace movements (and understandably so), the February 15 demonstrations were, first of all, specific protest events, as large and impressive as they were. As we know, the relationship between protest events and social movements is a complex one. Regardless of whether we define them as "sustained interactions between power holders and authorities," à la Tilly (see, e.g., 1995, 369; 1994), or as "informal networks linking individuals and/or organizations, engaged in a conflict on the basis of a shared collective identity" (Diani 1992, 13; Diani and Bison 2004), social movements are usually associated with collective action, displaying substantial continuity over time. Specific events, no matter how big, do not necessarily make a movement. Rather than the peak of long-term mobilization efforts conducted by peace campaigners, the February 15 demonstrations might have been instead the outcome of one-off efforts conducted by ad hoc coalitions, set up precisely for those events.

Therefore, looking at the composition of the coalitions that mobilized on February 15 may provide valuable insights about the nature of those marches. In general, those coalitions were highly heterogeneous, as their members ranged from established interest groups and political parties to environmental, human rights, development, women's, and ethnic minority groups; global justice organizations; churches; and so forth. But what was the relative presence of peace activists and peace organizations in the different marches? Did these mainly attract people with long-lasting commitment to peace activism? Or, regardless of their numbers, did those people and their organizations play a central role in promoting the demonstrations? If that was the case, then the February 15 events could be most plausibly seen as peaks in longer waves of peace-movement mobilization, following in the wake of the campaigns originated by the attack on Afghanistan in fall 2001. If, however, the demonstrators came overwhelmingly from other sectors of social and political activism, then an interpretation of the demonstrations as a major expression of broader political conflicts within the specific countries might be in order. Similar conclusions might be reached if one discovered that organizations without peace profiles were most prominent among those promoting the marches. For example, if one found this to be the case in Italy, it would not be difficult to link the February 15 demonstration in Rome to the larger protest wave against Silvio Berlusconi's right-wing government (della Porta and Diani 2005).

To address these questions, I will draw on our dataset from two different if integrated perspectives. First, I will look at the individual demonstrators' backgrounds in collective action and in associations. By doing so, it will be possible to present hypotheses about the sectors of civil society that contributed to the demonstrations, and their interdependence. Then, I will focus more specifically on demonstrators' involvement in the organizations promoting the demonstrations. This will enable me to assess what types of organizations played the most central roles in which country, as well as the extent to which organizations central to the promotion of the marches were actually connected to peace activism, and thus were expressions of a longer term peace activist agenda, rather than actors linking the peace issues to other types of collective agendas.

I shall also relate our findings to the characteristics of the political context in which the different mobilizations occurred. Since the 1980s, theories explaining the success and traits of social movements as a result of favorable "political opportunities" (della Porta 1995; Tarrow 1998[1994]; Kriesi 2004) have addressed at least three dimensions of the political context: the most permanent, structural features of a given polity. Among these are the institutional arrangements available to facilitate citizens' access to the political system, the established cleavages, or the cultural traits of a society that may facilitate or hinder the spread of certain interpretations of reality and/or of certain identities (Kitschelt 1986; Rucht 1990; Diani 1996; Koopmans and Statham 1999; see also chapter 2 in this volume). These properties are the ones most closely associated with the concept of "political opportunity structure" and are often differentiated from more volatile political opportunities (see, e.g., Gamson and Meyer 1996), such as those offered by changes in the configuration of political actors potentially supporting or opposing a certain movement (their alliance and conflict structure: Curtis and Zurcher 1973;

Klandermans 1990), as well as in social movements' "interaction context." This expression refers to the opportunities created by the interplay of elites' and policy-makers' strategies and social movements' strategies (Kriesi 2004, 70). The explananda for these theories have been similarly varied, ranging from the reasons accounting for specific episodes of collective action to large-scale changes in the levels of participation in contentious politics or in the spread of certain action repertoires (e.g., Tilly 1995). Chapter 3 in this volume presents an empirical assessment of the specific interaction context concerning the February 15 demonstrations in the eight countries under study.

In this chapter, I stay on the parsimonious side in my choice of both explanandum and of explanatory model. More specifically, I look at the composition of the coalitions challenging the attack on Iraq and at how it might be affected by a distinctive element of the "interaction context," namely, national governments' policies toward the war (see chapter 3 for details on these positions). As argued in chapter 2, it would make little sense to try to explain inherently variable traits such as the composition of coalitions converging on a specific event, in the light of the most permanent features of the polity. For example, while the United States could in general be regarded as a weak state offering many points of access to citizens' organizations (Kitschelt 1986; Kriesi 2004), such broadly structural factors are unlikely to have created a favorable opportunity structure for the 2003 peace protest. In contrast, one might plausibly suggest that policy options and political discourse combined to create most unfavorable opportunities in the countries that actively promoted the war and whose forces took the heaviest toll (the United States and the United Kingdom). We specified this in chapter 3 when we showed that politics, media, and public opinion in the United States and the United Kingdom were, indeed, most supportive of the war compared to the other countries. In war-initiating countries, only the organizations most committed to the peace cause might be expected to play a significant explicit role. The others might be discouraged from actively engaging in the demonstrations for fear of being somehow labeled as "antipatriotic." In contrast, in countries whose governments opposed the war, such as Belgium, Germany, or Switzerland, the demonstrations might have attracted a broader range of organizations. These might be expected to be broadly representative of the full spectrum of groups and associations, active in those center-left sectors of civil society most likely to criticize the military intervention. Finally, in countries where governments supported the war but with a limited military commitment, such as Italy, Spain, or the Netherlands, there might be the highest chances for conflicts opposing government and opposition about the war issue. Accordingly, a more substantive role within the coalitions for established left-wing political actors such as political parties and unions might be in order.

Demonstrators from Associations and Protest Communities

February 15 was the result of the mobilization of highly diversified sectors of civil society in the different countries. Therefore, to understand the position of the demonstrations in their national politics, it is necessary to explore their members' overall involvement in other types of collective action. Preliminary attempts to map civil society structures from this perspective have largely focused on multiple organizational memberships (Knoke and Wood 1981; Diani 1995; Carroll and Ratner 1996). However, one must recognize that participation in collective action participation takes at least two different forms: through associations and in the context of loosely structured protest communities (Staggenborg 1986; Taylor and Whittier 1992; Melucci 1996; Doherty, Plows, and Wall 2003; Diani 2005). The latter are usually regarded as less stable and more occasional forms of interaction, often associated with specific protest events or campaigns, unable to show the same capacity to last as formal organizations. When continuity in relation to informal networks is spoken of, it is often in reference to counter- and subcultural networks, seen as preconditions rather than as instances of collective action in their own right. However, even sustained participation in protest communities may be expected to create both the shared frames and the social connections that normally result from participation in associational life.

Accordingly, I look at participation in associations and at sustained participation in protest activities as two different practices that, for all their differences, nonetheless generate ties and solidarity among the people involved. For this reason, both may be expected to secure the continuity required for collective action to develop over time. For the same reasons, they may also be expected to have had a role in shaping the February 15 demonstrations. I will refer to these two sets of experiences as the associational field and the protest community. In this chapter, I consider part of the associational field those demonstrators that in February 2003 were active in at least one of fifteen different types of organizations. Apart from peace organizations, these included organizations active in transnational and global issues (antiracist or immigrant's rights organizations; global social justice organizations; third-world organizations; human rights organizations); political parties; labor unions and professional organizations; sociocultural organizations (art, music, educational, charitable, and church or religious organizations); new social movement organizations (associations for women's rights; environmental organizations); sport, leisure, and youth associations. As for the protest community,

I looked at people who in the previous five years had taken part in more than ten demonstrations regarding issues of peace, antiracism, human rights, the third world, social inequality and labor, the environment, global justice, and women's rights.

Combining high intensity of participation in demonstrations with active participation in associations at the time of the march, we get a more complete picture of the collective action settings in which the February 15 marches were embedded (Table 10.1). Overall, levels of active participation were very high. Only one quarter of the demonstrators were neither actively involved in associations nor in protest communities. At the other extreme, slightly more than one in ten demonstrators was involved in both. Over half were active in associations, while a mere 3 percent were participating in protest communities only. This profile changed significantly across countries:

1. In four countries (the United States, the United Kingdom, the Netherlands, and Switzerland), demonstrators came disproportionately from associations, while they had below-average levels of participation in protest communities.
2. Two countries (Spain and Germany) had the largest shares of demonstrators not involved in either type of collective action (52 percent and 49 percent).
3. The remaining two countries (Belgium and Italy) combined above-average levels of participation in associations (if slightly, as in Italy) with above-average involvement in protest communities.
4. All in all, Italy and the United States showed the most different profiles, with Italian demonstrators highly involved in protest communities (36 percent versus an average 16 percent) and with only average participation in associations, and Americans displaying exceptionally high levels of associational participation (85 percent versus 71 percent) and below-average involvement in protest (10 percent).

That the associational field and the protest community were actually distinct is demonstrated by the links created by overlapping memberships, that is, by those demonstrators who were active in more than one type of association or protest field. Grouping together types of associational and protest activities on the basis of the number of demonstrators simultaneously engaged in them always identified two main sets, one corresponding to associations and the other to protest communities. This suggests the convergence on the demonstrations of two fairly distinct sectors of civil society. This was by no means an inevitable outcome. In principle, one could have also expected stronger recurrent links between associations and protest communities focusing on

Table 10.1. People active in associations and/or with intense (more than ten times) recent protest involvement (percent)

	US	UK	SP	IT	NL	SW	BE	GE	Total
None	14	24	42	21	25	25	23	39	26
Associations only	76	70	44	42	70	62	59	51	58
Protest communities only	1	2	5	8	1	2	2	2	3
Associations and protest communities	9	4	9	28	4	11	16	8	12
N	696	542	445	973	531	625	498	762	5,072

similar issues (for example, between ecology organizations and ecology protest communities, or between women's organizations and women's protest
communities). Instead, data reduction procedures robustly showed that links
were stronger among associations on one side and protest communities on
the other, regardless of the issues addressed, than between associations and
protest communities interested in similar issues.

Promoting the Protests

Within that broad range of protest and associational activities, it is of particular interest to look at the demonstrators' involvement in the organizations that promoted the march. While innumerable organizations signed up
to march, their relative weights and contributions varied drastically. A closer
look at the relationship between protestors and the organizations promoting the marches may provide a better understanding of who played what
role in what country. Almost one-fifth of respondents claimed membership
in such organizations, and one-fourth reported acquaintances in some of
them; slightly over half reported no ties whatsoever (Table 10.2). One could
question the validity of these figures, as respondents might not have been
that informed about the involvement of their organizations in the promotion of the marches. This might be the case; however, the differences between
some membership figures, depending on whether we look at promoting organizations (Table 10.4) and organizations at large (Table 10.5), suggest otherwise. For example, while 27 percent of the Dutch demonstrators belonged
to unions or professional associations, only 1 percent of those claiming to
belong to one promoting organization did (consistent with the fact the unions
in the Netherlands were barely involved as march organizers). Other possible examples include membership in parties and unions in the United States
(Tables 10.4 and 10.5).

The discrepancy between general organizational membership and involvement in specific promoting organizations suggests that the demonstrations attracted a population that was not restricted to the membership and
constituency of their backing organizations. At the same time, however, such
a profile was not evenly spread across the different countries. The British
demonstrations attracted the highest number of people without any tie to
the organizers and also by far the fewest members of promoting organizations. At the other extreme, Italy was the only country with a very high proportion of demonstrators who were members and also the only one to have
a balance between members and people with no ties. The United States also
had a high number of people with no ties, while Spain was the closest to the

Table 10.2. February 15 demonstrators' relations to the promoting organizations (percent)

	War-promoting countries			War-supporting countries					War-opposing countries				Total
	US	UK	ALL	SP	IT	(IT)[a]	NL	ALL	SW	BE	GE	ALL	
No ties	63	82	73	46	31	(29)	59	45	51	50	60	54	55
Know member	24	12	18	37	38	(46)	19	31	28	26	24	26	26
Member	13	5	9	17	31	(25)	22	23	21	24	16	20	18
N	705	1,129	1,834	452	942	(74)	542	2,010	637	510	781	1,928	5,772

Note: [a]Figures in parentheses refer to the 74 marchers (out of 230) who responded to the questionnaires distributed in Rome rather than on trains. Exact and Monte Carlo tests showed no significant differences between the two groups.

Italian figure, as more than half of its demonstrators had some connection to the organizers. The other countries were closer to the average.

A clearer pattern emerges in looking at the distribution of these figures depending on the national governments' attitudes toward the war (Table 10.2). The percentage of people who participated without the incentives provided by close ties to some of the promoting organizations was highest among demonstrators from the nations that promoted the war (United States and United Kingdom), lowest among those whose governments supported the war (Italy, the Netherlands, and, at the time, Spain), and average in countries that opposed it (Belgium, Germany, and Switzerland). As I argue in the next section, these differences are likely to stem from the narrower range of promoting organizations in the United States and the United Kingdom than in other countries and from the greater range of organizations promoting the marches in countries where governments supported the war, such as Italy or Spain.

If this approach is extended to participation in associations and in the protest community at large, one might ask the extent to which the organizations behind February 15 managed to act as bridges between the different sectors of civil society that mobilized on that day. In all countries, the demonstrators connected with promoting organizations also showed much stronger connections to both the world of associations and protest communities (Table 10.3): the percentage of demonstrators active in both sectors was three times higher among members of promoting organizations than among people who knew somebody there, and nine times higher than that of people with no ties to the demonstrations promoters whatsoever. Beyond promoting and coordinating the marches by establishing coalitions of organizations, the organizations behind the demonstrations also linked the different sectors of civil society concerned with the Iraq War through the multiple involvements of their individual members.

Table 10.3. Current participation in associations and protest communities by contact with promoting organizations (percent)

	None	Know member	Member[a]	Total
None	37	24	0	26
Associations only	57	58	63	58
Protest communities only	3	6	0	3
Associations and protest communities	4	12	37	12
N	2662	1437	973	5072

Note: [a]This column includes both active and passive membership, whereas rows only refer to active associational memberships.

What Organizations Are Behind the Demonstrations?

What organizations were more frequently indicated as promoters of the marches by the demonstrators? We recoded the names of the organizations to which demonstrators belonged under seven headings, consistent with the types introduced earlier: political parties; unions and professional associations; peace organizations; organizations active on global justice issues; new social movement organizations; sociocultural organizations; sport, leisure, and youth associations. Parties and unions—the latter more than the former—were by far the most represented among demonstrators. The countries where the role of "old politics" actors in promoting the marches were most conspicuous included the Netherlands, Spain, Germany, and Italy. In particular, political parties were most prominent in the Netherlands (Groen Links and SP), even though Rifondazione Comunista in Italy and the socialist PSOE in Spain stood out in a context where parties were otherwise fairly minor players. As for unions, they are very important in both Mediterranean countries and in Germany (CGIL in Italy, the Comisiones Obreras and the UGT in Spain, and GEW and Ver.di in Germany).

In contrast, the role of interest representation organizations seemed negligible in both countries directly promoting the war, the United States and United Kingdom. There, peace organizations and peace coalitions, such as CND and the Stop the War Coalition in the United Kingdom, and SNOW in the United States, were the main players in promoting the marches. This seems related not to the shortage of party or union members among demonstrators (Table 10.5) but to those organizations' reluctance to engage directly with promoting the marches. In the United Kingdom, 28 percent of the demonstrators were actually current or former members of political parties, in line with the 30 percent recorded for the total sample, while in the United States the share was as high as 54 percent. Likewise, current and former union members amounted to 44 percent in the United States and 43 percent in the United Kingdom, versus a general figure of 37 percent.

Moving to other organizations, transnational organizations were strongly represented in Belgium and Germany, whereas they were hardly noticeable in other countries. The role of groups mobilizing on migration, human rights, and global inequality issues was particularly prominent (11.11.11 and Oxfam in Belgium, ATTAC in both countries). The presence of environmental and religious organizations appeared minimal across the board, with Belgian and (curiously, given the weakness of Spanish environmentalism) Spanish demonstrators slightly overrepresented among the former (particularly Greenpeace in both countries), Germans and Dutch among the latter.[1] Other organizations with recurring mentions included Amnesty International and—in Italy—ARCI, the umbrella cultural association of the Italian Left.[2]

If we look at countries' different approaches to war (Table 10.4), the picture is very clear: in countries promoting it, where government's opportunity to play the patriotic card was easiest to seize, specific peace organizations had to take up most of the organizing roles in the marches and to mobilize the largest share of demonstrators (this is also reflected in the highest share of demonstrators in those countries with previous experiences in peace organizations: 28 percent, versus 12 percent in the other two types of countries). The strength of patriotic feelings and of the rhetoric about "supporting the troops" may have discouraged many organizations from actively promoting the demonstrations, and participation in these may have been guided principally by strong personal motivations. For example, while many Labour Party members in the United Kingdom actually attended the demonstrations, their party was officially hostile to them, even though some local branches actually were involved in the organization of the marches.[3]

In countries that supported the war but were unable to play the patriotic card because of their lower commitment, like Italy or Spain, interest organizations played the largest organizing role. This further confirms the war issue in those countries being embedded in broader conflicts between the ruling coalition and its political opposition, as was detailed in chapter 6. This might have resulted in more demonstrators with links to the political organizations promoting the march (in particular, the organizations of the Left). This accounts particularly well for the Italian figure, showing a very high involvement with promoting organizations (even when controlled for different styles of data collection, as the figures in parentheses in Table 10.2 demonstrate). In Italy, the intensity of political conflict and mass protest had been particularly high in the two years preceding the march, that is, since 2001, when Berlusconi had taken over as prime minister.

Finally, in countries where government and opposition were both against the war and, thus, no domestic conflict about the war was present, actors that were difficult to locate with respect to the traditional left-right cleavage played a major organizing role. These included organizations close to the new social movements as well as operating on transnational issues or on moral and social issues, which, once again, could not be easily associated with left-right divisions (Table 10.4). In those countries, the chances of the demonstrations taking a more distinctively super- or transnational dimension may have been highest.

Of course, all the findings discussed above might simply be due to the fact that in different countries demonstrators were in general more involved

Table 10.4. Demonstrators' membership in organizations promoting the marches (percent)

	War-promoting countries			War-supporting countries				War-opposing countries				Total
	US	UK	All	SP	IT	NL	All	SW	BE	GE	All	
Political parties	2	8	5	23	20	74	33	26	17	15	20	24
Unions and professional organizations	2	5	3	44	44	1	34	29	22	42	31	28
Peace organizations	66	69	67	4	4	2	3	17	6	5	10	14
Transnational or global organizations	4	3	4	13	17	2	11	15	42	20	27	17
New social movements	0	3	1	8	0	3	3	4	6	1	4	3
Sociocultural organizations	25	13	21	15	14	18	16	40	18	25	27	21
Sport, leisure, and youth organizations	2	3	2	2	3	1	2	1	2	1	1	2
N	93	39	132	124	224	156	504	152	171	114	437	1073

Note: Because of multiple memberships, responses in this and following tables refer to dichotomous variables and are not mutually exclusive.

with certain types of organizations than with others, regardless of whether those organizations participated in the promotion of the demonstrations. However, a look at the distribution of organizational memberships at large among demonstrators suggests this not to be the case (Table 10.5). With the only exception of sport, leisure, and youth associations, U.S. demonstrators were significantly more involved than the others in all types of organizations; yet only peace organizations were overrepresented among organizers of the U.S. protests. As for the UK demonstrators, they were no more involved in peace organizations than the others, yet only peace groups, again, seemed to be playing the organizers' role.

Conversely, parties and unions had figures around the average in countries supporting the war, despite their overwhelming role as promoters of the demonstrations. Among the countries whose governments opposed the war, Switzerland and Belgium actually fit the pattern, as global justice, new social movement, and sociocultural organizations were as overrepresented among demonstrators in general as they were among those linked to promoting organizations. Germany, however, does not fit in, as the same organizations were consistently underrepresented among those who took to the streets. All in all, global justice, new social movement, and sociocultural organizations were not as present among the general demonstrators as they were among those demonstrators who were members of promoting organizations.

Explaining Membership in Promoting Organizations

I will now explore more in detail the relationship between membership in certain types of organizations and membership in the specific organizations that promoted the demonstrations. The latter may surely depend on the distribution of different types of organizational memberships in general, although the paragraphs above do not suggest this. It is also important to see the extent to which members of the promoting organizations differed from the others on a number of important dimensions.

As gender, education, and age have proved to have an impact on patterns of political participation at large, it might be worth exploring the possibility that they influenced involvement for the organizers of the February 15 marches. On the one hand, the organizations promoting the marches might be more established than the others (a reflection of their capacity to carry on a remarkable organizational effort), and this might result in their members having the traits usually associated with more established political participation: prevailingly male, with higher levels of education (i.e., in this context, holding degrees), and relatively old (i.e., in their thirties or forties rather than in their twenties). On the other hand, the strong association of

Table 10.5. Demonstrators' memberships in organizations at large (percent)

	War-promoting countries			War-supporting countries					War-opposing countries				Total
	US	UK	Al	SP	IT	NL	All	SW	BE	GE	All	
Political parties	51	13	34	13	19	25	19	19	20	10	16	22
Unions and professional organizations	33	30	32	25	29	27	28	30	31	24	28	29
Peace organizations	35	15	26	7	16	13	13	16	16	7	13	15
Transnational or global organizations	41	29	36	34	27	45	34	47	42	17	33	33
New social movements	49	26	34	13	18	44	24	53	32	18	33	30
Sociocultural organizations	71	59	66	21	35	46	35	53	41	36	43	41
Sport, leisure, and youth organizations	27	29	27	23	30	37	31	33	26	19	26	26
N	705	547	1252	437	1016	542	1999	637	510	781	1928	5175

the peace campaigners with the global justice movement might lead us to expect exactly the opposite profile, with relatively young demonstrators, a greater proportion of females, and a greater role for working-class and deprived people (hence, a smaller presence of degree holders than, say, in the typical new social movements of the 1980s and 1990s). Table 10.6 below illustrates results separately for each country. Sociodemographic traits only played roles in Italy, where members of promoting organizations were older and more frequently male than nonmembers, and in Switzerland, where older demonstrators were also overrepresented.

There are also reasons to expect differences between members of promoting organizations and the rest when looking at the demonstrators' attitudes and ideological orientations. The self-placement on the left-right scale could reflect either a more moderate position of the members of the promoting organizations vis-à-vis the other demonstrators or the capacity of more radical sectors to promote a broader agenda, capable of attracting relatively more moderate sections of the public. Similar remarks could apply to sympathy for the global justice movement or for the level of opposition to war (measured in terms of higher scores on the "opposition to war scale," see chapter 6 in this volume).

As it was, sympathy for the global justice movement only played a modest role in two countries (see Table 10.6), the United States and the Netherlands, while the strength of antiwar feelings did not at all distinguish members of promoting organizations from the other demonstrators. Previous recourse to radical protest was most important in the United States (a further confirmation of the very distinctive nature of the public mobilized in that country); it was also significant, but to a much smaller degree, in Italy and Switzerland. Consistently across continental Europe, members of promoting organizations were more left-leaning than the other demonstrators, despite the relative ideological homogeneity of the demonstrators, with Spain the only exception. Other than Switzerland, these were countries with "conservative welfare regimes" (Esping-Andersen 1990), where traditional political cleavages were more salient and the boundaries between institutional and protest politics seemed less stable. By contrast, the left-right divide seems less relevant in liberal democracies such as the United States and the United Kingdom, characterized by more individualistic styles of participation. Spain and Switzerland represented significant exceptions to this overall pattern.

Looking at the broader organizational memberships provides a consistent picture, yet one more articulated than the one I presented earlier. Being a member of a peace organization drastically increased one's chance of being associated with a promoting organization in the United States and the United

Table 10.6. Predictors of membership of promoting organizations (logistic B coeficients)

	US	UK	SP	IT	NL	SW	BE	GE
Organizational memberships								
Political parties	-.133	.809	1.98***	.968***	3.37***	2.16***	.849***	1.33***
Unions and professional organizations	.443	.228	1.43***	1.72***	-.376	.783***	.913***	2.03***
Peace organizations	2.14***	2.53***	-.197	.440	1.09***	1.13***	.475	1.02**
Global justice organizations	.547	.613	1.14*	.966***	.05	.774**	1.74***	1.70***
New social movements	.768**	-.557	-.261	.189	-.39	-.435	-.101	.140
Sport, leisure, and youth organizations	-.063	-.231	-1.02**	-.170	-.02	.267	-.487	.441
Social organizations	.089	-.478	.608	-.64***	-.47	-.065	.174	.17
Political attitudes and behavior								
Leftist position	.049	.132	.040	.11***	.15*	.145*	.25***	.29**
War opposition	-.229	.172	.657	.135	-.02	.182	.422	.134
Global justice sympathy	.599*	.329	.321	-.119	.74*	.378	.439	.04
Used radical protest	1.141*	.266	.654	.402*	.90	.737**	-.338	-.29
Sociodemographics								
Age	.017	.004	.007	.025***	.00	.021*	.008	.01
Male	-.254	.056	.774	.478***	.39	.166	.163	.324
University degree	.411	-.294	.326	-.166	.49	.362	-.403	.30
Nagelkerke R²	0.29	0.35	0.40	0.38	0.55	0.45	0.40	0.39
N	696	542	445	973	531	625	498	762

***: p<.001; **: p<.01; *: p<.05

Kingdom. It also did so, if to a more limited extent, in the Netherlands, Switzerland, and Germany, but not in Spain, Italy, or Belgium—a further proof that the association between peace demonstrations and peace organizations should not be taken for granted. By contrast, members of traditional parties and unions were more likely than nonmembers to be associated with the promotion of the marches in all countries but the United States. However, those chances were highest where the peace issue was mostly controversial given the governments' position, namely, Spain, Italy, and the Netherlands (although the impact of parties and unions was also strong in Germany, where the issue was not controversial). Global justice organizations' members were more frequently involved in organizing marches where I would expect them to be, according to my previous exploration, that is, in Belgium, Germany, and (if to a smaller measure) Switzerland. However, they were also heavily involved in both Italy and Spain.

Finally, membership in other organizations had no significant role in promoting the demonstrations, and when it did, it was a negative one. Members of sport, leisure, and youth associations in Spain and of sociocultural (i.e., cultural, charitable, and religious) organizations in Italy were indeed less likely than the other demonstrators to be connected to an organization promoting the marches. In the case of the organizations less directly associated with political action, like charities, cultural associations, or sport clubs, membership may have had an impact on individuals' predispositions to attend the demonstrations, but not on those demonstrators' involvement with the promotion of events. Remarkably, membership in the organizations active in environmental and women's issues, that is, those more directly associated with the new social movements, seemed to have hardly any effect (except in the United States, and even there, modestly so): surely important in terms of the political socialization of the individuals, it did not facilitate a more direct association with the demonstration promoters.

Conclusion

The February 15 demonstrations not only attracted substantial numbers of people with no previous experiences of collective action—which is made even more remarkable by their being national demonstrations, located in the capitals or in other major cities, and therefore more demanding to attend (see chapter 9 in this volume). They also mobilized very broad sectors of civil society, at least of its leftist sections. The organizers showed a complex relationship to peace activism. On the one hand, many organizations were not primarily oriented to peace issues; on the other, their members had a substantial background in peace activism. Not only that, they also had above-average connections to both the world of associations and to the protest communities operating within civil society. In this sense, members of promoting organizations acted as links between specific peace issues and much broader sectors of collective action, and they did so from a perspective that was only occasionally more radical than the other demonstrators' in terms of action repertoires, strength of opposition to war, or links to global justice movements. Members of promoting organizations, however, were more left-wing than the other participants in most European continental countries. In any case, the promoting organizations did not stand out for their moderation. If anything, when differences were significant, they suggested that promoting organizations were more radical rather than more moderate than the others.

Generally, the organizations that promoted the marches attracted quite different sectors of civil society in different countries, with political parties and unions underrepresented among their members (although not among the demonstrators in general) in the United States and the United Kingdom, and overrepresented in Italy and Spain, peace organizations dominant only in the Anglo-Saxon countries, and left-wing affiliation being a predictor of membership in those organizations in most of continental Europe but, once again, not in the United States or the United Kingdom. Although it would be difficult to identify specific explanations for all such differences, it seems plausible to suggest a link between governments' policies and the configuration of the coalitions that promoted the marches. This stresses the importance of the more contingent elements of the political context, in particular, of the interaction context in which social movement actors and their opponents (here, mainly national governments) engage in a struggle that involves both specific political resources and broader symbolic elements (Kriesi 2004). While coalitions were very heterogeneous in all countries, the political opportunities determined by the governments' approaches to the war, and by their variable inclinations to adopt specific patriotic discourses, contributed to shape the configuration of those coalitions. At the very minimum, they seemed to affect the relative weight of promoting organizations in the different coalitions. In countries that directly promoted and actively participated in the attack on Iraq, the strength of the call to national unity (as well as, in the United Kingdom, the fact that the government was a "left" one) made it very difficult for organizations other than those focusing on peace issues to engage explicitly in promoting the protests, even though their members were massively involved in the marches on an individual basis.

In contrast, in countries where governments supported the intervention but from a more cautious and noncommittal position, the issue became heavily politicized along traditional lines, which led to the peace protestors relying on much larger alliance structures. Accordingly, the coalitions promoting the demonstrations in countries such as Italy, Spain, or the Netherlands saw a huge role for oppositional forces, including both unions and parties. Finally, where there was no particular need to pressure national governments who were already hostile to the war, promoting coalitions emerged that were more representative of the overall spectrum of organizational backgrounds from which the demonstrators came. If anything, the organizations whose broad issues were most directly linked with peace issues, such as those active in global justice themes, consistently played a more significant promoting role in Germany, Belgium, and Switzerland. These conclusions should not be automatically generalized to explanations of coalitions promoting social movement activity on a longer and more sustained basis. They do offer, however, valuable insights for our understanding of mobilization dynamics in the context of specific large-scale protest events like the February 15 demonstrations.

Notes

1. One might be puzzled by the minimal role played, according to our data, by environmental or women's organizations in promoting the marches in countries like the United States or Germany, where those organizations are notoriously strong. As far as the United States are concerned, a possible explanation focuses on the central role played by ad hoc peace coalitions in promoting the marches; in Germany, however, the strong association of radical environmentalism with the global justice movement may have encouraged activists to define promoting organizations as such rather than as environmentalist—hence the low presence of the latter among promoting organizations.

2. Here are the frequencies for the most frequently mentioned organizations across all countries: Amnesty International 25, ARCI 15, ATTAC 59, CCOO 29, CGIL 83, CND 12, GEW 64, Greenpeace 27, Groen Links 53, GSOA 22, Oxfam 18, PSOE 26, Rifondazione 30, SNOW 20, SP 76, UGT 28, Ver.di 19.

3. This finding might also be the result of the UK (and, indeed, the U.S.) tradition of putting up specific umbrella organizations to coordinate specific campaigns. As a result, the UK and U.S. respondents might have felt encouraged to identify those peace (umbrella) organizations as promoters of the marches and to underestimate the role of other actors.

Works Cited

Carroll, William K., and Robert S. Ratner. 1996. "Master Framing and Cross-Movement Networking in Contemporary Social Movements." *Sociological Quarterly* 37: 601–25.

Curtis, Russell L., and Louis A. Zurcher Jr. 1973. "Stable Resources of Protest Movements: The Multi-Organizational Field." *Social Forces* 52: 53–61.

della Porta, Donatella. 1995. *Social Movements, Political Violence, and the State.* Cambridge: Cambridge University Press.

della Porta, Donatella, and Mario Diani. 2005. "'No to the War with No Ifs or Buts': Protests against the War in Iraq." In *Italian Politics Yearbook 2004,* ed. Sergio Fabbrini and Vincent Della Sala, 200–218. New York: Berghahn.

Diani, Mario. 1992. "The Concept of Social Movement." *Sociological Review* 40: 1–25.

——. 1995. *Green Networks: A Structural Analysis of the Italian Environmental Movement.* Edinburgh: Edinburgh University Press.

——. 1996. "Linking Mobilization Frames and Political Opportunities: Insights from Italian Regional Populism." *American Sociological Review* 61. 1053–69.

——. 2005. "The Structural Bases of Movement Coalitions." Paper presented at the ASA Annual Meeting, Philadelphia, August.

Diani, Mario, and Ivano Bison. 2004. "Organization, Coalitions, and Movements." *Theory and Society* 33: 281–309.

Doherty, Brian, Alex Plows, and Derek Wall. 2003. "The Preferred Way of Doing Things: The British Direct Action Movement." *Parliamentary Affairs* 56: 669–86.

Esping-Andersen, Gøsta. 1990. *The Three Worlds of Welfare Capitalism.* Princeton, N.J.: Princeton University Press.

Gamson, William, and David S. Meyer. 1996. "Framing Political Opportunity." In *Opportunities, Mobilizing Structures, and Framing,* ed. Doug McAdam, John D. McCarthy, and Mayer N. Zald, 275–90. Cambridge: Cambridge University Press.

Kitschelt, Herbert. 1986. "Political Opportunity Structures and Political Protest: Anti-Nuclear Movements in Four Democracies." *British Journal of Political Science* 16: 57–85.

Klandermans, Bert. 1990. "Linking the 'Old' and 'New': Movement Networks in the Netherlands." In *Challenging the Political Order: New Social and Political Movements in Western Democracies,* ed. Russell J. Dalton and Manfred Kuechler, 122–36. Cambridge: Polity.

Knoke, David, and James R. Wood. 1981. *Organized for Action: Commitment in Voluntary Associations.* New Brunswick, N.J.: Rutgers University Press.

Koopmans, Ruud, and Paul Statham. 1999. "Ethnic and Civic Conceptions of Nationhood and the Differential Success of the Extreme Right in Germany and Italy." In *How Movements Matter: Theoretical and Comparative Studies on the Consequences of Social Movements,* ed. Marco Giugni, Doug McAdam, and Charles Tilly, 225–51. Minneapolis: University of Minnesota Press.

Kriesi, Hanspeter. 2004. "Political Context and Opportunity." In *The Blackwell Companion to Social Movements,* ed. David A. Snow, Sarah A. Soule, and Hanspeter Kriesi, 67–90. Oxford: Blackwell.

Melucci, Alberto. 1996. *Challenging Codes: Collective Action in the Information Age.* Cambridge: Cambridge University Press.

Rucht, Dieter. 1990. "Campaigns, Skirmishes, and Battles: Anti-Nuclear Movements in the USA, France, and West Germany." *Industrial Crisis Quarterly* 4: 193–222.

Staggenborg, Suzanne. 1986. "Coalition Work in the Pro-Choice Movement: Organizational and Environmental Opportunities and Constraints." *Social Problems* 33: 623–41.

Tarrow, Sidney. 1998[1994]. *Power in Movement: Social Movements, Collective Action and Politics.* Cambridge: Cambridge University Press.

Taylor, Verta, and Nancy Whittier. 1992. "Collective Identity in Social Movement Communities: Lesbian Feminist Mobilization." In *Frontiers in Social Movement Theory,* ed. Aldon D. Morris and Carol McClurg Mueller, 104–32. New Haven, Conn.: Yale University Press.

Tilly, Charles. 1994. "Social Movements as Historically Specific Clusters of Political Performances." *Berkeley Journal of Sociology* 38: 1–30.

——. 1995. *Popular Contention in Britain, 1758–1834.* Cambridge, Mass.: Harvard University Press.

11

Crossing Political Divides: Communication, Political Identification, and Protest Organization

W. Lance Bennett, Terri E. Givens, and Christian Breunig

The February 15 anti–Iraq War protests mobilized demonstrators from a wide variety of political backgrounds. For quite a few people, it was the first demonstration they had ever attended. Others were associated with single issues or social movements, most notably peace organizations and related protest activities. Large numbers of demonstrators had been involved in global social justice protests against organizations such as the World Trade Organization (Walgrave and Verhulst 2003; and see chapter 10 in this volume). Within this broad context, there were many demonstrators with complex political histories that crossed multiple issue and movement lines; these activists may have been instrumental in establishing both the scale and the speed with which the February 15 demonstrations occurred. Chapter 10 presented some evidence making this point, and the idea in this chapter is that by participating in multiple political networks, these complex activists expanded the diffusion paths by which information, coordination, and encouragement to participate were passed through large numbers of people.

Conventional understandings of the diffusion of protest affiliations and repertoires of action suggest that the underlying protest diffusion mechanisms generally involve social relationships based on singular organizational or political identities. Diffusion along dominant identification paths results in mobilization that is typically bounded in scale along organization, ideology, or issue lines, often requiring brokerage mechanisms to bridge those lines of division (Tarrow and McAdam 2005; McAdam 1988). A new wrinkle in the idea of diffusion may be appearing in the form of individuals in various transnational protest contexts who display identifications with multiple issue and movement networks, permitting diffusion at a fine-grained individual level across a broad spectrum of issue networks. For example, della Porta describes the movement for global justice as cohering at the individual level via "heterogeneous, multiply faceted identities that reflect social complexity" with the result that an "identity shift from single-movement identity to multiple, tolerant identities has helped the movement in dealing with its heterogeneous bases" (2005, 186).

This conception of activists with complex or flexible political identities helps resolve a conceptual dilemma concerning whether the complex array of issues and organizations that have appeared in globalization demonstrations (and that, in some countries, played important roles in the antiwar demonstrations studied here; see chapter 10) can be reasonably called a movement, or whether they are so fragmented that they might better be thought of as representing multiple movements. The concept of multiple identities suggests that such diverse, large-scale mobilizations may be less fragmented than the multiplicity of issues and organizations make them appear. The formation of multiple or complex identities may also explain how individuals and organizations within networks can readily "transpose" their objects of protest or solidarity without losing their local issues and roots (Tarrow and McAdam 2005).

In the case of the February 15 protests, many of the diffusion paths for protest participation seem to have emerged from the transposition of global justice, or as we prefer to call it, the global social justice movement, into a vast antiwar network. Chapter 1 describes the role of global social justice activists in the European Social Forum and the World Social Forum in the early coordination and planning of the antiwar demonstrations. We propose in this chapter that some part of this networking capacity is related to the communication practices of particular types of activists. The basic idea is that activists with complex political identifications somehow communicate more broadly across different issue networks and are more likely than activists with single-issue or organizational identifications to build bridges across different issue communities. Our primary concern is to understand what communication practices enable this network-bridging to trigger mobilizations on the scale witnessed in these demonstrations.

Identification, Communication, and Protest Organization

To build and assess a model of complex political identification, communication practices, and the scale of protest mobilization, we define and explore several sets of related variables. First, we developed three separate measures of complex political identification, as stated here and explained more fully below: strength of affiliation with the global social justice movement, reported number of memberships in different kinds of organizations (including churches; human rights, peace, and labor organizations; and parties), and the number of diverse issues in the activist's demonstration history.

Next, to assess whether those with more complex identifications are closer to the core diffusion paths of protest organization, we measured whether or not each respondent was a member or personally knew a member of an organization responsible for the demonstration. Those who answered "yes" to either question were designated as being in the "organizing circle" of the demonstration and then assessed for the complexity of their political identifications. It is clear that organizations continue to matter in the production of large transnational demonstrations, helping to publicize, mobilize, coordinate, and otherwise support the participation of others (Fisher et al. 2004). However, less is known about the mechanisms that ripple out from these organizations to diffuse participation at the finer-grained levels of political identification and network-bridging communication that we have measured.

Finally, we assessed how those with complex political identifications communicated about both the demonstration in particular and politics in general. We also assess how the communication practices of those with more complex identifications differ from those with less complex identifications, such as those claiming membership in few different kinds of organizations, those with less sympathy for the global social justice movement, or those with thinner histories of demonstrations on different types of issues. We hypothesize that those with more complex political identities (as measured above) manage those identities and share information across their various networks with digital or electronic media channels such as e-mail, lists, text messages, or interactive political Web sites operated on appliances such as computers and mobile phones. (Hereafter, we use the term digital media to refer to these communication modes, while using the shorthand e-media in our data tables.)

Our surveys measured more conventional digital media applications such as e-mail, lists, and Web sites that are typically accessed via computers. However, we note that in some national and political contexts, other digital technologies such as text messaging using hand-held devices may be more important organizing tools (Rheingold 2002). The basic idea here is that the flexibility, density, hyperlinked, and network-bridging capacities of digital media enable complex activists to manage their multiple political identifications in ways that can ramp up the scale of protest activities via participation in more diverse political networks. These communication formats also enable activists to maintain personal coherence in what might otherwise seem a fragmented and stressful set of social and political relationships (which, to outward appearances, may seem burdened with information overload).

The strength of these communication and political identification patterns may vary from country to country, depending on the resources and membership strengths of conventional social movement (e.g., labor, church, and issue) organizations and the general accessibility and cost of digital media services, from computer-based Internet to text messaging on mobile phones. Despite these national differences, we anticipate that the general patterns predicted here will hold for activists in most of the countries surveyed in the February 15 demonstrations, because all of them are more or less similar postindustrial democracies.

Communicating Complex Identities

The proliferation of interactive digital media technology enables the spread of political news, mobilizing information, and action options, often packaged within the same e-mails, lists, and Web sites. Much has been written on how digital communication technologies—both hardware and software applications—facilitate activist network bridging in ways that go beyond the familiar claims that the Internet mainly reduces the speed and costs of communication, or merely amplifies the capacity of existing organizations (Bimber 2003; Flanagin, Stohl, and Bimber 2006; see also Center for Communication and Civic Engagement 2004). In addition to reducing costs and accelerating the speed of mobilization, electronic networks may also constitute loose organizational structures linking actors in decentralized campaigns, providing community protest calendars and planning sites, enabling activist news reporting and social forums, and otherwise linking diverse and often widely dispersed activists (Bennett 2003; 2005).

The distributed (flat, nonhierarchical) design of many activist communication networks—referred to by Coopman (2003) as "dissentworks"—also helps to explain their capacity to recombine and reconfigure around different issues, producing a steady stream of large-scale coordinated protests that have overcome impressive obstacles of geography, time, culture, resources, and ideology. For example, the importance of nonhierarchical digital networking practices and technologies in bridging issue networks may help account for the sustained transposition of organizational purpose and commitment noted by Tarrow and McAdam (2005) in describing the Zapatista solidarity network. In our case, these digital networking practices may help explain how initiatives that diffused through various world and regional social forum networks helped organize a wave of transnational antiwar protests.

At the core of this analysis is the idea that applications of digital technologies create network structures that are attractive to activists with complex or "tolerant" identities (della Porta 2005). These fluid, interactive, and individually calibrated interpersonal communication networks may explain a good deal about the scale and sustainability of recent transnational protest politics (Bennett 2005; Tarrow 2003). The importance of interpersonal networks here is not new; it has been well established in social movement research (Snow, Zurcher, and Ekland-Olson 1980; McAdam 1986; della Porta and Diani 1999). However, recent research by Shah and colleagues on digital media and activism suggests that these communication technologies and the networks they enable can transform both the substantive scope and the scale of interpersonal political relationships as they move people to interact more widely both on and off line (Shah et al. 2005; Nah, Veenstra, and Shah 2006; Hwang et al. 2006).

New communication technologies would not likely be used to bridge diverse activist networks unless the underlying political identities of many activists were suited to such flexible political exchanges. Recent analyses suggest that political identity patterns in contemporary Western societies continue to shift away from ideologically based identifications anchored in mass social organizations (e.g., party, class, or church) and toward more self-directed political affiliations driven by lifestyle values (Giddens 1991; Beck 2000; Inglehart 1997; Bennett 1998). Putnam (2000) finds in the United States that traditional civil society relations (e.g., group memberships) continue to decline, a trend that is most pronounced among younger citizens who are least engaged by conventional group membership and political participation patterns.

These broad political trends indicating more complex political identity formation raise a series of questions about the relationship between individual-level consciousness and social organization. How do multi-issue activists—particularly those operating in transnational movements—manage complex political identities on their own with fewer cues and less leadership from conventional groups, leaders, and institutions? Of equal interest is the question of how these relatively autonomous activists engage in sustainable collective action with others. We propose that a place to start answering these questions is to explore whether, and how, activists with more complex political identifications differ in their communication behaviors from citizens with simpler, or more conventional, political profiles.

Identification, Organization, and Media Use: Hypotheses and Measures

As explained earlier, we suspect that activists with multiple political identifications are likely to be key diffusion links in large-scale protest networks both because they operate close to the organizing circles of demonstrations and because they are more likely, compared to the other activists, to acquire and exchange information, maintain commitments and identifications, and sustain contacts with diverse social networks through various uses of digital media. In particular, we predict that high levels of reliance on digital media (our survey measured e-mail, lists, and Web sites) will be positively associated with various measures of complex political identity, including identification with the global social justice movement, participation in past demonstrations for diverse issues, and affiliation with diverse organizations. Conversely, we predict that reliance on conventional mass media channels (radio, television, newspapers, and magazines) will be more characteristic for first-time demonstrators and for more experienced activists whose political profiles are defined by fewer issues or demonstration types and organizational memberships.

Measures of Complex Political Identification

Identification with the global social justice movement was measured in two ways, which are reported in the analyses below as either sympathy or identification with the movement. The sympathy measure was a simple yes/no response to the question "Do you sympathize with the movement against neo-liberal globalization?" Identification strength was assessed by asking how much the demonstrators identified with the movement along a five-point scale: not at all, a little, somewhat, a lot, very much. We created two measures: a binary, yes/no sympathy or support measure with values 0 and 1 based on the sympathy question, and a three-point strength of identification scale where 1 = no identification (either no on the sympathy question or not at all on the identity question), 2 = a little or somewhat, and 3 = a lot or very much. The resulting identification patterns for the different countries are presented in Table 11.1.

Demonstrators were also asked whether they were active, inactive, or former members of sixteen kinds of organizations, ranging from political parties; labor, environment, and human rights groups; to charitable organizations. Our organizational diversity measure is based on the summation of active membership in various kinds of organizations. Using this raw data, we created a scale where all missing values are coded as no active membership and organization diversity is divided into three categories (0, 1–3, and 4+). The resulting organizational diversity patterns across the investigated countries are also displayed in Table 11.1.

To measure protest diversity, the questionnaire asked the respondents who had participated in other demonstrations in the last five years to indicate what different types of demonstrations they had participated in by checking as many as applied from the following list: peace demonstrations, antiracism, human rights, third world, social issues (including labor), environmental, antiglobalization, women's rights, regionalist, and other. The level of protest diversity is determined by the number of different types of demonstrations a respondent checked. All blank, unchecked types are counted as zero (i.e., not attended). Utilizing these answers, we constructed a scale measure of protest diversity with the following four groups: 0, 1, 2–5, and 6+. Table 11.1 reports the levels of demonstration diversity across our cases.

As indicated in Table 11.1, the overall levels of identification with the global social justice movement were fairly high, but substantial differences existed across the nations in the study. Sympathy and identification with the movement appear to be especially prevalent among Italian demonstrators (.93) but are still widespread among demonstrators in the "least sympathetic case," the United States (.63). For most countries, the average level of organizational diversity involves being an active member in between one and three different kinds of organization. In Belgium, Spain, and the United Kingdom the average person was active in less than one type of organization. Regarding protest diversity, it appears that across all cases respondents had participated in roughly two different types of protests. Nevertheless, variation regarding protest diversity exists among the cases. Italian demonstrators are the most diverse, with an average of more than three types of protests, and those in the United Kingdom are the least diverse. On average, respondents had engaged in a considerable number of protests in the last five years. The cross-national average of participation in protest is between two and five. Italians on average attended six to ten protests and thus are the most active protestors, whereas the antiwar demonstrations in the Netherlands drew a considerable number of people who were protesting for the first time in the last five years (54 percent of all protestors).

Measuring Proximity to the Core Demonstration Organizations

To assess whether those with complex political identifications occupied strategic positions in the protest diffusion network, we asked whether respondents were members of or personally knew members of a group responsible for organizing the demonstration. Answering "yes" to either question was scored as 1, and no was scored as 0, forming a variable that we have labeled "association" in the "organizing circle" for the demonstrations. Scores on this measure (proportion belonging to organizing circle) varied from one national sample to another as follows: United Kingdom (.38), United States (.38), Netherlands (.41), Germany (.41), Sweden (.50), Belgium (.51), Spain (.55), Italy (.72). It is of course impossible to tell how much these differences reflect either different national organizational structures or sampling differences, such as the existence of multiple protest sites in some national samples and single sites in others. In any event, the tests we impose on the data

Table 11.1. Descriptive statistics of key political identification variables

	Maximum	US	UK	SP	IT	NL	CH	BE	GE	Total
Global justice sympathy (percent)[a]	0/1	.63	.87	.82	.93	.72	.87	.86	.75	.81
Globalization movement[b] identification (median score)	1/3	2	2	3	3	2	2	3	2	2
Organization diversity ($\bar{x}$)[b]	0/16	3.1	1.3	.9	1.2	1.2	1.2	1.1	0.9	1.5
Organization diversity[c] (scaled) (median score)	0/2	1	0	0	1	1	1	0	1	0
Protest diversity ($\bar{x}$)	0/10	2.3	2.1	2.1	3.4	1.2	1.8	1.9	2.4	3.0
Protest diversity (scaled)[d] (median score)	0/3	2	0	2	2	2	1	2	2	1
Protest frequency (median score)[e]	1/4	2	2	2	3	1	2	2	2	2
First-timers (percent)	0/1	.30	.32	.21	.09	.54	.27	.23	.22	.27
N		705	1,633	452	1,016	642	818	706	781	6,753

Notes: The following central tendencies are displayed: percentage answering "yes" (percent), mean ($\bar{x}$), and median (m). The total number of cases for each country is also displayed, but the number of valid cases varies among variables.

[a] No = 0; yes = 1.

[b] Median score five-point strength of sympathy scale: 1 = low, 2 = moderate, 3 = high.

[c] Scaled: 0 = 0; 1 = 1–3; 2 = 4+.

[d] Scaled: 0 = 0; 1 = 1; 2 = 2–5; 3 = 6+.

[e] Scaled: 1 = first time; 2 = 2–5; 3 = 6–10; 4 = 11+.

are designed to assess patterned relationships and are not likely to be affected by these differences.

Measuring the Media and Communication Variables

The core questions of how those with relatively more and less complex political identities manage the flow of information and political communication required asking a number of questions about media use and communication practices. Most generally, respondents were asked a battery of questions about how they received general political information, information about the Iraq crisis and how they learned about the February 15 demonstration. These items covered a range of information sources: television, newspaper, magazines, radio, other people such as family or friends, Web sites, e-mail lists, and others. For the general political information measure, respondents were asked how often they utilized each source (on a four-point scale). These sources are displayed separately, as they were measured in the top portions of the core data tables in the analyses below and then combined into broader information or media categories to simplify the analyses. The bottom portions of the media and information source tables contain these summary measures of mass and digital media, which were constructed by combining TV, radio, newspaper, and magazine into a mass media category variable and combining Web sites and e-mail lists into a digital or e-media variable. Friends and family as information sources are identified as social networks.

As we expected, media-use patterns varied from nation to nation. For example, there was wide variation in reliance on television for general political information (recall that 1 = never, 2 = monthly, 3 = weekly, and 4 = daily): United States (2.7); Sweden (3.1); Belgium (3.4); Germany, Italy, and the United Kingdom (3.5); Spain (3.6); Netherlands (3.7). These differences, particularly in the case of the United States, may well reflect the quality of available television news sources and the degree to which political issues are presented in terms that interest activists. By contrast, newspaper use for general political information was fairly similar, ranging from a low of 3.3 in Belgium to a high of 3.7 in the Netherlands. As should be expected, e-mail use for general political information was generally low (in the 1.5–1.8 range) and only exceeded an average of 2 in Italy and the United States (which was highest at 2.6, perhaps reflecting the popular trend of using automated news services that come through e-mail). By contrast, a far larger portion of the entire sample (.45) reported using e-mail for purposes of achieving social change. The national differences on this measure were considerable: Germany (.30); United Kingdom (.36); Sweden and Spain (.41); Netherlands (.42); Italy (.45); Belgium (.50); United States (.73).

Analyzing the Different Measures of Complex Identification

We begin by examining the basic relationships among the different measures of complex political identities. Since all variables of interest are measured on an ordinal scale, we rely on Spearman's rho as our test statistic. Global social justice movement identification is strongly related (.29) to protest diversity in the cross-national sample. This correlation is also significant at the .001 level when each country is examined individually. The test statistic for this relationship is the lowest in Italy (.20) and the highest in Switzerland (.33).

Although there is some overlap among the three measures of complex political identification, the three variables clearly measure different types of orientation that may operate differently. For example, the relatively weak association between global social justice identification and organizational diversity (.06) suggests, as many observers have noted, that many activists who support the global social justice movement are not strongly identified with organizations. Even though the relationship between globalization movement identification and organizational diversity is significant at the .05 level in the Belgian, Dutch, Swiss, Spanish, and German cases, the strength of the associations is not great. The Belgian case displays the strongest relationship, at just .20, and no significant associations between global social justice identification and organizational diversity were found for the United States, Italy, or the United Kingdom. By contrast, organizational diversity is more strongly related (.33) to protest diversity, with all the national samples registering significance levels of .05 or greater. There was, however, considerable variation in the strength of the relationship, ranging from .53 in Belgium to .09 in Spain.

There was also an anticipated high correlation (.64) between scores on protest diversity and protest frequency, which is measured as the respondent's estimate of total times she or he had participated in local, national, or international demonstrations or public protests in the last five years. However, as we expected, the correlations between protest frequency and organizational diversity (.16) and global social justice identification (.34) are far lower than the protest frequency–protest diversity correlation, indicating that the theoretical explanatory value of frequency alone would be confounded with the measure of protest diversity and not with the other two measures of complex political identification. We point the reader to the strong correlations reported below between all three measures of complex political identity and the communication variables in the later analyses, which suggest that the interpretation is consistent with our theoretical construction, and not a simple function of protest frequency. In general, the different levels of association among our complex political identification measures enable us to consider media use through a rich set of activist identification measures.

The proposition that activists with more complex political identifications will be close to the organizing circles of the antiwar demonstrations was supported overwhelmingly for all measures of complexity in all national samples, as shown in Table 11.2. There were, of course, national differences, due to both the organizational structures of national demonstrations and properties of the distributions of scores on various measures. For example, in the Italian case, the relatively lower associations between all three measures of complexity and organizing circle membership were caused by a combination of Italy having by far the highest percentage of respondents in the demonstration organizing circles (.65) and the highest scores on two of the three measures of complex political identifications.

Complex Political Identification and Communication Practices

We can now assess our major prediction that activists with more complex political identities (by all three measures) are more likely to use digital media to manage their political communication. The following analyses examine several different media-use patterns: which media sources different types of demonstrators use for general political information, which sources different political types used for information about the Iraq War in particular, and what kinds of activists use digital media for creating social change.

General Political Information

We know that activists in recent years have developed impressive digital networking capabilities, and in some cases have even succeeded in reaching broader publics with news and political messages of their own design through such Internet platforms as Indymedia (Pickard 2006; Peretti and Micheletti 2004; Jordan, Houser, and Foster 2003). This said, the framing of protest activities by mass media outlets clearly remains an important concern in the strategic calculus of many activists, and thus we do not expect electronic media use to displace reliance on mass media for information and communication, although as indicated in Table 11.3, digital media comes close to displacing conventional media for high global social justice movement identifiers.

In general, our findings show that reliance on Web sites and e-mail lists is significantly and positively associated with all three measures of political complexity in all countries (with the exception of e-mail lists in the United Kingdom, which contained a high number of missing values on these variables). Diagnostic regression analyses show that the described patterns hold when controlling for a host of sociodemographic variables (age, sex, education,

Table 11.2. Associations between organizing circle membership and three measures of complex political identification for each nation

	US	UK	SP	IT	NL	SW	BE	GE
Global social justice	.192***	.207***	.192***	.146***	.294***	.224***	.291***	.202***
Protest diversity	.223***	.120*	.132***	.163***	.187***	.187***	.273***	.136***
Organizational diversity	.176***	.134**	.184***	.175***	.264***	.227***	.210***	.261***

*p<.05, **p<.01, ***p<.001

Note: The values represent Somer's d coefficients between the political identification variables in the top row and organizing circle membership scores. N values for countries are found in Table 11.1.

etc.). These findings represent perhaps the most difficult test of our main hypothesis, since they pertain to the media sources used for general political information, rather than for information about specific issues such as the Iraq War, or for promoting change.

In the interest of saving space, we report in Tables 11.3 and 11.4 the relationships between media information sources and just two of the identification complexity measures, global social justice identification and organizational membership diversity, since the protest diversity findings strongly resemble the organization diversity findings. They both clearly indicate that in most countries digital media are more important than conventional mass media sources for general information among demonstrators with complex identifications. As a guide to interpreting the data, the various information sources we measured are displayed down the left column in the top half of Tables 11.3 and 11.4, with the results based on significance levels of the cross tabs assessing the relationship between the complex identification scale and the four-point media-use scale. The bottom half of each table offers summary measures of mass and digital media by combining TV, radio, newspaper, and magazine into a "mass media" variable and combining Web sites and e-mail lists into an "e-media" variable. For example, daily use of an information type (mass, digital, or social networks) is based on respondents indicating daily reliance on at least one of the component information sources that make up the type. The summary "e-media" measure detects whether respondents indicated any use of either Web sites or e-mail as sources of political information. E-media dominant means weekly or daily reliance on any combination of digital media sources with only monthly or no use of mass media sources. Similarly, mass media dominant means weekly or daily reliance on any combination of mass media sources combined with only monthly or no digital media use.

As Table 11.3 indicates, high global social justice identifiers not only rely disproportionately on digital media for general political information, but in some countries they are even averse to mass media use in their general information-seeking behaviors. (The test statistic for both the direction and significance of these associations is Somer's d.) By contrast, our other two measures of complex identification reveal higher reliance on both mass media and digital media sources, suggesting that there is some difference in whether the basis of complex political identification is transnational or national activism (see Table 11.4 for comparison of digital and mass media use by those with high levels of organizational diversity). We suspect national media simply do not feature the issues or perspectives global social justice identifiers care most about, while they are aware of online information sources that

Table 11.3. Relationship between strength of global social justice movement identification and general political information sources

	US	UK	SP	IT	NL	CH	BE	GE
TV	-**							
Newspaper	-**	-*						
Magazine	+		+**	+**				
Radio				+*	+**			
Social network		+						
Web sites	+*	+	+*	+**	+***	+*	+**	+**
E-mail lists	+**		+**	+	+***	+**	+***	+***
Social Networks daily					+°			
Mass media daily	-**	-***	-*	-**	-***	-°	-*	
Mass media dominant		-***						
E-media use	+**	+*	+**	+**	+**	+*	+***	+***
E-media daily	+***		+**	+**	+*	+**	+°	+***
E-media dominant	+***		+*	+°		+**		+*

p<.1; * p<.05; ** p<.01; *** p<.001

Note: Notation of + or – specifies the direction of the association as indicated by Somer's d. The top half of the table is based on 4 x 3 crosstabs between globalization identification scale and four-point media-use scale in which 0 = never, 1 = monthly, 2 = weekly, 3 = daily. The bottom half is based on 2 x 3 crosstabs based on binary summary media variables indicating reliance or no reliance on indicated media source type. N values for countries are available in Table 11.1.

can satisfy those concerns. Also interesting is the finding that social networks play less central roles in the general information networks of global social justice activists than for demonstrators who scored high on the organizational membership (shown in Table 11.4) and protest diversity measures, suggesting, not surprisingly, that the face-to-face experiences implied in participation in organizations and demonstrations involve enduring personal information networks.

As Table 11.4 illustrates, demonstrators with diverse organizational memberships use a mix of digital and conventional media sources for their general political information, with the notable general exception of television. Those with complex organization and demonstration profiles tend to be multimedia information seekers. This said, our main hypothesis is supported for all three types of complex political identification: Web sites and e-mail lists top any single conventional media source of general political information for complex activists in most nations in our sample. Moreover, for general political information daily e-media use is stronger among complex identifiers in more national samples than daily mass media use.

Complex Political Identification and Information about the Iraq Crisis

Since there is remarkable similarity across nations in the patterns of media and information associated with complex political identities, we can step back and take a different look at these relationships by pooling and weighting the country data and displaying two striking trends across the entire set of demonstrators. This time we will look not at general political information habits but at specific sources of information on the Iraq crisis itself. First, we calculated the distribution of responses across the entire eight-nation sample for a question about all activists' (not just those with complex political profiles) most important sources of information on the Iraq crisis. As common sense might lead us to think, mass media sources are far and away the most important for the demonstrators as a whole: more than 35 percent of the respondents say that newspapers were the most important source of information regarding the Iraq crisis; TV follows with 27 percent, and then radio, with 20 percent. However, electronic media sources are most important for those scoring highest on all of our measures of complex political identification. Put differently, those who listed e-mail lists (2 percent) and Web sites (7 percent) as the most important sources of information on the Iraq crisis scored highest on all three measures of complex political identification. (By contrast, those who found TV most important had the lowest scores on all three measures of complex political identification.) Those who cited e-mail lists as most important scored highest on organizational and demonstration

Table 11.4. Relationship between strength of organizational diversity and general political information sources

	US	UK	SP	IT	NL	SW	BE	GE
TV		–*						–*
Newspaper	+*			+*	+**	+***	+*	+*
Magazine	+**	+**		+**	+***	+*	+	
Radio	+**				+***	+***		
Social network	+***		+*		+**		+	+*
Web sites	+***	+**	+	+***	+	+*	+***	+**
E-mail lists	+***	+**		+**	+***	+***	+***	+***
Social networks daily	+*	+***	+	+*	+***	+***	+***	+**
Mass media daily	+*	+***		+*	+***	+***	+***	
Mass media dominant	–***	+***		–***	+***	+***	+***	
E-media use	+**	+**	+*	+***	+	+**	+***	+**
E-media daily	+***	+***	+***	+***	+***	+***	+***	+***
E-media dominant	+**	+***		+*		+*	+*	+**

p<.1; * p<.05; **p<.01; ***p<.001

Note: Notation of + or – specifies the direction of the association as indicated by Somer's d. N values for countries are available in Table 11.1.

diversity, while Web sites were most important for high global social justice identifiers. Since space prohibits displaying all of these relationships, Figure 11.1 illustrates the most important Iraq information sources across the range of demonstration diversity scores found in the eight-nation sample.

Complex Political Identification and Use of the Internet for Social Change

The inclusion of multiple information, communication, and media variables in the questionnaire enabled us to develop multiple indicators of electronic media and mass media use. Table 11.5 shows relationships between all of our complex identification measures (including both sympathy and strength of identification with the global social justice movement) and a yes/no answer to a question about whether the respondent had used the Internet in various activities aimed at promoting societal change in the past twelve months. The list of change-oriented activities included, among other things, contacting a politician, organization, or local or national official; displaying a pin, poster, flyer, or sticker; signing or gathering signatures for a petition, initiative, or referendum; strike; boycott; fundraising; donation; contacting media; sit-in, occupation, squatting; violent action; and "use the Internet for any of the above activities."

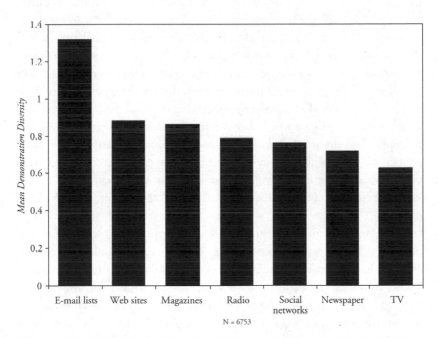

Figure 11.1. Average level of demonstration diversity for each most important source of information on the Iraq crisis

As shown in Table 11.5, there are strong associations in all countries between high scores on all of our measures of complex identification and the use of the Internet for some activity aimed at social change. We also note for comparison that those who were attending their first demonstration on February 15 indicated that they had not used the Internet for social change purposes in the past twelve months. This pattern held for all nations in the sample.

Conclusion

Our data support a simple model of how the transnational coordination and the immense scale of the February 15 demonstrations may have occurred. Activists with complex political identifications may occupy critical positions in diffusion networks that connect the organizations responsible for mobilizing and supporting protests with larger numbers and types of issue and organizational networks. This is not to deny the importance of the many social movement groups (labor, peace, women's organizations) that surely mobilized their constituents through conventional means. Nor do we overlook the remarkable number of first-timers who found the demonstrations through more conventional media channels and sought out local demonstrations to express their opposition to war. What we do suggest is that to different degrees in each nation, there was an additional factor at work: activists who bridged organizational affiliations with their own diverse networks, which they managed through digital media channels. These complex activists manage the information, and communication flows across their networks through substantial reliance on digital media. Indeed, the activist types who are most reliant on digital media and least reliant on conventional media are the global social justice identifiers whose movement played an early role in planning and spreading the word about the demonstrations. This capacity for fine-grained network bridging may help explain how the scale of transnational protest such as the February 15 demonstrations can be organized within such short periods of time and occur nearly simultaneously across such global distances.

The processes observed here may also help explain how transposition of purpose occurs in activist networks, as in the relatively fluid repurposing of social forum networks into antiwar networks, which, in turn, connected readily with local and national peace organizations, trade union and political party grassroots social movement networks, and large numbers of first-time demonstrators. Such transposition may well entail brokerage between organizations, as Tarrow and McAdam (2005) observe, but it also seems to involve network bridging at the individual level among activists who demonstrate

Table 11.5. Relationship between measures of complex political identification in the use of the Internet for social change

	US	UK	SP	IT	NL	SW	BE	GE
Global justice movement sympathy[a]	+*	+***	+	+	+***	+**	+**	+***
Global justice movement identification[b]	+***	+***	+***	+**	+***	+***	+***	+***
Organizational diversity[c]	+***	+*	+**	+***	+**	+***	+***	+**
Protest diversity[d]	+***	+*	+**	+***	+***	+***	+***	+***
Protest frequency[e]	+***	+*	+*	+***	+***	+***	+***	+***
First timer	−***	−**	−*	−**	−***	−**	−**	−**

p<.1; * p<.05; ** p<.01; *** p<.001

Notes: Chi-square levels of significance; + or − indicates direction of the association, as shown by Somer's d. N values for countries are available in Table 11.1.

[a]Binary scale no = 0; yes = 1.

[b]Rescaled 5 point strength of sympathy scale – 1 = low, 2 = moderate, 3 = high.

[c]Scaled: 0 = 0; 1 = 1–3; 2 = 4+.

[d]Scaled: 0 = 0; 1 = 1; 2 = 2–5; 3 = 6+.

[e]Scaled: 1 = first time; 2 = 2–5; 3 = 6–10; 4 = 11+.

the capacity to identify and communicate across issues, organizations, and geographical space.

The political communication styles observed here among activists with these complex network identifications or affinities are important for understanding both the diversity of their political action repertoires and the capacities of their networks. In particular, our findings suggest that digital media applications are not just more convenient for some activists than conventional communication channels, or that digital media use merely reduces the cost of communicating across diverse networks or great distances, although these properties of digital communication are surely true. Digital communication technologies are also important because they enable activists to constitute new organizational forms (e.g., large-scale, weak-tie network bridges) that reflect—at the collective level—the principles of political consciousness inscribed at the individual level: inclusiveness, diversity, and commitment to radical democracy—with fewer leaders, fewer binding group memberships, and less obligation to share specific ideological collective identity frames. Again, this is not a generalization about all the demonstrators. It applies to notable subsets in each nation that appear to operate with somewhat different mechanisms for mobilization and participation and who rely on digital media to manage often surprisingly complex personal political networks. Their behavior reflects principles of inclusiveness and diversity that represent an increasingly visible meta-ideology in global protest—an ethos that has been adopted in the charter of the World Social Forum, for example (World Social Forum Bulletin 2004). It is also clear that the large populations who demonstrated against the Iraq War reflected highly diverse positions, demands, and political histories (Bennett 2005), findings that concur with previous chapters in this volume (see in particular chapters 6, 8, and 10).

If rethinking the nature of communication among these activists (i.e., as organizational, not just informational) helps to explain the scale, the diffusion speed, and the coherence of transnational protest, some conventional understandings about social movements and political action may have to be adjusted. For example, in his impressive historical analysis of social movements, Charles Tilly (2004) has raised compelling concerns that these activist networks may be less sustainable or effective because of their thin organizational ties and seemingly weak activist commitment levels. As the story of transnational protest unfolds, these concerns may eventually prove well founded. However, there is also a possibility that such concerns about sustainability and effectiveness reflect perspectives on social movement organization that have been forged through observation of more conventional social protests focused within national cultural and institutional contexts. To the extent that observers view the protests such as the antiwar demonstrations studied here (or the globalization protests to which they were loosely linked) through the lenses of conventional movement organization and collective identity frameworks, something important may be missed: there may be considerable intentionality and strength in the design of flexible communication networks that nest loosely within larger, dense, multi-issue networks in which individual activists frequently shift commitments and action repertoires (Bennett 2005; Surman and Reilly 2003).

A core organizational principle running through these repertoires of transnational protest is the creation of self-organizing networks based on personal relationships that are sustained at least partly by online information exchanges and interactions (Jordan, Houser, and Foster 2003). The idea of self-organizing networks in which each new technology release reflects the political learning from the last release puts communication in a constitutive relationship to social movement organization. To cite just one example, what we conventionally think of as news (e.g., about the Iraq crisis) is now commonly produced, edited, rated, and distributed by activists themselves. The movement slogan for this kind of information relationship was coined by Indymedia: "Be the media."

While conventional mass media communication remains important, as indicated in our data, new communication repertoires enable the integration of information and action, marking a departure from the idea of a two-stage mass communication model in which information comes, first, from distant sources to passive individual receivers, who may then use that information in developing action plans at a subsequent stage of the political process. It is now common for information to become integrated with the action process in real time, as activists report on events as they are happening and incorporate those reports in the evolving coordination of the event itself. For example, demonstrators commonly report on their own actions via mobile phones or digital video cameras linked to streaming technologies, enabling information to be interpreted and fed back to participants who are able to then make tactical decisions in real time that can shape the course of a protest action. Rheingold (2002) has described these digitally assisted collective intelligence and organizational capacities as smart mobs.

If it is time to begin to think differently about movement organization and effectiveness, a place to start is with individual-level consciousness, action repertoires, and communication preferences. The activists with complex political identifications in this study seem able to sustain multiple commitments precisely because of the flexible, interactive communication systems that facilitate their creating durable (yet fluid) organizational networks. Even if access to technologies is neither widely nor well distributed in the general populations of most societies, our look at eight nations suggests that there seems to be enough digital communication capacity to reach enough people in enough different places with common cues about times, locations, themes, and practices, to make a difference in how protests are organized and how activists themselves think about their places in them. With political organization and identification codes embedded in communication technologies, activists with complex political identifications can maintain self-organizing networks advancing diverse causes, all with little apparent conflict of commitment.

Works Cited

Beck, Ulrich. 2000. *What Is Globalization?* Cambridge: Polity.

Bennett, Lance W. 1998. "The Uncivic Culture: Communication, Identity, and the Rise of Lifestyle Politics." *Political Science and Politics* 31: 41–61.

———. 2003. "Communicating Global Activism: Strengths and Vulnerabilities of Networked Politics." *Information, Communication, and Society* 6: 143–68.

———. 2005. "Social Movements beyond Borders: Understanding Two Eras of Transnational Activism." In *Transnational Protest and Global Activism*, ed. Donatella della Porta and Sidney Tarrow, 203–26. Lanham, Md.: Rowman & Littlefield.

Bimber, Bruce. 2003. *Information and American Democracy: Technology in the Evolution of Political Power.* New York: Cambridge University Press.

Center for Communication and Civic Engagement. 2004. "Democratic Applications of Internet Technology." http://depts.washington.edu/ccce/digitalMedia/demonet.html.

Coopman, Ted. 2003. "Dissentworks: Identity and Emergent Dissent as Network Structures." Paper presented at the Association of Internet Researchers, October. Toronto, Canada.

della Porta, Donatella. 2005. "Multiple Belongings, Flexible Identities, and the Construction of 'Another Politics': Between the European Social Forum and the Local Social Fora." In *Transnational Protest and Global Activism*, ed. Donatella della Porta and Sidney Tarrow, 175–202. Lanham, Md.: Rowman & Littlefield.

della Porta, Donatella, and Mario Diani. 1999. *Social Movements: An Introduction.* Oxford: Blackwell.

Fisher, Dana R., Kevin Stanley, David Berman, and Gina Neff. 2005. "How Do Organizations Matter? Mobilization and Support for Participants at Five Globalization Protests." *Social Problems* 52: 102–21.

Flanagin, Andrew J., Cynthia Stohl, and Bruce Bimber. 2006. "Modeling the Structure of Collective Action." *Communication Monographs* 73: 29–54.

Giddens, Anthony. 1991. *Modernity and Self Identity: Self and Society in the Late Modern Age*. Stanford, Calif.: Stanford University Press.

Hwang, Hyunseo, Michael Schmierbach, Hye-Jin Paek, Homero Gil de Zuniga, and Dhavan Shah. 2006. "Media Dissociation, Internet Use, and Anti-War Political Participation: A Case Study of Political Dissent and Action against the War in Iraq." *Mass Communication and Society* 9: 461–83.

Inglehart, Ronald. 1997. *Modernization and Post-Modernization: Cultural, Economic, and Political Change in Forty-three Societies*. Princeton, N.J.: Princeton University Press.

Jordan, Ken, Jan Houser, and Steven Foster. 2003. "The Augmented Social Network: Building Identity and Trust into the Next Generation Internet." White Paper for the Planetwork Linktank. http://asn.planetwork.net/whitepaper.html/.

McAdam, Doug. 1986. "Recruitment to High Risk Activism. The Case of Freedom Summer." *American Journal of Sociology* 92: 64–90.

———. 1988. *Freedom Summer*. Chicago: University of Chicago Press.

Nah, Seungahn, Aaron S. Veenstra, and Dhavan Shah. 2006. "The Internet and Anti-War Activism: A Case Study of Information, Expression, and Action." *Journal of Computer Mediated Communication* 12: 230–47.

Peretti, Jonah, and Michele Micheletti. 2004. "The Nike Sweatshop Email: Political Consumerism, Internet, and Culture Jamming." In *Politics, Products, and Markets: Exploring Political Consumerism, Past and Present*, ed. Michele Micheletti, Andreas Follesdal, and Dietlind Stolle, 127–44. New Brunswick, N.J.: Transaction.

Pickard, Victor W. 2006. "Assessing the Radical Democracy of Indymedia: Discursive, Technical, and Institutional Constructions." *Critical Studies in Media Communication* 23: 19–38.

Putnam, Robert D. 2000. *Bowling Alone: The Collapse and Revival of American Community*. New York: Simon & Schuster.

Rheingold, Howard. 2002. *Smart Mobs: The Next Social Revolution*. Cambridge, Mass.: Perseus.

Shah, Dhavan, Jaeho Cho, William P. Eveland, and Nojin Kwak. 2005. "Information and Expression in a Digital Age: Modeling Internet Effects on Civic Participation." *Communication Research* 32: 531–65.

Snow, David A., Louis A. Zurcher, and Sheldon Ekland-Olson. 1980. "Social Networks and Social Movements: A Microstructural Approach to Different Recruitment." *American Sociological Review* 45: 787–801.

Surman, Mark, and Katherine Reilly. 2003. "Appropriating the Internet for Social Change: Towards the Strategic Use of Networked Technologies by Transnational Civil Society Organizations." Version 1.0. New York: Social Science

Research Council. http://mediaresearchhub.ssrc.org/appropriating-the-internet-for-social-change-towards-the-strategic-use-of-networked-technologies-by-transnational-civil-society-organizations/attachment.

Tarrow, Sidney. 2003. "The New Transnational Contention: Social Movements and Institutions in Complex Internationalism." Revision of a paper presented at the 2002 Annual Meeting of the American Political Science Association, Boston.

Tarrow, Sidney, and Doug McAdam. 2005. "Scale Shift in Transnational Contention." In *Transnational Protest and Global Activism,* ed. Donatella della Porta and Sidney Tarrow, 121–50. Lanham, Md.: Rowman & Littlefield.

Tilly, Charles. 2004. *Social Movements, 1768–2004.* Boulder, Colo.: Paradigm.

Walgrave, Stefaan, and Joris Verhulst. 2003. "Worldwide Anti-War-in-Iraq Protest: A Preliminary Test of the Transnational Movement Thesis." Paper presented at the European Consortium for Political Research, Marburg, Germany, September 17.

World Social Forum Bulletin. 2004. March 19. http://www.modkraft.dk/phorum/read.php?f=7&i=7222&t=7222.

12

The Framing of Opposition to the War on Iraq

Dieter Rucht and Joris Verhulst

Wording matters when it comes to influencing people's hearts and minds. Many words and catchphrases are value-loaded. Because they have or evoke positive, negative, or ambivalent connotations and feelings, they are often carefully chosen by actors in a political struggle, thus becoming part of a contest over naming, blaming, and framing (Gamson 1992). It seems that the more morally loaded a conflict is and the higher the stakes, the more the actors engage in a framing contest to win support and discredit their opponents. Just consider the discursive struggles over abortion, in which each side deliberately chooses terms and slogans: "unborn baby" or "fetus," "pro-abortion" or "pro-choice," "anti-abortion" or "pro-life," "abortion is murder" or "my body belongs to me," and so forth (Ferree et al. 2002). When it comes to the protest against an imminent war in Iraq, we can also expect that the actors on both sides place much emphasis on the words and slogans they want to communicate to both their constituency and the audience at large. In part, they have control over the phrasing of their messages. This applies, for example, to the protesters' banners and speeches during a rally. Another—and politically probably more relevant—part of the communication, however, is beyond the direct control of authors and speakers: their messages, if covered at all, are mediated by the mass media (Bennett and Entman 2001). As has been demonstrated repeatedly, the media are highly selective in what and how they report (Hilgartner and Bosk 1988), whom and what they cite literally or indirectly, whether they explicitly express their own views in commentaries and side remarks. In short: naming, blaming, and framing are crucial in the case we are analyzing. Accordingly, this chapter concentrates on the communicative dimension of the demonstrations against the imminent war on Iraq. To this aim, we are using three kinds of materials: First, since we are interested in how the "ordinary" participants in the demonstrations expressed their views and motives, we analyze mainly quantitatively their responses to the open-ended survey questions. Second, we investigate qualitatively and illustratively how organizers, representatives of movement groups, and speakers expressed their views and claims during the demonstrations. Third, in addition to the analysis provided in chapter 3 dealing with mass media reports and governmental positions, we look more specifically at the media coverage of the expected war on Iraq. In methodological terms, depending on the material and the specific question in which we are interested, we use both a more conventional, quantitative content analysis and a more qualitatively oriented frame analysis, as has been developed in social movement studies in the 1980s and 1990s (Snow et al. 1986; Snow and Benford 1988; Gamson and Modigliani 1989; Gerhards and Rucht 1992).

The Voices of "Ordinary" Protest Participants

In a public protest, mere participation is a message in itself. Therefore, not all participants feel the need to explicitly voice their views during the event. Moreover, there are forms of protest—for example, a silent march or a silent prayer—where words are deliberately avoided. However, in the mass demonstrations against the war in Iraq, explicit messages in various forms were abundant. Many people were carrying handmade signs, standardized placards, or large banners. And they were shouting slogans or singing peace songs, giving interviews to journalists, and discussing the issue of war in small groups during the marches and rallies. Whereas a look at the many signs and banners unveils in an extremely condensed form what the most committed people in the crowd wanted to say (e.g., "Bush—Terrorist No. 1"; "No blood for oil"), analyzing the International Peace Protest Survey questionnaire, as done in several chapters in this volume, can give a more systematic picture of the participants' views. While the questionnaire mainly included lists of preformulated, that is "closed," answers, we also asked a key question that had no standardized answer options: "Why did you participate in the demonstrations on February 15, 2003? (Write down your answer in the box below)." The box provided space for about seven lines. Some demonstrators responded by writing down only one single word; most gave one or two short sentences; a clear minority completely filled the space provided. The answers to this open-ended question are, in our view, the most comprehensive and authentic data on the motives of the antiwar protesters on this particular day.

While it was already amazing to see that relatively few protesters refused to accept the questionnaire (see appendix A), we were even more surprised to learn how many of those who had completed their questionnaires had also answered the open-ended question. After all, this usually takes more time and reflection than to tick a box and is therefore often omitted by respondents in other research contexts. In our case, however, out of the 5,772 questionnaires that we received, a total of 78 percent included answers to this particular question. The response rates ranged from 44 percent in London to 97 percent each in Spain and the United States. This readiness to speak out confirms our general impression based on many conversations held while distributing the questionnaire: people were strongly motivated to express their views.

Exemplary Voices

We will first look at a few examples of how demonstrators have expressed their motives. Quite a number of protesters categorically rejected war ("War is no means to solve problems"; "Because I am convinced that war is always the wrong instrument to solve conflicts, regardless when and where"; "I am a pacifist"; "violence only breeds counterviolence").

Others rather rejected this particular war under the given circumstances ("I am opposing this war because it serves the hegemonic interest of the USA"; "This war is for the control of oil"; "I don't want my country, the U.S., to become the bully of the world"; "This war is absurd"; "Think this is about global domination"; "Because war is the last resort, not a first resort. After four years without inspections the inspectors have only been at work for 11 weeks"; "Because a war of pre-emption is immoral and illegal under international law and I'm worried we're setting a terrible precedent, not only for us, but the world"; "I feel a diplomatic solution is appropriate. I am not a pacifist"; "Because I think U.S. pre-emptive war is morally wrong, illegal, unconstitutional and un-American. Our government is betraying our ideals in a much more flagrant way than ever before").

A minority of respondents framed their opposition to war as part of a broader political struggle. For instance, a London demonstrator stated the "need for [a] vibrant anti imperialist movement in the metropolis of capital." Others defined the war as an act of "neo-colonialism," "imperialist politics," and the like. Still others expressed their solidarity with the Iraqi people or more generally with those who suffer from war and exploitation ("To prevent the killing of innocent Iraqi civilians"; "To save the life of Iraqis").

A substantial number of protesters made clear that they equally opposed the United States government and the government of Saddam Hussein ("No doubt that Saddam & his sons are worse than animals but killing innocent people will not remove them"). Most European protesters who criticized the U.S. position in particular emphasized that they were not against "America," the "USA," or "the American people" in general, but against Bush ("Bush is an asshole"), the U.S. government, the U.S. elites. Contrary to the views of many commentaries to be found mainly in conservative newspapers, very few respondents expressed views that could be interpreted as outright anti-American (see also Table 12.1), such as "USA is shit," "Because I am a confessing opponent of America," or "Hatred toward America and war." Demonstrators also referred to the particular situation in their home country ("I want to support Chancellor Schröder and Foreign Minister Fischer in their clear 'no' to this war"; "To protest the UK being the USA's lapdog").

A small minority commented on their personal situations to explain their opposition to war: "Because my nine-year old son asked me whether there will be war and what we could do against it"; "I have experienced World War Two and know about the consequences"; "Because I am a mother. Because I am a teacher . . . Because I am a human being . . ."; "I was representing my six small grandchildren"; "To show her [my daughter] an example of how to be an engaged citizen. To show her the beauty of being active in a community effort"; "I fear the draft").

Often along with more specific reasons, many demonstrators stated that they felt a moral obligation to express their dissent, that they didn't want to be counted among those who were indifferent, or that participation in the rally was the only means they had ("I felt a need to express my dissent. It's my right"; "I feel I have a civic duty to express my hope for a peaceful resolution"; "A need to 'stand up and be counted' in the effort to deflect our administration's policy versus Iraq"; "I felt I had to swell the numbers in the hope that PM [Prime Minister] would take notice of public opinion"; "Because it's the only action, within my reach, to try and stop this war"; "I demonstrated in hopes that this would send a message to other countries via news media"). These and many similar statements underscore that people not only protested for instrumental reasons but also wished to express their feelings of anger and frustration—and hope.

Indeed, in some responses hope was articulated that protest could eventually be successful ("We made a difference when we marched against war in Vietnam—we can do it again"; "Because I believe that the pressure of millions of people in the streets can have an impact"; I felt it was time to put my feet where my mouth is. I feel strongly and truly believe one can make a difference"). Yet a few respondents expressed doubts over whether protest could prevent war but still felt a need at least to try it, or, as one of them noted, "to be counted as a voice + body against the war and the policies of Bush and his war-mongers." Another demonstrator wrote: "To forget my desperateness because of our powerlessness and to make clear: This war, which cannot be prevented, shall not be fought in my name."

In addition, a marginal proportion of respondents said they were primarily or only present not to protest against war but for more mundane reasons ("To take pictures"; "To spend time with friends"; "Because my boyfriend organized a trip from Boston to take part in the rally") or on professional grounds ("Freelance journalist, interested in social movements"; "To document this event, I am a photographer").

While these selected statements give us a taste of the range and kind of individual reasoning behind participation in protest, they do not provide a systematic picture of the relative weight of different reasons and how these are related to certain characteristics of the protesters.

Quantitative Results

To process the total of 4,514 non-standardized answers, we categorized them according to our research interests. Because of different language capacities, we conducted the categorization at three different places. The coding was done on the basis of general explanations but without a joint training of the coders, let alone a test of intercoder reliability. Nevertheless, we believe that the data are acceptable, as long as we refer to the big picture and ignore both small numbers and small differences across categories.

In a first step, we inductively developed a classification of the various reasons to take part in the protest, ending up with seventeen categories. The results are displayed in Table 12.1. Because respondents often provided more than one reason to protest, the percentages add up to more than one hundred.

As it can be seen in the far right column of Table 12.1, in the aggregate of all countries, pacifist beliefs were the most frequent reason to protest (24 percent), followed by general criticisms against this war (22.1 percent), and a number of more specific reasons. Almost 14 percent mentioned the desire to express their views in front of the public. Anti-Americanism was entirely marginal, with an average of 0.3 percent across all countries. Substantial cross-national differences exist regarding attitudes toward the protesters' own countries' governments. Almost 10 percent of the Belgian demonstrators and almost 8 percent of those in Germany mentioned support of their government as a reason to take to the streets.[1] Yet substantial cross-national differences in the motives of protest also become apparent with regard to some other categories. Pacifism, for example, is rarely mentioned in the United States and the United Kingdom, by only 8.2 and 8.5 percent, respectively, but frequently in Italy,

Table 12.1. Reasons to participate in antiwar protest (percent)

	US	UK	SP	IT	NE	SW	BE	GE	Total
1. Pacifism	8.2	8.5	34.4	50.2	33.9	14.5	30	26.7	24
2. Criticism of reasons for war	23.9	40.2	18.9	8.9	22.9	14.2	23.6	20	22.1
3. Active policy-making or responsibility of civil society	18.9	16.7	8.3	12.3	9.9	26.2	7.2	11.5	14.9
4. Proclaiming own opinion	15.9	7.2	6.9	17.5	5.4	18.8	10.6	16.8	13.6
5. Criticism of Bush government	17.3	4	6.5	3	11.4	17.4	14.5	12.5	10.1
6. War breaks international law	4.4	5.5	26.6	1.7	5.6	2	4.8	6	6.2
7. Criticism of own government supporting Bush	–	12.5	16.9	5	7	–	0.2	0.5	5.1
8. Against political-military hegemony	2.8	3	2.8	2.2	6	5.4	9.5	6.7	4
9. Against capitalistic economic order	1.5	4.5	3.9	6.7	1.4	5.4	6.2	3.3	4
10. Danger for democracy	5.6	8	11.5	0.2	1.2	1.2	1.9	0.5	3.9
11. Support social movements	5	2.1	0.7	1.1	3.7	3.9	7.9	7.2	3.7
12. Personal worries	2.8	3.2	0.5	0.4	3.3	1.9	0.4	8.3	3.1
13. Solidarity with Iraqi people and Muslims	0.6	2.3	10.4	0.4	3.9	4.4	4.6	1.7	2.5
14. Social incentives or curiosity	2.9	1.3	0.5	2.6	2.9	2.5	1	3.5	2.4
15. Support governments against war	0.1	0.2	–	0.2	0.6	2	9.9	7.9	2
16. Anti-Americanism	–	0.2	0.5	0.4	1	0.5	0.6	0.3	0.3
17. Other reasons	11.3	9.1	0.9	9.3	12.2	6.9	6.6	7.9	8.6
Total	121.3	128.4	150.1	122.3	132.2	127.2	139.5	141.2	130.4
N	4,956	4,746	2,600	4,520	1,364	2,259	674	5,295	26,414

at around 50 percent. Considerable differences also become apparent regarding the category "War breaks international law," brought up frequently in Spain (26.6 percent) but rarely in Italy (1.7 percent) and Switzerland (2 percent). In Italy and Belgium, opposition to war was most often linked with a more general struggle against the capitalist economic order (6.7 percent and 6.2 percent), while in the United States, this was not the case (1.5 percent).

In a second step, we recoded applicable categories listed in Table 12.1 according to one dimension that we found to be of particular interest. We call this "type of reasoning," based on a "moral-affective" versus "cognitive" dichotomy.[2] While some items could not be classified according to this criterion, there were also the instances that the same respondents gave two or more reasons, of which one was "moral-affective" and another "cognitive."

Considering this "type of reasoning" dimension, we find that "cognitive" reasons to protest war have a significantly greater weight (33.5 percent) when compared to "moral-affective" reasons (16.0 percent; see Table 12.2). The gap is particularly big in the United States, with a difference of about 37 percent. Only among the Italian demonstrators did moral-affective reasons outnumber the cognitive ones.

Moreover, we can also study the correlation between the type of reasoning and several other characteristics of the protesters (figures not displayed). The relative weight of cognitive reasons increases with the level of education and age. Also, men mentioned cognitive reasons to a greater proportion than women did. But, contrary to common expectations, religion seems to be unrelated to the kind of reasoning. Also, there appears to be no significant correlation between the kind of reasoning on the one hand, and the position in the working sector, and the satisfaction with democracy on the other hand. Fewer protesters who claimed having taken part (only or also) in disruptive

Table 12.2. Type of reasoning, by country (percent)

	Moral-affective	Cognitive	Both	None
United States	8.5	45.4	2.7	43.4
United Kingdom / London	4.1	26.5	0.9	68.6
United Kingdom / Glasgow	4.4	30.2	3.4	62.0
Spain	22.1	45.4	18.8	13.7
Italy	20.7	9.0	2.5	67.9
Netherlands	26.4	34.3	11.1	28.2
Switzerland	14.4	33.9	4.2	47.4
Belgium	21.2	42.0	11.6	25.3
Germany	22.5	35.1	10.4	32.0
All countries (average)	16.0	33.5	7.3	43.2

actions in the past provided cognitive reasons when compared to those protesters who had participated only in moderate actions.

The Voices of Protest Organizers and Speakers in Public

In a second step, we shed some light on how the groups that organized the protest framed the antiwar cause in leaflets, calls for action, brochures, and speeches of group representatives and other individuals during the demonstration. While the above answers to the open-ended question had to be brief due to limited space, the written texts and the speeches were, of course, much longer and more elaborate.

The constituencies of groups and movements participating in the antiwar protest of February 15 were exposed to a flood of written material before and during the event. Among this material were various texts distributed within protest groups such as the "Anti-War Call" launched by the European Social Forum, and the "Platform against War on Iraq" issued at the preparatory meeting in Copenhagen (see chapter 1), public advertisements such as the one initiated by the U.S.-based Artists United to Win without War, the Business Leaders for Sensible Priorities, the Internet-based network MoveOn.org, and the speeches held wherever masses took the streets. Because we only have selective material from these various sources and cannot assume representativeness, we aim neither at a quantitative analysis nor at a comparison across countries. Rather, we present some examples we find interesting and noteworthy (see also Cortright 2004).

Many written signs of protest had straightforward messages. The shortest could be seen on a banner presented at London's Trafalgar Square: "No!" Flyers and calls for action often were headlined by "No war on Iraq," "Europe against the war," and the like. Such brief messages were occasionally accompanied by expressions of urgency as directly stated, for example, in an "URGENT world-wide call to action from CITIZEN to CITIZEN" distributed by the U.S.-based group United for Peace. This sense of importance comes from the perception of being "on the verge of a major disaster" that can only be prevented by "the world public." Another example was an advertisement entitled "Prime Minister Blair, It Is Two Minutes before Midnight," published in five UK newspapers: the *Guardian,* the *Independent,* the *London Times,* the *Telegraph,* and the *Financial Times.* Combined with this dramatic gesture, activists often assured that protest would matter, as indicated in both the first and the final sentence of the "Anti-War Call" by the European Social Forum: "Together we can stop this war" and "We can stop this war."

A further characteristic of such written documents was signaling to the public that this war is "Not in our name," a message that could be made specific by adding a particular addressee, such as "Not in our name, Mr. Blair" (Scottish Campaign for Nuclear Disarmament) or sender "Not in Iraqis' names: Exiles thank the worldwide peace movement" (petition).

Besides slogans and catchy headlines, many texts stressed specific reasons for opposing the war in Iraq. The three-column advertisements sponsored by the New York–based Business Leaders for Sensible Priorities presented four arguments in bold letters: "Warning—War Will Wreck Economy"; "Warning—War Will Breed Terrorism"; "Warning—War Will Discredit America"; "Warning—War Will Take a Terrible Toll on Human Life."

While many texts exclusively focused on the war and its immediate consequences, others related the opposition to war with other kinds of struggles. This is illustrated by a flyer from the ANSWER (Act Now to Stop War and End Racism) Coalition in the United States. The group announced a Week of Anti-war Resistance, starting on February 13, with "youth and student action, teach-ins and forums" on the twelfth anniversary of the Gulf War bombing of a shelter in Iraq and ending with a "Students and Youth Action on the anniversary of the assassination of Malcolm X, a Coordinated Day of Resistance including student walk-outs from hundreds of high schools and colleges—and other acts of non-compliance" on February 21.

Quite a number of flyers and other texts emphasized the massiveness and worldwide character of the resistance to war. This is stressed in both the European Social Forum's "Anti-War Call"—"There is a massive opposition to war in every country in Europe. Hundreds of thousands have already mobilised for peace"—and the December 15, 2002, Copenhagen declaration: "It is clear that there is majority to war in almost every country in Europe and across the world. This is why this war cannot be fought in our name." In the advent of the February 15 protest, organizers further encouraged potential participants by confronting them with lists of countries or cities in which protest activities had been scheduled. For example, at the bottom of a call for action distributed by the UK Stop the War Coalition, some eighty cities are listed, starting with Adelaide and ending with "Wollongong and many more (total over 600)." Thus, contrary to Mancur Olson's theory that individuals would be reluctant to participate in mass collective action when their own contributions would not make a difference (Olson 1965), the organizers of the February 15 protests were right in assuming the opposite: the bigger the forthcoming event seemed to become, the more it would attract additional people who otherwise would be reluctant to participate—as theoretically expected in the threshold model proposed by Granovetter (1978). In other words: beyond the substantive arguments to oppose the war, the mere size of the expected protests was also considered a motivator for participation in protest, as expressed in such answers to the open-ended questionnaire as "I want to be counted" or "To be another body in a mass of bodies." In a similar vein, organizers not only pointed to the (expected) mass of people but also to the broad variety of different groups and social strata opposed to war, ranging from U.S. veterans of the Vietnam War to the UK "Dog Owners against War Stunt" (as mentioned in a flyer of the Stop the War Coalition) to the Marxist-Leninist Bolshewik Partizan, a group of Kurds aiming at building a Bolshevist Party in Germany.

Furthermore, the various speeches and performances of the February 15 demonstrations were deliberately chosen to exhibit the variety of protest groups and reasons to protest. Consider, for example, the program of the Berlin event, which consisted of two gatherings earlier in the day (in old East and West Berlin) from which marches led to the main site of the rally. The whole event was coordinated by the Netzwerk Friedenskooperative (Network of the German Peace Movement), which was part of a much broader Action Alliance February 15. Besides a variety of music (e.g., drums, Soul and Gospel Choir Berlin, and well-known singers), poems, theater, and recitation, the program included speeches by representatives of the East German citizen movements that had toppled the communist regime and from members of trade unions and, among others, peace, Christian, immigrant, youth, and medical groups. Their speeches, whose transcripts were distributed on the Internet in the aftermath of the event, offered a broad range of arguments against the war: moral, social, political, juridical, social, and environmental. Also, they indicated hidden agendas behind the official declarations of politicians ready to engage in warfare; pointed to disastrous consequences; appealed to the demonstrators and the worldwide public to take action; linked this struggle to struggles in other periods, places, and policy areas; emphasized the unique character of this protest as part of a worldwide event; supported—in the German case—the position of their own government; and expressed hope that war could be prevented if millions of people said "no." All shared the belief that war in principle, or at least this war, under the given circumstances, is immoral and wrong. The declaration from the Netzwerk Friedenskooperative read by one of its speakers at the very end of the main rally concludes by stating: "Peace is not everything, but without peace there is nothing!"

On the eve of the antiwar demonstration in Berlin, several more-or-less prominent critics presenting themselves as the Coalition against Anti-Semitism, in an open letter to the media, had accused the antiwar groups of being "anti-American" and "politically naïve." Probably in reaction to this, several speakers at the antiwar demonstration expressed their sympathy with "peace-loving Americans" while at the same time opposed not only the Bush administration but also the repressive regime of Saddam Hussein and his Bath Party. The criticism of being "anti-American" is also rejected in a written statement entitled "The Peace Movement Is Anything but Anti-American." The authors maintain their opposition to the war plans of the Bush government while defining their protest even as pro-American insofar as they endorse "one of the greatest achievements of the United States: The rule of law" (Bundesausschuss Friedensratschlag, 2002).

Reviewing numerous written and oral statements by the antiwar protesters, it is obvious that the lowest common denominator is that this war is morally and politically wrong. However, the various motives of and reasons for this opposition vary considerably, so that we cannot identify a single overarching ideological master frame (for this concept, see Snow and Benford 1992) shared by all participants. Whereas outspoken leftist participants tended to interpret the war as an expression of imperialism, other groups perceived it more as the consequence of misperception of a number of factors, such as Iraq's weapons arsenal, its contribution to international terrorism, and the chances of establishing a peaceful and democratic order after the war. Clearly, the imminent war offered platforms to a broad variety of issue-specific groups for relating their cause to the opposition to war, thereby providing many examples of frame-bridging and frame-extension, as discussed in the literature (Snow at al. 1986). Also, we found clear examples of the three components of collective action frames that Gamson (1992, 7) has identified, namely injustice, agency, and identity.

For the most part, however, mass protest is not an end in itself. As expressed by many participants, it is meant to send a strong signal to a large, possibly worldwide, audience that, ultimately, may have an impact on decision-makers. To this aim, it is necessary to attract media attention and, if all goes well, positive media coverage (Molotch 1979; Walgrave and Manssens 2000; Verhulst and Walgrave 2006).

Media Coverage of the Iraq Crisis and the February 15 Demonstrations

Most of our knowledge of current affairs in the world stems from television, radio, and/or newspapers. This news is not an unbiased reflection of reality but is selected according to news values and news routines, framing preferences and political positions. Studies have documented the U.S. media's agenda-setting, priming, and framing impact on mass opinion during the 1991 Gulf War (Iyengar and Simon 1994). With regard to the 2003 Iraq War, Kull, Ramsay, and Lewis (2004) showed that a large segment of the U.S. public, during and after the war, held misperceptions. These people thought weapons of mass destruction had actually been found in Iraq, that there was indisputable proof of the link between Saddam Hussein and Osama bin Laden, and that the majority of world public opinion supported the U.S intervention. Kull and his colleagues found these misperceptions to be strongly associated with media use. For example, Fox News viewers held more misperceptions than CNN viewers, regardless of their educational or professional backgrounds. Clearly, news sources do matter. And, as seen in chapter 3, they also matter at the national level. In different countries, the Iraq crisis was framed differently, which was likely to affect mobilization potential and, ultimately, the kind of people that actually took the streets. This brings us to social movements. For them, mass media coverage can be a matter of life and death (Walgrave and Manssens 2000; Verhulst and Walgrave 2005). Media can validate and legitimize social movements' existence (Gamson and Wolfsfeld 1993; 'Smith 1999). Mass media link social movements to their mobilization potential and can help movements recruit new adherents and attract additional financial resources (Barker-Plummer 2002). Positive coverage of movements can enhance their impact on political decision-making. But the relationship between social movements and mass media is fundamentally asymmetrical, with the former much more dependent on the latter (Gamson and Wolfsfeld 1993; Verhulst and Walgrave 2005; Rucht 2005). Movements have a tough job in competing with other societal actors and events to gain media attention (selection bias). And once a message or event is in the media, the question remains of how the media report on it (description bias) (Smith et al. 2001; Verhulst and Walgrave 2005; McLeod 1995; Cooper 2002). This is what we want to find out in the remainder of this chapter: Did the antiwar movements manage to get some of their arguments and frames on the Iraq conflict into the press? How were the February 15 protests covered, and how did the nationwide newspapers portray the demonstrators?

Chapter 3 explored the relationships among national governments' positions on the Iraq conflict, public opinion on the eventuality of war, and how the media reported on the Iraq crisis. In summary, in those countries where the governments were trying to engage in war, both national media and public opinion were basically supportive of the government's stance. Where the national governments strongly opposed the war, the media and public opinion tended to share this position. Finally, in countries where the government's position on the eventuality of war was limited to lukewarm and/or merely oral support, the newspapers and (eventually) public opinion tended to not support the government's stance. In all countries, national press coverage and public opinion on the eventuality of war converged.

Framing of the Iraq Conflict

As we did in chapter 3, we will use original media data. In each of the eight countries, we analyzed three newspapers: the major left-leaning broadsheet, the major right-leaning broadsheet, and the most popular national (or local) newspaper. All papers were scrutinized for articles on the Iraq conflict, using the neutral search term "Iraq," between January 21, 2003, that is, three weeks preceding the February 15 protests, and March 21, 2003, the day after the invasion of Iraq began. We aimed at obtaining three articles per day and per newspaper. In sum, 3,968 articles were selected and coded. Additional methodological information can be found in appendix A.

An initial question is whether the antiwar sentiments of the February 15 demonstrators were reflected in the different national newspapers and to what degree these papers report on reasons why a war should not (yet) be waged. Out of all articles, 1,521 (38 percent) mentioned at least one reason not to go to war. Similar to the variety of responses of the protesters to the question why they took part in the demonstration, the reasons not go to war mentioned in the newspapers were quite diverse (see Figure 12.1). The disregarding of the UN procedures, and the work and views of its weapons inspectors, constituted the lion's share of the reasons mentioned why war should not be waged (yet). When all UN-related reasons are cumulated, the

Reason	Percent
UN inspectors doing a good job; no evidence of weapons of mass destruction	48.6
Lack of UN war mandate; damage to United Nations; illegality of preemptive strike	45.2
Pacifism: no war as a political tool	14.2
Economic interest or oil	10.0
War will fuel (religious) terrorism or be perceived as West-Islam aggression	8.2
Destabilization of Middle East	6.1
Lack of link between Iraq and al-Qaeda	5.3
Double standards (invasion only of Iraq, no other country)	4.8
Iraqi regime no threat to world peace	3.5
Cost of war to tax payers or to country's resources	3.6
War fought for religious reason	2.8
No hope for democratization	2.5
Lack of after-war strategy	2.4
War as dangerous precedent	2.4
Bush administration or family wanting to finish job of Gulf War	1.7
(Future) casualties among own troops	1.5
War as distraction from bad domestic policy	1.3
N	1,512

Figure 12.1. Reasons for not going war, as mentioned in newspapers

second most important reason is pacifism, in the sense that war can never be accepted as a political tool. Remarkably, this reason is more often mentioned than, for example the economic interests in war (control over oil) or the fact that war will raise the chance of religiously based terrorism. This is consistent with the motivations made explicit by the February 15 demonstrators, who mentioned cognitive reasons more frequently than moral-affective reasons, including pure pacifism.

Regarding the newspaper reports, pacifism is the most frequently mentioned reason not to go to war (as it was for the February 15 protesters). In cross-national comparison, pacifism was least mentioned in the United States and the United Kingdom (as was also the pattern for the protesters from those countries) and most frequently stated in Spain. In general, the rank order for pacifism across countries is the same for newspapers and protesters (see Figure 12.2).

When looking from a cross-national perspective at the weight of various topics and issues as reported in the newspapers under study here, the first striking finding is the differential reference to the domestic government in the context of the Iraq conflict (figures are not displayed). By far the most references to the domestic government were found in the U.S. press, followed by the UK and German press. This is understandable for the war-leading countries for which the government plays a crucial role. However, we have no explanation for why Germany and Belgium, as war-opposing countries, differ so widely in terms of references to the own government. Divisions within the press's own government were most salient in the United Kingdom, and, accordingly, were reported in almost every fifth article. German newspapers mentioned a divided Europe most often; they also covered the

	Percent of articles
United States	6.5
United Kingdom	7.2
Spain	27.2
Italy	16.0
Netherlands	10.0
Switzerland	16.2
Belgium	14.4
Germany	18.2
Total	14.2
N	1,559

Figure 12.2. Mentions of pacifism ("war is no political tool") in newspapers per country

divided opinions within the United Nations (as did U.S. papers). In Switzerland and the United States, overall opposition to war was mentioned least frequently. In sum, the German press was most frequently referring to various kinds of actors opposing the war, while the papers in Spain and the United Kingdom reported most frequently on opposition among the populace. The costs of war were most often referred to in the United States and in the United Kingdom, the two countries that were the most determined to engage in warfare. The idea that war cannot be prevented, however, was not as widespread in the news outlets of these two countries as it was in the Italian press. The opposite idea, that war could still be prevented, was most frequently found in the Spanish and German presses. In the United States, which can be considered the most crucial player, the press highlighted the domestic government's role and aspects of war preparation and war costs but remained relatively silent on dissident voices.

Coverage and Framing of the February 15 Protests

In the two-month period around February 15, protests were mentioned in 270 articles (about 7 percent of all articles), with the Belgian and German press far above average (16.5 and 13 percent, respectively) and all other countries at about 4 percent. The actual protests mentioned in the articles add up to 414 different events, of which most were referred to in Germany and Belgium, followed by the United States and the UK. Hence, protest is of greatest interest to the press in the countries that range at the far ends of the pro-antiwar scale. Nonetheless, the way protests were covered might have been different, more critical on the one end and more supportive on the other.

Because we are especially interested in how the February 15 protests were covered, we will only focus on protests mentioned between February 14 and 22 and only those in the Western countries or that were reported as "worldwide." We counted 130 protests mentioned in the selected period, the most in the United Kingdom (36) and the fewest in Switzerland (2).[3] Many of the titles of the articles referring to the protests or public opinion on war, especially those in the United States, featured an antiwar voice: "French See Bush as the Ugly American" (*USA Today*, February 14); "From New York to Melbourne, Cries for Peace" (*New York Times*, February 16); "US Builds War Coalition with Favors—and Money" (*USA Today*, February 15), and "Blair Under Siege Over Stance on Iraq. Opposition Up, Poll Numbers Down" (*Washington Post*, February 19).

In the UK press, the titles were more upfront, with some of them pointing to the dwindling popularity of the country's prime minister: "Blair's Popularity Plummets" (*Guardian*, February 18); "Blair Hasn't Even Won the

Establishment Round to War" (*Times,* February 20), or "This Government no Longer Speaks for Me. Voices of Protest" (*Guardian,* February 17). In other titles, the prime minister was mentioned as holding the line in spite of the loud antiwar voices: "Blair to Defy Anti-War protests: Million-Strong Demonstrations Will Not Deflect Iraq Policy as Ministers Rally around Prime Minister" (*Guardian,* February 17); "The Peace Marches: Blair's Warning: 'Weakness Will Be Paid in Blood.' Impassioned Prime Minister States the 'Moral Case' for Ousting Saddam" (*Guardian,* February 16). And finally, some titles directly referred to the expected mass protests. For example, two articles in the *Times* predicted: "Glasgow March May Be Biggest since World War 2" and "Protests Will Reach Every Continent" (both February 14). Similar titles can be found in other papers: "The Peace Marchers: One Million" and "People Power Takes to the World's Streets" (both in *Guardian,* February 16). The *Sun,* the tabloid that openly backed the government's position on war (e.g., "Blair Can See Big Picture" [February 28]; "Selfish Chirac Shows France's True Colors" [March 3]) did not mention any kind of protest in articles we found for this period, providing a stunning example of a selection bias.

For Spain, we only had *El Mundo* reporting on the protests in this period—for example, "The Old Europe Does Not Want a War" (February 16). *La Stampa,* in Italy, provided a similar picture: "Five Kilometers of Protest" (February 16). These papers exhibited a positive attitude toward the antiwar voices. As said, in Switzerland, only two protests, both in the *Tages-Anzeiger,* were mentioned in the articles we selected for the period from February 14 to 22. In Belgium, protests mentioned in this period were always reported in a neutral way, for example "Human Chain against War in Iraq" (*Het Laatste Nieuws,* February 19). In Germany, except for "Scholar Does Not Believe in Continuation of Protests" (*Frankfurter Rundschau,* February 18) and a negative report, "Who Demonstrated against Saddam" (*Bild,* February 14), all relevant article titles were neutral or supportive of the protest.

Moving beyond the titles, we looked at how the protests were portrayed in the text body. The total of 130 articles in the nine-day period does not really allow for a meaningful quantitative analysis. Yet some quotes and references provide us with an idea of how the February 15 protests and protesters were presented in the press. Demonstrators' characteristics were referred to in one out of five articles in this period. With one or two exceptions, all stressed the participants' amazing diversity: "college students, middle-aged couples, families with small children, older people, environmental, and religious groups, business and civic organizations" (*New York Times,* February 16). In the UK press, with the exception of one reference to "anarchists," the demonstrators were described as "people with an astonishing variety of backgrounds and political viewpoints" (*Guardian,* February 17); or "nuns, CND, social workers, anarchists, Walthamstow Catholic Church" members (ibid., February 16) or "a mixture of pacifists, nuclear disarmers and hard-leftists. Many of the people were not pacifists or ultra-leftists (though they naively gave credibility to the latter impressions) but part of the United Kingdom's liberal conscience" (*Times,* February 20). In the Spanish *El Mundo* (February 16), the February 15 demonstrators were portrayed as being a mixture of "Catholics, pacifists, immigrants, members of the Green Party, religious minorities, parliamentarians of all the parties of the left-wing." Papers in Italy, the Netherlands, Belgium, and Germany provided similar descriptions. Yet, the German press also disproportionally referred to the presence of ministers and members of parliament "[German politicians] Thierse, Trittin, Wieczorek-Zeul" (*Frankfurter Allgemeine Zeitung,* February 17), or "[ministers] Wieczorek-Zeul, Künast, Trittin, and [head of parliament] Thierse" (*Frankfurter Rundschau,* February 15). It seems that German politicians were well aware of the popularity of their antiwar stance. In all countries, the media tended to stress the astounding diversity of the February 15 protesters, thereby painting a picture that did not match reality, as the results of our survey have shown (see, in particular, chapter 5).

By and large, the demonstrations received newspaper coverage of which most organizers only can dream: protests were said not just to be the largest ever seen, but in addition, to have attracted ordinary people from all parts of the country and all layers of society. It seemed that the world had said no to war on February 15.

Our final question concerns the ultimate challenge for protest organizers: In addition to positively framing the demonstrations, did they also succeed in getting their substantive message across? The answer, again, is mostly positive. Slogans such as "the world says no to war," "no blood for oil," "we can stop the war," "don't attack Iraq" and "not in my name" were mentioned in almost all countries. In Italy, Spain, and the Netherlands, these general catchphrases were complemented by those targeting the leaders of both war-initiating and war-opposing countries. In Spain, for example, one could read "USA Stay Home" (*El Mundo,* February 17); "Schröder Be Strong. Don't Go to War" and "The Old Europe Doesn't Want a New War" (both in *El Mundo,* February 16). Italian and Dutch papers echoed such messages. In Belgium, the demonstrators were described as applauding their minister of foreign affairs: "Thanks Michel—Merci Michel" (*Het Laatste Nieuws,* February 17) for his efforts to block a war-favoring NATO decision (see chapter 1). Yet in Germany, apart from more general statements for peace, only one cited slogan indirectly addressed the UK government: "Make Tea, Not War!" (*Frank-furter Allgemeine Zeitung,* February 17).

To summarize, the newspaper coverage of the Iraq crisis was far from uni-form. Again, this proves that national context matters. The UK and especially the U.S. press regarded the war as a national issue, with much attention paid to its "practical" side, in terms of preparation, tactics, and costs, and with relatively little emphasis on pacifism as a reason not to go to war. In the UK press, considerable attention was given to the antiwar opposition within Prime Minister Blair's Labour ranks. German press, however, reported on the Iraq crisis as an international issue in which many countries were involved and where many war-disapproving voices could be heard. A reflection of this atti-tude is the importance given the concept of pacifism in German newspaper articles. In all other countries' presses, too, the crisis was portrayed as an internationalist issue, with Italian and Spanish newspapers paying much atten-tion to opinions that disapproved of the war and to pacifism as a reason not to go to war. Yet, regarding the coverage of the February 15 protests in par-ticular, differences are much smaller. In all countries, the protests tended to be portrayed as positive events that brought onto the streets masses of diverse people that could not be ignored. And, finally, the protesters also got their messages and main slogans across.

Conclusion

In this chapter, we have used three kinds of sources—the voices of the "ordi-nary" demonstrators, the organizers and speakers of the protests, and the newspapers—to see how opposition to the (then imminent) war against Iraq was communicated and framed. We highlight three general findings. First, opposition to war was based not on a one-dimensional view but on a broad variety of arguments, ranging from principal opposition anchored in uncon-ditional pacifism to very specific reasons. Pacifism was the reason against war most frequently mentioned by both the protesters and the newspapers. Al-though all protesters agreed that the war was unjust and unfounded, we were unable to identify an overarching interpretative ideological master frame for this opposition. Rather, we found a broad array of reasons to protest, among which, contrary to the views of some observers, anti-Americanism was ex-tremely marginal.

Second, the various arguments and frames regarding the war were not evenly distributed across countries. Context mattered even in cases where countries seemed similarly affected by the (potential) war. The single factor with the biggest impact on the pattern of communication was whether gov-ernments were actively willing to, or would eventually, engage in warfare (the United States and the United Kingdom) or reject it outright (Germany and Belgium). Countries somewhere in between these extreme positions tended to exhibit a more inconsistent pattern.

Third, while there seems much congruence in the views of the "ordinary" protesters and the protest organizers and speakers, the media, not surprisingly, were more selective in what exactly they reported about reasons for objecting to the war. Again, variation across countries is significant, reflecting not only the position of the governments and public opinion toward war and protest, but also specific political constellations, for example, a divided government in the United Kingdom. By the same token, the newspapers in the United States, the country bearing the brunt of the costs of war, tended to downplay the scope of opposition in other countries and international institutions as well as in their own country. Overall, however, the protesters were taken seriously by most newspapers and covered in a neutral or even positive manner. Also, unlike in many other instances of protest, where media tend to focus on side aspects rather than protesters' views and motivations, the protesters were able to get their basic messages across. In part, this might be explained by media and public opinion that sympathized with their cause. To some extent, however, this relatively favorable way of reporting may also be a function of the protest's sheer size and perceived—but actually much more limited—social heterogeneity. While relatively small groups of protesters, even when covered by the mass media, can be easily presented in a disrespectful and distorted way, such a characterization is hardly advisable when millions of supposedly ordinary citizens (and media consumers!) take to the streets. By and large, through media, the public in the eight countries under study could get a clear idea of the scope and reasons of opposition to war, though some analyzed newspapers tended to ignore or misrepresent the protest altogether.

Notes

1. Note that in the German case, for example, protesters even criticized their own war-opposing government, because this government tended to tolerate logistic support to the war by allowing U.S. troops on German soil.

2. Items 1, 12, and 13 were classified as "moral-affective." Items 2 and 5 to 10 were classified as "cognitive."

3. Note that this is not a protest event analysis. We did not systematically gather press articles reporting on protests. Rather, when any protest was mentioned in an article we had found using search word "Iraq," our encoders filled out a separate encoding form for it.

Works Cited

Barker-Plummer, Bernadette. 2002. "Producing Public Voice: Resource Mobilization and Media Access in the National Organization for Women." *Journalism and Mass Communication Quarterly* 79: 188–205.

Bennett, Lance W., and Robert M. Entman, eds. 2001. *Mediated Politics: Communication in the Future of Democracy*. Cambridge: Cambridge University Press.

Bundesausschuss Friedensratschlag [Federal Committee on Peace Discourse]. 2002. "Die Friedensbewegung ist alles andere als 'antiamerikanisch.'" *AG Friedensforschung an der Uni Kassel: Veranstalter des Friedenspolitischen Ratschlags*. February 18. Kassel, Germany. http://www.uni-kassel.de/fb5/frieden/bewegung/antiamerikanismus.html.

Cooper, Alice H. 2002. "Media Framing and Social Movement Mobilization: German Peace Protest against INF Missiles, the Gulf War, and NATO Peace Enforcement in Bosnia." *European Journal of Political Research* 41: 37–80.

Cortright, David. 2004. *A Peaceful Superpower: The Movement against War in Iraq*. Goshen, Ind.: Fourth Freedom Forum.

Ferree, Myra Marx, William A. Gamson, Jürgen Gerhards, and Dieter Rucht. 2002. *Shaping Abortion Discourse: Democracy and the Public Sphere in Germany and the United States*. Cambridge: Cambridge University Press.

Gamson, William A. 1992. *Talking Politics*. Cambridge: Cambridge University Press.

Gamson, William A., and Andre Modigliani. 1989. "Media Discourse and Public Opinion on Nuclear Power: A Constructionist Approach." *American Journal of Sociology* 95: 1–37.

Gamson, William A., and Gadi Wolfsfeld. 1993. "Movements and Media as Interacting Systems." *Annals of the AAPSS* 28:114–25.

Gerhards, Jürgen, and Dieter Rucht. 1992. "Mesomobilization: Organizing and Framing in Two Protest Campaigns in West Germany." *American Journal of Sociology* 98: 555–95.

Granovetter, Mark. 1978. "Threshold Models of Collective Behavior." *American Journal of Sociology* 83: 1420–43.

Hilgartner, Stephen, and Charles L. Bosk. 1988. "The Rise and Fall of Social Problems: A Public Arenas Model." *American Journal of Sociology* 94: 53–78.

Iyengar, Shanto, and Adam Simon. 1994. "News Coverage of the Gulf Crisis and Public Opinion." In *Taken by Storm: The Media, Public Opinion, and U.S. Foreign Policy in the Gulf War*, ed. W. Lance Bennett and David L. Paletz, 167–85. Chicago: University of Chicago Press.

Kull, Steven, Clay Ramsay, and Evan Lewis. 2004. "Misperceptions, the Media, and the Iraqi War." *Political Science Quarterly* 118: 569–98.

McLeod, Douglas M. 1995. "Communicating Deviance: The Effects of Television

News Coverage of Social Protest." *Journal of Broadcasting and Electronic Media* 39: 4–19.

Molotch, Harvey. 1979. "Media and Movements." In *The Dynamics of Social Movements: Resource Mobilization, Social Control, and Tactics,* ed. Mayer N. Zald and John D. McCarthy, 71–93. Cambridge, Mass.: Winthrop.

Olson, Mancur. 1965. *The Logic of Collective Action: Public Goods and the Theory of Groups.* Cambridge, Mass.: Harvard University Press.

Rucht, Dieter. 2005. "Appeal, Threat, and Press Resonance: Comparing Mayday Protests in London and Berlin." *Mobilization* 10: 163–81.

Smith, Jackie, John D. McCarthy, Clark McPhail, and Augustyn Boguslaw. 2001. "From Protest to Agendabuilding: Description Bias in Media Coverage of Protest Events in Washington, D.C." *Social Forces* 79: 1397–424.

Smith, Paul. 1999. "Political Communication in the UK: A Study of Pressure Group Behaviour." *Politics* 19: 21–27.

Snow, David A., and Robert D. Benford. 1988. "Ideology, Frame Resonance, and Participant Mobilization." In *From Structure to Action: Comparing Social Movement Research across Cultures,* ed. Bert Klandermans, Hanspeter Kriesi, and Sidney Tarrow, 137–96. Greenwich, Conn.: JAI Press.

———. 1992. "Master Frames and Cycles of Protest." In *Frontiers in Social Movement Theory,* ed. Aldon D. Morris and Carol McClurg Mueller, 133–55. New Haven: Yale University Press.

Snow, David A., E. Bourke Rochford, Steven K. Worden, and Robert D. Benford. 1986. "Frame Alignment Processes, Micromobilization, and Movement Participation." *American Sociological Review* 51: 464–81.

Verhulst, Joris, and Stefaan Walgrave. 2005. "Gezien worden of Gezien zijn? Over Nieuwe en Oude sociale bewegingen in de Vlaamse pers." *Mens en Maatschappij* 80: 305–27.

Walgrave, Stefaan, and Jan Manssens. 2000. "The Making of the White March." *Mobilization* 5: 217–40.

Conclusion:
Studying Protest in Context

Stefaan Walgrave and Dieter Rucht

On February 15, 2003, an unprecedented mass of people publicly expressed their indignation in hundreds of cities around the globe. About one month later, the United States and its allies did what the demonstrators had sought to prevent: they invaded Iraq because of its alleged possession of weapons of mass destruction. At least to the invaders, it seemed that this war would soon come to an end. On May 1, 2003, aboard the aircraft carrier *Abraham Lincoln*, President Bush declared "one victory." Behind him hung a banner reading "Mission Accomplished." However, as we write these lines in April 2008, the war in Iraq is still not over. The large contingent of troops mainly from the United States and United Kingdom seems incapable of controlling the situation even after the Bush administration increased the contingent of in Iraq. In hindsight, it appears that the fears of the February 15 demonstrators were largely warranted—no wonder the fifth anniversary of the beginning of the war provoked another wave of protest in many countries.

This volume, however, does not discuss whether the reasons for war were legitimate, which course the war took, or what consequences it had. Rather, we have engaged in analyzing who those demonstrators against imminent war were, why they took to the streets, and how they were mobilized. We drew on exceptional empirical evidence based on thousands of answers to a questionnaire that was distributed in eleven cities in eight Western countries. Our main aim was to compare the demonstrators in the eight nations to make headway in understanding how the protest events on February 15 were set up with relation to a specific environment, and how they were determined by their specific context. The apparently homologous nature of the protest events under study—timing, slogans, action type, platform, and so forth were almost identical—gave us the unique opportunity to investigate the similarities and differences of these protests and the reasons that may account for them.

Our Ambition, Theoretical Framework, and Assumptions

The central idea for our endeavor was that the protests on February 15 must be studied in their political, social, and cultural context. We set ourselves apart from the classic political participation studies, as they entirely decontextualize protest participation and do not allow the examination of how protest motivation and eventual actual participation are molded by the structural and situational environment. We also argue that most social movement studies, even when taking a comparative perspective, have difficulties in identifying and weighing causal factors because too many variables come into play (see Kolb 2007). In our cross-national research setting, however, the issue, time frame, and form of protest is held constant. In this regard, we had an ideal research setting—a kind of "natural experiment" that allows us to study the impact of contextual factors.

The available macro- and meso-level theoretical perspectives do not offer clear clues as what to expect of individual protesters, their sociostructural features, attitudes, and behaviors. The political opportunity structure approach, for example, which seems to be well suited for comparative analysis, does not make inferences about individual protesters. Rather, it was designed to explain meso-level variables (social movements, social movement organizations, and campaigns and their successes) or even macrolevel variables (the amount and cycles of protest in a given society). Therefore, in the introductory chapter, we suggested five different context layers that may determine or predetermine what individual participants may look like.

First and very generally, we assumed that the sociodemographic composition of the population at large has an impact on the composition of the protester populations. If people in a country are generally highly skilled, we expect a large proportion of protesters in that country to be highly skilled as well, at least in a protest that does not recruit a particular social group such as farmers or workers. Second, stable structural features of the political system may also play a role, as they may determine the strength of the general movement sector on which specific protest events can build. We hypothesized that certain political structures foster a strong progressive movement sector, which, in turn, is likely to produce a high turnout in peace protest. Third, we introduced the concept of the issue-specific context, referring to the particular political and social environment in which a certain protest event is staged. How do government and opposition position themselves on the issue? Is there support on part of the mass media? What does the public at large think about the issue? Probably more so than general political opportunities, the issue-specific context matters in terms of the size and kind of protest and the characteristics of the protesters. Fourth, we assumed that, additionally, social movements and their structures, goals, and strategies affect the profiles of the protesters. In countries with a strong peace movement, for example, we expected the February 15 protests to be populated to a greater extent by peace movement activists than in other countries. Finally, we also expected demonstrators' characteristics to be influenced by the specific mobilization strategies and processes that the organizers used to incite people to take to the streets.

Main Descriptive and Explanatory Findings

In this volume, we were not able to systematically test the preliminary model, which, at any rate, should be considered more of a toolbox or heuristic device than the result of an integrated theory. In particular, we could not assess the relative weight of these five contextual layers. Yet, looking at the empirical evidence presented in this volume, we believe we can safely state that at least parts of the model seemed to have worked quite well and therefore offer valuable insights for better understanding the factors and mechanisms of protest participation.

One of our key findings is that quite substantial differences exist among the February 15 protesters in the eight countries studied. This holds in spite of the fact that we chose to investigate protesters from similar countries (regarding the logic of a most-similar-systems design, see Przeworski and Teune 1970) focusing on the same issue, responding to the same call issued in a prior social movement meeting, and, finally, protesting on the same day. Yet it was only at first glance that the protesters might have appeared very similar— with the same slogans, appearance, et cetera. As a matter of fact, contrary to our initial expectations, the protesters in the eight countries exhibited considerable cross-national differences in their sociodemographic profile, their attitudes, and their behaviors.

Regarding the sociodemographic profiles, of course, the average demonstrator, in the aggregate of all countries, resembled the typical new social movements' activists with high levels of education, a relatively large proportion of whom were women, belonged to the younger age cohorts, and predominantly worked in the human service sector. But beneath this aggregate profile we found notable differences. Just two examples: demonstrators were much younger in Switzerland, and in Belgium, an extremely large percentage of demonstrators had high educational levels and a disproportionately large number of them were male (see chapter 5).

In a cross-national perspective, attitudes varied as well. To be sure, all who protested on February 15 were strongly opposed to the war. Nearly all participants thought that it was fought for political control and/or control over oil, and that war without UN approval was unjustified. But apart from this general rejection of war on Iraq, we came across significant differences among countries in the degree of unconditional pacifism, the embeddedness of antiwar positions in broader opposition to the government, or general feelings of political dissatisfaction (see chapter 6). The protesters, when asked an open-ended question about their reasons and motives to participate, offered a broad range of arguments, again showing significant differences across countries (see chapter 12). Neither in their answers nor in written pamphlets and speeches held during the demonstrations did we find evidence of an overarching ideological master frame as a driving force to protest, apart from general statements, as expressed in the joint call for action, to "fight . . . for social rights and social justice, for democracy and against all forms of oppression." Interestingly, anti-Americanism, an important reason underlying the protest according to some commentators, was almost completely absent in these many answers.

We also found significant variation in the extent of membership in political groups and previous protest activity. In general, many respondents to our questionnaire had considerable protest experience, and many were active in voluntary associations and social movements. But in some countries—the Netherlands, for example—the clear majority of the demonstrators had taken to the streets before. And in other countries, the United Kingdom, for instance, protesters were much less engaged in civil society groups (see chapters 7 and 10). Participation in the antiwar protest is strongly correlated with a leftist orientation and identification with the global justice movements and similar groups focusing, for example, on labor and social issues, or third-world solidarity (chapter 7). However, many of the organizations running the protest were not primarily oriented toward peace issues (chapter 10). In other words, the protesters, characterized by "complex political identifications," according to the analysis in chapter 11, were recruited from a broad spectrum of political and social groups. Again, the range of these groups varies across countries, with broader alliances, for instance, in Italy, Spain, and the Netherlands, where governments were supporting the war from a more cautious and less committed position, and smaller alliances in the war-leading United States and United Kingdom (chapter 10). In line with earlier research findings (e.g., Dalton 2002), the demonstrators, when asked about their previous political activities, tended to mention both unconventional and conventional forms of action. As chapter 8 shows, they were not turned off completely from the electoral process and party politics. Yet, this chapter also provides evidence that the protest had little effect on subsequent voting behavior.

Most of the chapters tried to explain the many cross-national differences among the protesters found in our data, by drawing on one or more of the five context layers presented above. Given certain problems of measurements on the side of independent variables as well as the complexity of the task, some authors could not fully explain the cross-national differences they found.

The most valuable tool by far to account for cross-national differences in sociodemographic characteristics, attitudes, and behavior was what we have called the issue-specific context of the protests—which Kriesi (2004, 70) has labeled the interaction context. Regarding this context, several more specific dimensions come into play. First, the position of established political actors is of crucial importance. Whether the national government participated in, supported, or opposed war, and how the oppositional parties reacted to that official stance, made a sizeable difference regarding the profile of the (potential) protesters. The classification of countries presented in chapter 3 by rank-ordering countries on a simple pro-war to antiwar scale proved to be the best overall predictor of demonstrators' cross-national differences. Although an analysis based on only eight countries limits the reach of our conclusions, in many cases the simple fact that demonstrators lived in a country participating or not participating in war had a considerable impact on their profiles when it comes to their sociodemographic characteristics, range of motives to participate in the demonstration, and embeddedness in civil society groups.

More or less the same applies to the second dimension of the issue-specific context: public opinion on the issue of war. Whether the public in a country rejected or approved of war—to be precise, the extent to which it rejected war—affected the protests and the protesters. Though there is strong evidence that both factors of the "issue-specific context"—the stance of government or opposition and the population's stance on war—do matter, we can assess neither the differential effect of these factors on the protesters nor how the factors are related. On theoretical grounds, we believe that the political positions of governments or oppositional parties affect public opinion rather than vice versa. Accordingly, public opinion can be seen as an intermediary variable (strongly influenced by the stance of the government, yet not necessarily in accordance with this stance) that affected the composition of the protesters.

The media, the third dimension, act as intermediaries connecting established political actors and opinions of the populace. After all, almost all the information people receive about the war is presented via mass media. Moreover, we can assume that both the kind and distribution of speaker mentioned in the media and the media's own positions regarding war, as expressed, for example, in commentaries, also influence people's views and attitudes.

At a closer look, it appears that the main factor affecting the sociostructural characteristics, attitudes, and behavior of the demonstrators was not merely governmental (or oppositional) stances on a continuum from participation in war (United States and United Kingdom) to support (Spain, Italy, and the Netherlands) to opposition (Switzerland, Belgium, and Germany). Rather, it was whether or not the country was or would be militarily engaged in fighting the war. Indeed, the United States and United Kingdom demonstrators stood out in most analyses and differed most from those in all the other countries. We found that, in some respects, the Spanish, Italian, and Dutch demonstrators—their governments supporting the war only with words—differed from the rest as well. Yet, the actual participation in war clearly was most consequential for the composition of the protesters. It appears that "rally around the flag" mechanisms and "support our troops" discourses substantially affected which kinds of movements, organizations, and people publicly mobilized against war. Moreover, in both countries with war-promoting administrations, even the main opposition parties were not able to raise a strong and consistent argument against war; instead, they were marginalized in a spiral of pro-war discourse. Consequently, in these two countries, the media and public opinion were also by far the least opposed to the idea of ridding the world from Saddam Hussein and his supposed "weapons of mass destruction" by engaging in warfare. In the United States in particular, the newspapers, and perhaps the media in general, tended to downplay the extent of opposition to war in other countries and in international institutions such as the United Nations (see chapter 12). The situation was entirely different in the merely war-supporting—but not war-leading—countries (Spain, Italy, and the Netherlands), where the left-wing opposition noisily and forcefully argued against war, and the entire left-wing social movement sector unambiguously mobilized against war. In these countries, demonstrators, for the most part, did not differ that much from the protesters present in the war-opposing countries (Switzerland, Belgium, and Germany). Also, the media in these countries tended to provide a more complete and fair account of the opposition to war than the media in the United States did.

However, our argument that especially active engagement in warfare made a difference to people who ended up demonstrating may be challenged by the observation that both belligerent countries also differed in other respects: they are Anglo-Saxon nations not belonging to continental Europe, unlike the rest of the nations in our sample. How can we be sure that the systematic differences we found are a result of their governments engaging in war and not an expression of Anglo-Saxon political culture? Again, in operational terms, we cannot separate the impact of these factors. But we believe it is difficult to conceive that public opinion and media in these two countries dislike war less than they do in the six other countries. Unfortunately, we do not have at our disposal systematic evidence regarding general war-and-peace attitudes of the population in our sample of countries.

Let us briefly summarize when and how the position of governments and political opposition (and likely linked media coverage and public opinion) made a difference, as shown in various chapters of this book. Considering the sociodemographic traits of the demonstrators, chapter 5 showed that their "normalization"—the extent to which they were heterogeneous and resembling the population at large in a given country—was by far the least obvious in the United States and the United Kingdom. In these two countries, protesters formed a more homogeneous crowd, while in Switzerland and the Netherlands, they were the most diverse. Chapter 6 studied the attitudes of the demonstrators and, not surprisingly, established that those in the bellicose countries were more opposed to their governments. More significant, perhaps, this chapter showed that these protesters were also more skeptical about the general functioning of democracy in their countries and that they were more politically dissatisfied. In short, in countries engaging in or rhetorically supporting the war, resistance to war was embedded in broader oppositional sentiments, bringing different kinds of people to the streets. Chapter 8, focusing on political parties, revealed that although the protesters were mainly left-wing party supporters, there were interesting cross-country differences in their partisan makeup depending on the stances of the countries' government and opposition. Regarding mobilization patterns, chapter 9 demonstrated that the official governmental position, translated into public opinion vis-à-vis the war, affected the dominant type of mobilization in the different countries. The more the public endorsed the antiwar cause, the more the mobilization relied on open channels. Chapter 10 presented evidence of the significance of issue-specific political context. Different kinds of organizations promoted the marches or rallies in the eight sampled countries, and, consequently, participants had quite different organizational relationships with the protest organizers. In the United States and the United Kingdom in particular, the ties of participants with organizing groups were weaker than in the other countries.

Dramatically different issue-specific national political contexts—the government's position on the war—almost consistently affected most dependent variables. This finding raises questions about the prevalence and importance of national versus international political contexts for protest participation. Since for the majority of the eight countries, the war on Iraq was a "foreign" issue, and they were not actively engaged in waging it, one might assume that their national contexts are of little relevance. In fact, however, the specific national context seemed to have molded the protests most. We conclude that international political opportunity structures do not directly affect protests and protest participants, but, rather, the latter are mediated by national opportunity structures, power structures, conflict constellations, media coverage, and public opinion. If the international context had been primary, we would not have found as many substantial cross-national differences among the protesters as we did.

Various chapters showed that the issue-specific context explains quite a few differences among demonstrators. Thus, it is a useful analytical tool. What about the other explananda or "layers" in our heuristic model? Chapter 5 documented that the composition of the demonstrators in terms of age and education is associated with a country's general sociodemographic pattern, the most general factor in our model. None of the chapters found a clear link between the protesters' features and the general properties of the national political context—the stable institutional arrangements and the subsequent strength of the progressive social movement sector. While this is not surprising, because the political opportunity structure approach was never meant to explain the characteristics of individual participants in specific protest events, chapter 2 did not locate a consistent link between structural access for all kinds of challengers and the strength of the progressive movement sector. Thus, based on general properties of political systems, it was impossible to generate clear and unambiguous hypotheses about the number and kind of demonstrators in the different countries.

Also the massiveness of previous antiwar demonstrations and the power of the peace movement in the past, as explored in chapter 4, did not prove to be a good predictor of the composition of the February 15 protesters. Comparing the protest against the deployment of nuclear missiles in the 1980s with the resistance against the Gulf War in the early 1990s, we found major discrepancies, with some countries mobilizing strongly in the 1980s and much less so in the 1990s, and vice versa. This also made us uncertain as to the turnout we might expect on February 15. However, as documented in chapter 10, general levels of political participation, protest patterns, and features of the social movement sector seem to have affected the organizational basis of the demonstrations. In countries that had strong global justice mobilizations prior to February 15, 2003, like Italy and Belgium, antiwar protesters appeared to exhibit the traces of this past. In countries with strong and active unions, the protesters more frequently were trade union members. And in countries with strong mass political parties, the protest participants were more active in parties than in countries with fewer party members.

The final layer in our heuristic model comprised the specific patterns and channels of mobilization adopted by the organizations staging the protest. Did mobilization affect the differential organizational composition in the eight countries? This clearly was the case. The open or closed character of the mobilization had significant consequences in recruitment, as chapter 9 demonstrated. Sociodemographic characteristics, attitudes, and political behavior all were affected by the mobilization pattern. When laying out our heuristic model in the introduction to this volume, we considered mobilization pattern an intermediary variable. Indeed, while directly affecting the dependent variables, that is, the characteristics of the protesters, the typical mobilization pattern in the eight countries was, in turn, affected by two independent variables of the model. The issue-specific context—in terms of the public opinion regarding war and the strength of the social movements in a country—membership in organizations and patterns of protest were directly associated with the openness or closedness of the mobilization process in the eight nations. Mobilization seemed to work as an intermediary factor, translating more structural dimensions of the political context into the specific composition of the protesters.

Concluding the evaluation, we think our heuristic model proved to be a theoretically reasonable and empirically plausible tool. Admittedly, we are unsure about precise interaction of the independent and intermediary factors. And we cannot, at this stage, examine the net effect of the various factors. Yet we have evidence that four of the five proposed factors that hypothetically influence the specific composition of the protests and the protesters did play roles and determined or codetermined the sociodemographic profile, attitudes, and behaviors of the participants. Above all, the issue-specific context, in particular the stance of government and opposition on the issue of war, seems to make a great difference regarding the kind of protesters that took to the streets. The sociodemographic composition of the population appears less influential. Also, the strength of the social movement sector seems to affect the makeup of the demonstrations. Mobilization processes do have the expected effect: they turn structural context factors into a specific composition of protesters. Only the political system variables did not yield substantial findings; we could not even use them to make concrete predictions about the strength and shape of progressive movement sectors. Though we cannot rule out that the most general and stable characteristics of a given political system might ultimately have some effects on the individual-level composition of protest events, we assume that such effects are very indirect and probably mediated by many additional variables. Political opportunity structure approaches are simply too abstract and too general to account for specific protest events and even more so for profiles of protesters. Therefore, we advocate for the elaboration of middle-range theories that link macro structures to micro behavior. In the social sciences in general, macro-micro bridges (see Dogan and Rokkan 1969) are one of the weakest and most underdeveloped areas. This is also reflected in studies on social movements and, more generally, political participation. We hope we highlighted some factors and variables that might be helpful in building such a bridging theory, though we are fully aware that this is no more than a first step.

Lessons for Further Research

In this volume we had not only theoretical aspirations; we also sought to test whether large-scale surveying of protest participants is feasible and, more importantly, whether it is useful. Surveys of protesters on the spot are not very common, and they have never been used on such a large scale as in our comparative endeavor. Conducting simultaneous surveys in eight countries and eleven protest venues is not an easy task. Yet it is possible, as our collective effort shows. It is, of course, up to the reader to judge whether protest surveys are useful to better understand the dynamics of protest events and protest participation. We hope we have shown that surveying protesters by questionnaire offers valuable and hard data that can put existing theories to the test and contribute to developing new theoretical insights.

Surveys of protesters necessarily imply a shift from the thus far prevailing focus on the meso- and macrolevel aspects of social movements and political protest to the micro level. The individual and his or her individual participation are put on center stage. For social movement research, this is quite a change, asking for better linking of meso- and macrolevel contexts on the one hand, with individual characteristics and behaviors on the other. In fact, this entire volume has been a constant struggle to adjust existing theories and insights to the individual level of analysis. Methodological innovation, thus, has theoretical consequences. The main limitation of surveys of protesters is that they cover only people who were successfully mobilized. Accordingly, we cannot directly compare participants with nonparticipants. In a sense, such surveys sample on the dependent variable. One way of dealing with this inherent problem of the research design is to resort, as we did, to comparisons of the participants in a given event and in different nations.

Our focus was to explore the links among three groups of variables: first, the relatively inert political structures; second, the—thus far largely neglected—issue-specific context, including issue-specific stances of political actors and the populace, but also channels of mobilization; and, third, the characteristics of those participating in a specific act of protest. We were lucky to rely on a quasi-experimental comparative research design: held constant was not only the very specific issue but also the day of the protest. Moreover, we studied one of the largest coordinated single protest actions in history by using the same questionnaire distributed on the spot, which produced a large data set that we analyzed according to analytical questions rather than offering country-by-country chapters. Taken to together, this resulted in a unique enterprise that involved dozens of researchers and their assistants. Nevertheless, when we look at the wider field of research of social movements and collective protest, it is obvious that we covered only limited ground. Only two of the many limitations: We did not study in much detail the planning of the protest, its logistics, or the concrete mobilization process as it occurred in the eight countries and eleven cities where we distributed our questionnaire. Nor did we study the impact of these protests on public opinion, public debates, and policy makers.

Though we consider cross-national comparison, as applied extensively in this volume, to be a fruitful research strategy, we also think that surveys of protesters yield even more insights when different protest issues are compared within a country or across countries. On such a basis, we also expect to find further evidence for the crucial relevance of issue-specific political opportunities, mobilization structures, and collective action frames.

Works Cited

Dalton, Russell J. 2002. *Citizen Politics: Public Opinion and Political Parties in Advanced Industrial Democracies,* 3rd ed. New York: Chatham.

Dogan, Mattei, and Stein Rokkan, eds. 1969. *Quantitative Ecological Analysis in the Social Sciences.* Cambridge, Mass.: MIT Press.

Kolb, Felix. 2007. *Protest and Opportunities: The Political Outcomes of Social Movements.* New York: Campus.

Kriesi, Hanspeter. 2004. "Political Context and Opportunity." In *The Blackwell Companion to Social Movements,* eds. David A. Snow, Sarah A. Soule, and Hanspeter Kriesi, 66–90. Oxford: Blackwell.

Przeworski, Adam, and Henry Teune. 1970. *The Logic of Comparative Social Inquiry.* New York: Wiley.

Acknowledgments

This book studies collective action, and it largely draws on collective action. The volume is the result of efforts by many people, not only those authoring or coauthoring chapters. They were helped by a host of other people in their respective countries. Although not authoring a chapter here, Manuel Jimenez coordinated the data collection in Madrid; we are grateful to him for letting us use the Spanish data. In the United States, main researchers Lance Bennett and Terri Givens had a hand from people who helped get this study into the field in Seattle and San Francisco: Victor Pickard, David Iozzi, Lisa Horan, and Edith Manosevitch. Lars Willnat organized the team that went into the field in New York. In the United Kingdom, Catherine Eschle organized the fieldwork in Glasgow, and Derek Wall in London. In other cities, numerous other people, most of them students, were also engaged in collecting data.

Similarly, media data were not collected only by the authors of the media chapters. More concretely, we thank Claudia Schmidt for collaborating on the design of the coding scheme and letting us use the German media data she collected.

We are grateful to the Forum Trentino per la Pace, and its president Roberto Bombarda, for generously funding a public event at the Faculty of Sociology in Trento on October 4, 2004, when some of our preliminary findings were presented. We thank Maria Fabbri and Enzo Loner for assisting with the organization of our meetings there.

Two anonymous reviewers and Sidney Tarrow read earlier versions of the manuscript and provided useful commentaries. We thank them for their suggestions.

Finally, the European Consortium for Political Research deserves our gratitude for the funding it provided the authors and editors to organize working meetings and finalize the book.

Appendix A:
Methodology of Protest Surveys in Eight Countries

Stefaan Walgrave and Claudius Wagemann

This book draws largely upon a central dataset comprising data collected in the eight countries under study. The main source is a survey conducted on the same day, February 15, 2003, based on a sample of almost six thousand demonstrators participating in massive protest events against the upcoming war on Iraq. This survey was conducted by eight local country teams using (nearly) identical questionnaires and a similar fieldwork method. The Belgian team, directed by Stefaan Walgrave, took the initiative for this endeavor. This team also provided the funding for data input and preparation. When the United States and the United Kingdom started to make clear in December 2002 that they would wage war on Iraq, the Belgian team began forging a network of social movement and political participation scholars to survey the potential demonstrations against the war. At that point, February 15 was still relatively far away. The international team adapted the questionnaire that the Belgian members had developed for previous protest surveys (Van Aelst and Walgrave 2001; Norris, Walgrave, and Van Aelst 2005), as well as their sampling procedure. Surveying is not a conventional or widely used method for analyzing protest events; rather, techniques such as participant observation, (qualitative) in-depth interviews, protest event analyses, life histories, text analysis, and so forth have been applied. So the application of survey techniques—widespread in other subdisciplines of political science and sociology—is rather novel for social movement research.

Opting for such a method also has quite a substantial effect on the logic of our research. Whereas previously applied methods mostly point to the motivations, behavior, and attitudes of individual participants in demonstrations, the individual person here disappears in an N survey and becomes a row in a data matrix. At the end of the day, variables interest us much more than cases. The methodological literature has called this a "variable-oriented approach" rather than a "case-oriented approach" (Ragin 2004). The positive effect of such a method is that a concentration on variables, using large datasets, helps us increase causal leverage and obtain broader generalizations of our results. Indeed, we might be able to draw conclusions about how different variables work in different countries (or in our aggregated dataset as a whole). However, we also risk the negative effect that correlations lead us to conclusions based only on covariations instead of a rigidly performed in-depth causal analysis of a few cases. If we find, for example, that first-timers in demonstrations are more reluctant to use violence as a means of expressing their political opinions, then this is nothing other than a (possibly non-randomly appearing) covariation of two distinct variables, and we can include the causal nexus only with other analytical techniques. However, since the February 15 demonstrations offered us the (perhaps) unique opportunity to collect data from large samples in comparatively similar settings (similar slogans and aims in all countries; same date and, therefore, same current state of international politics; same issue, namely, the war in Iraq; etc.), we decided to expose the domain of protest events analysis—which has long been case-oriented in its methodology—to a rather new methodological perspective, namely, the variable-oriented one.

As the following discussion will show, this did not work entirely neatly. However, it was not the lack of previous experience with survey techniques in protest research that led to problems in the application of the method, but rather the inherent characteristics of our object of research, that is, mass demonstrations. Indeed, mass demonstrations are embedded in different contexts (usually highly emotionalized ones, with fluid issues, that combine rather heterogeneous sets of actors and so forth) from consumer behavior or voting patterns. Therefore, they are analyzed in very specific circumstances, so we first had to adopt strategies for coping with these specificities. In the following, we will explain our procedure and sampling method in more detail. Note that the method we have sketched out here has not been followed in great detail in all countries; sometimes, specific circumstances made it almost impossible to stick to the fieldwork method guidelines explained below, in particular.

As mentioned, interviewing participants at protest demonstrations cannot build on much previous methodological knowledge. Favre and colleagues even speak of "a strange gap in the sociology of mobilizations" (Favre, Fillieule, and Mayer 1997). To the best of our knowledge, protest surveying has only been used in a few studies (see, for example, Jasper and Poulsen 1995; and Waddington 1988). Most elaborate is the work of the French research team including Favre, Mayer, and Fillieule, who developed a technique designed to offer all participants an equal opportunity of being interviewed (Fillieule 1997). Stefaan Walgrave and Peter Van Aelst refined their method further (2001).

The actual process of surveying demonstrators applied in this study, based on a random sample, was twofold. First, two fieldwork supervisors (each accompanied by a team of questionnaire distributors/interviewers) counted the rows of participants in the moving cortege, selecting every n-th row, to ensure that the same number of rows was skipped throughout the demonstration, and that the whole procession was covered. This should guarantee that all groups, no matter whether their members preferred to walk in the first or last part of a march (this issue is also linked to questions of visibility of a group in a march), have an equal chance to be part of the sample. One of the two groups of fieldwork supervisors and distributors started at the first row of demonstrators in the march and then gradually moved to the back, counting and skipping rows until the last one. The other group of fieldwork supervisors and distributors, the athletic ones (as they had to overtake the entire marching crowd), started at the end and gradually worked their way to the head of the march. Each time a row was selected by the fieldwork supervisor, the distributors selected every n-th person in that row and handed out questionnaires to these individuals. Ideally, the distributors alternated among demonstrators at the left side, at the right side, and in the middle of a row, again taking into account that some participants would prefer to march at the margins or in the center, respectively, of the crowd. Questionnaires were distributed in an addressed envelope, with postage paid by addressee. This sampling method, as simple as it may seem, aimed at guaranteeing an even distribution of the questionnaires over the demonstrating crowd and at giving every participant the same chance of being selected, no matter where and with whom she or he marched.

The selected participants were asked to complete a ten-page questionnaire at home and to mail it back. The questionnaire used for February 15 in each of the countries had a common core, including questions on the participants' profiles, the mobilization context, and political attitudes and behavior, plus a few specific items in some of the countries. The answers had to be short and succinct and were very often formulated in a multiple-choice format, in yes/no responses or in coded evaluations of opinions. In addition to the mail survey, a random sample of other demonstrators in Belgium, the Netherlands, Switzerland and the United Kingdom were interviewed face-to-face before the start of the demonstration. To do this, before the start of the demonstration the gathering crowd was divided into sectors, and each interviewer randomly, often following a specific procedure, selected a set number of respondents in his or her sector. These short interviews were used as a crosscheck to evaluate how far the different attitudes in responding to the mail survey might have biased the result of the postal interviews. Confidence in the reliability of this comparison was strengthened by the fact that hardly anyone refused to participate in a face-to-face interview: Rüdig assessed this systematically in the Glasgow part of the survey and found that the response rate there was no lower than 95.3 percent (2006). However, in this volume we have only drawn on respondents from the postal surveys, since these questionnaires cover more variables, we did not carry out face-to-face interviews for all the countries under research, and face-to-face data are only used to test the representativity of the postal answers.

As all surveys, those used here for demonstrations also raise important questions about the reliability and the representativity of sampling procedures. Since this is unknown territory, this is even more so: we do not have any information whatsoever about how sociodemographic factors or political attitudes might influence the response behavior. An undesired effect could be, for example, that demonstrators with more radical opinions and/or attitudes would be more likely to refuse a response than others (alternatively, they might be even more motivated to participate in a survey—but this would also cause a bias). This is further exacerbated because we had reason to believe that the February 15 demonstrations were not routine events. Indeed, this was many demonstrators' first protest experience (see chapter 8).

However, there are also practical difficulties in conducting a truly random sample: first, if a demonstration is large and fairly static and the streets are congested with people, it becomes difficult for the interviewers to get through the whole march and cover all kinds of groups, since they are simply immobilized. Second, it is impossible to get a good sample of respondents in violent and/or irregular demonstrations (or in violent sectors of an otherwise peaceful demonstration), even if we know that these forms of protest are usually small in number. Third, in some exceptional cases, extremist groups of demonstrators within a peaceful event refuse to accept the questionnaires—something that, of course, lowers the degree of representativity and biases the result. Yet again, this is rare, and, in general, demonstrators who have deliberately chosen to express their political opinion on the street are likely to collaborate and may even be anxious to share their views with researchers. Fourth, the weather conditions also play a role when one is conducting research literally "in the streets": when it is raining cats and dogs, for example, the distributed questionnaires can become soaking wet and can no longer be filled out and returned. Additionally, if it only starts raining when a demonstration has already started, questionnaires that were distributed before the rain shower are much more likely to be sent back than the others.

In terms of the February 15 sampling, the weather in the cities we surveyed was mild. We can assume that the differences in temperatures did not play any important role. Furthermore, the demonstrations we covered were not irregular, nor were they violent, nor had they violent sectors. Instead, they were for the most part orderly processions without running or accelerating segments. There were hardly any extremist demonstrators around, so this did not pose a problem, either. However, it turned out that the unexpectedly high numbers of demonstrators in some of our city cases made it simply impossible to strictly follow our field survey method. For example, some interviewers got stuck on the stairs in subway tunnels, or the crowds in the streets did not move at all and the interviewers became completely stuck because of the enormous attendance. When either the interviewers or the crowd were static, the sampling procedure could not always be applied. This was the case in London, Madrid, and, for the most part, Berlin: in these cities, the static sampling procedure of dividing the standing crowd in sectors was also adopted for the distribution of the postal questionnaires, which implies fewer guarantees that a representative sample of demonstrators was drawn. Furthermore, not all interviewers and supervisors had previous experience with the fieldwork method developed by the Belgian team; this also caused some confusion and misunderstandings here and there. Although in many instances we managed to follow the fieldwork procedure and sampling method quite in detail, this was not always the case. We are unsure about the effects different modes of application of the method had on our sample, and we cannot test them. Yet, since we know that the disturbances to the strict application of our sampling methods were not very big, we have reason to believe that our samples in the different demonstrations are, by and large, comparable. Social science often is forced to look at dynamic, spontaneous forms of behavior and activity—not systematically evolving ones—so that the methods it uses cannot be "exact," as in the natural sciences or as in more experimental settings of social science research. This is even more the case for demonstrations, which are, by definition, fast moving, hardly controllable, quickly changing objects of research: even the strictest method has to be applied flexibly. Nonetheless, we believe that the distortions in the sample should not make us worry too much, since the high number of questionnaires and the dominance of cases in which we were able to apply the method in

STEFAAN WALGRAVE AND CLAUDIUS WAGEMANN

an ideal setting might outweigh the practical problems that occurred in some instances.

In one case, the national team opted for a different sampling method. In Italy, the team, led by Donatella della Porta and Mario Diani, decided to draw mainly on face-to-face interviews, conducted before the Rome demonstration. Because the Italian team feared that response rates for the postal surveys would be too low, they interviewed the demonstrators on trains on their way to the protest in Rome. Of course, this might pose serious challenges to the comparability of the Italian sample with the other national samples. Interviewing on the spot might indeed lead to different answers than would filling in a questionnaire quietly at home. Moreover, on packed trains, it is very difficult to conduct interviews in private. Hence, social desirability and group pressures may affect the answers. Interviewing on trains might also lead to a bias since only demonstrators who travel by train have a chance to be part of the sample. Whether a demonstrator opts for the train or another means of transport (or whether she or he simply lives close enough to the venue) might also correlate with other sociodemographic and attitudinal factors that could influence the representativity of the sample. For example, we expect people traveling by train to be more likely to be members of an organization and to come from farther away (see chapter 9), which, consequently, might be an indicator of their high motivation.

In short, the differing sampling procedure in Italy might have substantially affected the Italian sample. However, the team also distributed a limited number of postal questionnaires at the Rome demonstration. In fact, a comparative analysis of differences between the train face-to-face surveys and the Rome postal ones did not reveal any statistically significant differences between the two groups with regard to either their sociodemographic characteristics or other variables. Thus, although it is still to some extent a leap of faith, we are confident in including the Italian sample in our systematic comparison with the other countries. However, especially when it comes to comparing the mobilization patterns of the Italians with those of the Belgians, Germans, and so forth—as we do in chapter 9 of this volume—we think it is important to take the differential recruitment of respondents into account and to be very cautious, as our sampling is quite likely biased on the dependent variable (mobilization pattern).

We conducted surveys in eleven major cities in the eight covered countries. Apart from including the major demonstrations in the capitals of these countries in most cases (London, Rome, Madrid, Berlin, Amsterdam, Brussels, and Bern), or in a major metropolis in the United States (New York), we also fielded our survey in Seattle and in San Francisco (United States) and in Glasgow (United Kingdom). As we wanted to analyze these data at the country level, the variation of the political and societal context is our main independent variable. Therefore, we checked whether we could detect any significant differences in the main variables between the different cities in the United States and the United Kingdom. This proved not to be the case: the Seattle demonstrators are very much like those in New York and San Francisco, and the London and Glasgow protesters hardly differed, either. That is why we consider it safe to merge the respective city datasets into one single set for the United States and one single set for the United Kingdom. In most chapters we use these (merged) country datasets, but in some chapters, for specific reasons, the authors split up the UK sample and dealt with the London and Glasgow demonstrations separately.

We relied on a double sampling strategy in some countries: we distributed postal questionnaires using our strict sampling method during the march and asked people to send them back (we had paid the postage beforehand); and we selected a smaller number of people, using a less strict sampling procedure, which gave the interviewers more leeway as they conducted a short interview on the spot. In this volume, we only use the completed postal questionnaires. We used the face-to-face interviews to test the representativity of the questionnaires that were sent back. As mentioned, we used face-to-face interviews in Belgium, the Netherlands, the United Kingdom, and Switzerland. In Italy, almost all surveys were conducted face-to-face, but since that has been done in an entirely different way, we do not include the Italian data in our test of representativity.

What can be learned from the systematic comparison of both interview types? Overall, the results tell us that there are, indeed, a few differences between the two interview types (even statistically significant ones) but that these differences remain limited. They are, of course, not surprising. The associations between the interview type and the responses can be traced to three diverging methodological biases: mail survey non-response bias, face-to-face survey selection bias, and face-to-face versus mail survey social desirability effects. As we cannot determine for sure which method effect is causing which kind of bias, we can only undertake an informed guess about what causes these differences.

First, men and younger people are significantly overrepresented among the face-to-face interviews. It seems that our interviewers, also young and predominantly male, tended to select more male and younger conversation partners, or, perhaps, that female and older respondents sent back the questionnaire more reliably. Thus, the observed gender and age differences between interview types might be due either to a response (mail) or selection (face-to-face) bias. Second, some variables regarding the company in which the interviewee attended the demonstration yielded significant differences, all pointing toward a selection bias in the face-to-face interviewing: directly interviewed people attended the demonstration to a lesser extent with family, colleagues, and comembers than mail respondents did. It makes sense that interviewers tended to address participants who came on their own rather than those who were part of a group. Third, we noticed that the face-to-face interviewees were more likely to agree with the Likert items they were confronted with; this is commonly known as the acquiescence effect of face-to-face interviews. This was especially observable for four statements in the questionnaire ("War is always wrong"; "War on Iraq is waged to secure national oil supply"; "I am satisfied with my government's efforts to prevent war on Iraq"; "War to bring down a dictatorial regime is justified"). Finally, we did not find any significant differences between the two interview types for many variables. There is no difference, for example, in the level of political interest, previous type or frequency of protest participation, political left-right self-positioning; perceived political efficacy of the demonstration. By and large, we did not find strong evidence of a systematic response bias in the mail sample. However, we found traces of a probable selection bias and of a social desirability effect in the face-to-face sample. Hence, we think we can rather safely consider the mail survey respondents a fair sample of the population. Similarly, Wolfgang Rüdig, the leader of the UK team, has carried out an extensive in-depth analysis comparing postal and face-to-face questionnaires in the Scottish (Glasgow) subsample (2006). His results also show that there are no substantial differences between the two interview types and reinforce our confidence in the reliability of the mail survey data.

Response rates for the February 15 mail survey vary between countries, but an overall response rate of almost 47 percent is clearly quite satisfying for a postal survey for which no reminders were sent out. In previous protest surveys covering a variety of demonstrations on very diverse sets of issues in Belgium, we got, on average, a response rate of nearly 44 percent. Thus, the February 15 rates are by no means exceptional or disturbing for this kind of research. We can say that peace demonstrators or anti–Iraq War demonstrators tend to send back their questionnaires after they got home to about the same extent as antiracist, anti-drug, global social justice, education, or social security demonstrators. Figure A.1 contains the February 15 response rates by country.

As we can see, differences among countries appear substantial. In the United Kingdom only a bit more than one out of three selected demonstrators sent back a completed questionnaire. At the same time, more than half of the sampled protesters answered our questions in the Netherlands, Switzerland,

	Number of mail survey respondents	Response rate for mail survey (percent)	Number of face-to-face respondents
United States	705	47.0	–
United Kingdom	1,129	35.9	503
Spain	452	37.7	–
Italy	1,016	–	–
Netherlands	542	54.2	100
Switzerland	637	53.1	181
Belgium	510	46.4	196
Germany	781	52.1	–
Total	5,772	46.6	981

Figure A.1. Response rates in the eight nations

and Germany. At this point, we have neither a clue as to where these inter-country differences come from nor a way to look systematically for an explanation. It could well be that the sociodemographic composition of the marches in the different countries led to different levels of conduciveness to this kind of survey research; as shown in chapter 5, we did find significant differences in the sociodemographic profile of the demonstrators across countries. Also, the mood and radicality of the demonstrators and the political position of government and opposition in the eight countries might have made a difference. In general, political cultural differences between the countries could have caused diverging response rates. Residents of the United Kingdom, for example, might in general be less willing to participate in survey research than Dutch citizens. Still, we believe that the response rates in the different countries are similar enough that we can systematically compare the covered demonstrators across nations.

Finally, we are aware that the method employed in this study raises questions that we might not have been able to answer all of them satisfyingly. After all, survey techniques are a fairly new method for the analysis of protest events, and they must be explored further and tested more profoundly than has been the case until now. The Belgian team that developed the protest survey method is currently working on a much more thorough test of the reliability and representativity of the fieldwork method. We hope to make further headway with this approach in the very near future.

Works Cited

Favre, Philippe, Olivier Fillieule, and Nonna Mayer. 1997. "La fin d'une étrange lacune de la sociologie des mobilisations: L'étude par sondage des manifestants:

Fondements théoriques et solutions techniques." *Revue Française de Science Politique* 47: 3–28

Fillieule, Olivier. 1997. *Stratégies de la rue: Les manifestations en France.* Paris: Presses de Sciences Po.

Jasper, James M., and Jane Poulsen. 1995. "Recruiting Strangers and Friends: Moral Shocks and Social Networks in Animal Rights and Anti-Nuclear Protests." *Social Problems* 42: 493–512.

Norris, Pippa, Stefaan Walgrave, and Peter Van Aelst. 2005. "Who Demonstrates? Anti-State Rebels or Conventional Participants? Or Everyone?" *Comparative Politics* 2: 251–75.

Ragin, Charles. 2004. "Turning the Tables: How Case-Oriented Research Challenges Variable-Oriented Research." In *Rethinking Social Inquiry: Diverse Tools, Shared Standards,* ed. Henry E. Brady and David Collier, 123–38. Lanham, Md.: Rowman & Littlefield.

Rüdig, Wolfgang. 2006. "Assessing Nonresponse Bias in Activist Surveys: A Study of 2003 Anti-Iraq War Protesters in Scotland." Unpublished paper, Glasgow.

Van Aelst, Peter, and Stefaan Walgrave. 2001. "Who Is That (Wo)man in the Street? From the Normalisation of Protest to the Normalisation of the Protester." *European Journal of Political Research* 39: 461–86.

Waddington, David. 1988. *Flashpoints of Public Disorder.* London: Methuen.

Appendix B:
Media Content Analysis

Joris Verhulst

We decided to restrict the media analysis to the two and a half months prior to the outbreak of war: from January 15 till March 21, 2003. In that period, the worldwide war debate was most vivid; it focused on the justification for the imminent war and on the potential approval of war by the UN Security Council. Also, the February 15 protest took place somewhere in the middle of this time period. This time span is well suited to test our propositions, since in exactly these few months countries fought a bitter battle about the justification of war, and most were forced to take a clear stance regarding the U.S.-UK war plans. Therefore, we expect country variations to be high in this period.

For the media analysis we selected two or three newspapers per country. For each, we tried to include, if applicable, three articles per day, using the broad search term "Iraq" in online search engines. In total, we used 3,968 news articles, which were encoded by trained researchers. We included twenty-two different papers. Their attention to the Iraqi crisis differed, but we had at our disposal sufficient articles per newspaper to carry out reliable analyses for all twenty-two. Figure B.1 lists the newspaper titles and the numbers of articles used for each.

The selection of so few newspapers per country is probably the trickiest aspect of the research design. We always took the major left- and right-leaning broadsheet newspapers, then, in most cases, we added the most popular newspaper, often a tabloid. Are these two or three newspapers representative of the written press in the eight countries? For some countries, we are rather confident that they are; for others, we are much less sure. Our U.S. sample, especially—with the *New York Times*, the *Washington Post,* and *USA Today*—

		Left/right/ popular	Number of articles
United States	*New York Times*	right	189
	Washington Post	left	193
	USA Today	popular (right)	90
United Kingdom	*Times*	right	206
	Guardian	left	210
	Sun	popular (left)	72
Spain	*El Mundo*	right	209
	El Pais	left	178
Italy	*Il Giornale*	right	299
	La Reppublica	left	259
	La Stampa	center	77
Netherlands	*NRC Handelsblad*	right	96
	De Volkskrant	left	402
	De Telegraaf	popular (right)	141
Switzerland	*Neue Zürcher Zeitung*	right (center)	170
	Tages-Anzeiger	left (center)	152
Belgium	*De Standaard*	right	206
	De Morgen	left	166
	Het Laatste Nieuws	popular (right)	142
Germany	*Frankfurter Allgemeine*	right	171
	Frankfurter Rundschau	left	173
	Bild	popular (right)	165
Total			3,968

Figure B.1. Description of newspaper sample

might be not entirely representative. Some might argue that it is too liberal and left-leaning to represent the average U.S. written press outlet. In Italy, we took *La Stampa* as a third paper, which is not the most popular paper in the country and has a centrist position. We were not able to get electronic access to the archives of the Switzerland's most popular tabloid, *Blick*. In Spain, the most popular national newspaper is the high-quality *El Pais,* and the selection of a third, more tabloid-like, newspaper was hindered because of a lack of electronic database access.

A final methodological remark concerning the media dataset relates to the actual coding of the media content. Our encoders read each article in its entirety and did not rely on electronic indexes provided by the news companies. Our encoders were all Belgian graduate students able to speak the language of the newspapers they read. Yet, because we encoded newspapers

in five different languages, overlaps between encoders could not be easily organized, and intercoder-reliability measures could not systematically be calculated. To preclude possible problems, the graduate students were briefed and
trained extensively beforehand, and their work was thoroughly controlled and
checked by the supervisor of the encoding project.

Contributors

W. LANCE BENNETT is professor of political science and Ruddick C. Lawrence Professor of Communication at the University of Washington.

MICHELLE BEYELER is lecturer and research fellow at the Institute of Political Science, University of Berne, Switzerland.

CHRISTIAN BREUNIG is assistant professor of political science at the University of Toronto.

DONATELLA DELLA PORTA is professor of sociology in the Department of Social and Political Sciences at the European University Institute, Florence. She is coauthor of *Globalization from Below: Transnational Activists and Protest Networks* (Minnesota, 2006).

MARIO DIANI is professor of sociology at the University of Trento in Italy. He is coauthor of *Social Movements: An Introduction.*

TERRI E. GIVENS is vice provost and associate professor in the government department at University of Texas, Austin. Her books include *Voting Radical Right in Western Europe.*

BERT KLANDERMANS is professor of applied psychology at Free University in the Netherlands. He is coauthor of *Methods of Social Movement Research* (Minnesota, 2002).

289

DIETER RUCHT is professor of sociology at Wissenschaftszentrum Berlin für Sozialforschung and the Free University of Berlin.

WOLFGANG RÜDIG is reader in government at University of Strathclyde, Glasgow. His books include *Anti-Nuclear Movements*.

SIDNEY TARROW is Maxwell Upson Professor of Government and Sociology at Cornell University. He is coeditor of *Silence and Voice in the Study of Contentious Politics*.

PETER VAN AELST is assistant professor of political science at the University of Antwerp.

JORIS VERHULST is assistant professor of political science at the University of Antwerp.

CLAUDIUS WAGEMANN took his PhD at the European University Institute, Florence, where he collaborated on a project studying the extreme right. He has been lecturer in methodology and scientific secretary at the doctoral program in political science at the Istituto italiano di scienze umane, Florence.

STEFAAN WALGRAVE is professor of political science at the University of Antwerp.

Index

abstaining, 152 (table), 154

action, 120, 128, 197, 262; antiwar, 1–2; collective, 171, 196, 198, 210, 211, 249, 271; direct, 121, 137n3; disruptive, 122, 125; information and, 235; mobilization, 170; political, xiv, 29, 121, 123–26, 143; semi-conventional forms of, 124; sociodemographic characteristics and, 128 (table); youth, 47, 247

Action Alliance, 248

activism, 120, 123, 126, 129, 144, 154, 195, 210; collective, 136–37; commitment to, 194; degrees of, 38n2; dynamics of, 136–37; kinds of, 80; market of, 143; persistent, 130; potential, 92

activists, 164, 194, 195; anti-racist, 10; complex political identifications and, 225; left-wing, 34–35, 34 (table); potential/actual, 90; protest history of, 217; social characteristics of, 128; social justice, 229; sociodemographic characteristics of, 90, 91 (table); socioeconomic centrality of, 120; young, 92

advertisements, 172, 176, 178, 246, 247

Afghanistan, attack on, 13, 195

age, 90, 92, 115, 160, 182, 225, 281; activism and, 120; mobilization and, 159, 183; overrepresentation for, 86 (table); participation and, 186, 206, 208; underrepresentation for, 84, 86, 86 (table)

al-Qaeda, vii, 7

Amnesty International, 204, 212n2

ANSWER (Act Now to Stop War and End Racism), 10, 12, 247

anti-Americanism, 242, 243, 249, 256, 264

antiglobalization movement, 166n4, 220

antinuclear movement, 142, 144, 148

antipartyism, 143, 154

antiracism, 126, 136, 197, 198, 220

"Anti-War Call," 9, 11, 246, 247

antiwar campaigns, 10, 30–31, 246, 266, 267

antiwar coalitions, 12, 38, 170

antiwar issue, 9–10, 95, 145, 162, 208

antiwar movement, ix, 22, 146, 174, 232, 250; downplaying, 266; party politics and, 142